TOYOTA KATA

TOYOTA KATA

MANAGING PEOPLE FOR IMPROVEMENT, ADAPTIVENESS, AND SUPERIOR RESULTS

MIKE ROTHER

New York Chicago San Francisco Lisbon London
Madrid Mexico City Milan New Delhi San Juan
Seoul Singapore Sydney Toronto

23 LCR 23

ISBN 978-0-07-163523-3
MHID 0-07-163523-8

McGraw-Hill Education books are available at special quantity discounts to use as premiums and sales promotions, or for use in corporate training programs. To contact a representative, please visit the Contact Us pages at www.mhprofessional.com.

This book is printed on acid-free paper.

Library of Congress Cataloging-in-Publication Data

Rother, Mike.

Toyota kata : managing people for improvement, adaptiveness, and superior results by mike rother.

p. cm.

Includes bibliographical references and index.

ISBN 0-07-163523-8 (alk. paper)

1. Total quality management. 2. Personnel management. I. Title.

HD62.15.R685 2010

658.3'01—dc22 2009016344

Contents

Foreword

Mike Rother's *Toyota Kata* is a rare and exciting event — a book that casts entirely new light on a much heralded set of management practices, giving those practices new significance and power. Countless people in the past 20 or more years have studied and written about Toyota's wildly successful management thinking and practice. But paradoxically, despite the vast amount of knowledge presented in these works, no organization outside Toyota's family of companies has ever come close to matching Toyota's stellar performance. There is a widespread feeling that something Toyota does is still not understood and put into practice by non-Toyota companies.

Toyota Kata will change all that. In this book, Mike Rother penetrates Toyota's management methods to a depth never before reached. In doing so, he offers a set of new ideas and practices that enables any organization, in any business, to do what it takes to match Toyota's performance.

This is not the first book in which Mike Rother presents pathbreaking insights into Toyota. He advanced the business world's understanding of Toyota's methods light-years in his 1998 book *Learning to See*, coauthored with John Shook. A brief look at the message of

Learning to See explains how *Toyota Kata* advances that understanding yet another order of magnitude.[1]

Learning to See describes and explains a mapping tool Toyota uses to "see" how work moves from the start of production to delivering finished product to the ultimate customer. Known inside Toyota as "material and information flow mapping," Rother, Shook, and publisher Jim Womack renamed Toyota's tool "value-stream mapping" and explained it for the first time in their book. Thanks to the enormous success of *Learning to See*, value-stream mapping became one of the most widely used tools to teach and practice Toyota's vaunted production system.

With the value-stream mapping tool, Rother and Shook show how to use many of Toyota's well-known techniques systematically to change a conventional batch-oriented mass-production factory flow — replete with countless interruptions and massive delays—into a flow resembling what one finds in a typical Toyota factory. Familiar names for some of these techniques are *takt time, andon, kanban, heijunka,* and *jidoka.* For most students of Toyota, *Learning to See* was the first extensive and clear explanation into how to use Toyota's techniques to improve across an entire facility.

That book, however, does not explore why and how these techniques evolved, and continue to evolve, at Toyota. Although *Learning to See* provides a monumental step forward in understanding how Toyota achieved the remarkable results it has enjoyed for over 50 years, it does not reveal why others, after implementing Toyota-style techniques, still seem unable to emulate Toyota's performance. How does Toyota develop its solutions? What specific process do they use? Now, in *Toyota Kata: Managing People for Improvement, Adaptiveness, and Superior Results*, Mike Rother shows us this next vital layer of Toyota practice.

The central message of *Toyota Kata* is to describe and explain Toyota's process for managing people. Rother sets forth with great clarity and detail Toyota's unique improvement and leadership routines, or *kata*, by which Toyota achieves sustained competitive advantage. The transformative insight in *Toyota Kata* is that Toyota's "improvement kata" and "coaching kata" both transcend the results-oriented level of thinking inherent in the management methods still used in most companies in the Western world.

The findings in *Toyota Kata* confirm my own interpretation of what I observed so often in Toyota operations since my first study mission to Toyota's giant facility (TMMK) in Georgetown, Kentucky, in 1992.[2] What distinguishes Toyota's practices from those observed in American and other Western companies is their focus on what I call "managing by means," or MBM, rather than "managing by results," or MBR. As far back as 1992, I learned from President Fujio Cho and members of his management team at Georgetown that Toyota steadfastly believes that organizational routines for improvement and adaptation, not quantitative/financial targets, define the pathway to competitive advantage and long-term organizational survival.

In this era, business organizations also have a great influence on the nature of society. How these organizations operate and, especially, the ways of thinking and acting they teach their members define not only the organizations' success but great swaths of our social fabric as well. While a rapid advance of knowledge about human behavior is now under way, those scientific findings are still too far removed from the day-to-day operation of our companies. Business organizations cannot yet access and use them to their benefit in practical ways. Because *Toyota Kata* is about developing new patterns of thinking and behavior in organizations, it provides a means for science to find application in our everyday lives. The potential is to reach new levels of performance in human endeavor by adopting more effective ways of working, and of working together.

In my opinion, the greatest change Mike Rother's *Toyota Kata* can bring to the non-Toyota business world is to replace traditional financial-results-driven management thinking with an understanding that outstanding financial results and long-term organization survival follow best from continuous and robust process improvement and adaptation —not from driving people to achieve financial targets without regard for how their actions affect processes. What has prevented this change from happening before now is the lack of a clear and comprehensive explanation of how continuous improvement and adaptation occur in Toyota, the only company I know in the world that truly manages by means, not by results. That explanation is now available to anyone who studies Mike Rother's findings and message in *Toyota Kata*.

H. Thomas Johnson
Portland, Oregon
Spring 2009

Notes

1 Mike Rother and John Shook, *Learning to See: Value Stream Mapping to Add Value and Eliminate Muda* (Cambridge, Massachusetts: Lean Enterprise Institute, 1998).

2 I recount my findings from these study missions in Chapter 3 and other parts of H. Thomas Johnson and Anders Broms, *Profit Beyond Measure: Extraordinary Results Through Attention to Process and People* (New York: The Free Press, 2000; and London: Nicholas Brealey Publishing, 2000 and 2008).

Acknowledgments

Thank you to the many dozens of people who have given me access to their companies and factories, who worked with me or in parallel in testing ideas, engaged in discussion about what we were learning, critiqued my thoughts, and were happy to keep going.

This book also reflects an ongoing dialogue with an ardent group of fellow experimenters, whom I count as colleagues, mentors, and friends. Thank you to: John Shook (who was coincidentally preparing a book on a related topic), Professor H. Thomas Johnson (Portland State University), Dr. Ralph Richter (Robert Bosch GmbH), Gerd Aulinger (Festool), Jim Huntzinger, Professor Jochen Deuse (Technical University Dortmund), Dr. Andreas Ritzenhoff and Dr. Lutz Engel (Seidel GmbH & Co. KG), Tom Burke and Jeff Uitenbroek (Modine Manufacturing Company), and Keith Allman (Delta Faucet Company).

Thank you also to a few exceptional people who over the years have given me support, input, or guidance that opened doors, moved my horizons, and created new possibilities: my wife, Liz Rother, Dr. Jim Womack (Lean Enterprise Institute), Professor

Daniel T. Jones (Lean Enterprise Academy), Mr. Kiyoshi Suzaki, Professor Jeffrey Liker (University of Michigan), and my daughters, Grace and Olivia.

And, last but not least, a deep bow to Toyota for giving us such an interesting subject about which to learn.

Introduction: Transforming Our Understanding of Leadership and Management

Imagine you have a way of managing that generates initiative among everyone in the organization to adapt, improve, and keep the organization moving forward. Imagine that although this method is different from how we currently manage, it is ultimately not difficult to understand. That is the subject of this book, which describes a way of bringing an organization to the top, and keeping it there, by influencing how everyone in it, yourself included, thinks, acts, and reacts.

In many organizations there is an unspoken frustration because of a gap between desired results and what really happens. Targets are set, but they are not reached. Change does not take place.

The music industry's major labels, for example, were broadsided by digital music downloads, even though the widespread popularity of compiling homemade mix cassettes, starting over 30 years ago, indicated that the market was there. For several decades Detroit's automakers chose not to focus on developing smaller, more efficient vehicles for their product portfolios, despite repeated signals since the 1970s that there was a growing market for them. More recently, PC industry giants were late to develop compact, Internet-oriented laptops tailored for Web surfing, e-mail, sharing photos, downloading music, and watching videos, even though many people, sitting in plain view in coffeeshops, use their laptop primarily for these tasks.

Our reaction to the fate of the music industry, the automakers, the PC companies, and hundreds of organizations like them is predictable: we blame an organization's failure to adapt on poor decision making by managers and leaders, and we may even call for those leaders to be replaced. Yet can there really be so many managers and leaders who themselves are the problem? Is that the root cause? I can assure you that we are on the wrong path with from-the-hip assertions about bad managers, and that hiring new ones, or more MBAs, is not going to solve this problem.

So what is it that makes organizations fall behind and even totally miss the boat, and what can we do about it? What should we change, and *to* what should we change it? Once you know the answers to these questions, you will be even more capable of leading and managing people, and of ensuring that your organization will find its way into the future.

Most companies are led, managed, and populated by thoughtful, hardworking people who want their organization, their team, to succeed. The conclusion has become clear: it is not the people, but rather the prevailing *management system* within which we work that is a culprit. A problem lies in how we are managing our organizations, and there is a growing consensus that a new approach is needed. But we have not yet seen what that change should be.

Business authors sometimes suggest that well-established, successful companies decline, while newer companies do well, because the new companies are not encumbered by an earlier, outmoded way of thinking. On the surface that may seem true, but the important lesson actually lies one step deeper. The problem is not that a company's thinking is old, but that its thinking does not incorporate constant improvement and adaptation.

Drawing on my research about Toyota, I offer you a means for managing people, for how leaders can conduct themselves, that is demonstrably superior to how we currently go about it. I am writing for anyone who is searching for a way to lead, manage, and develop people that produces improvement, adaptiveness, and superior results. You may be an experienced manager, executive, engineer, or perhaps you are just starting to learn about or practice management. Your organization may have only a few people or it may have thousands. You are successful, but you want to be better and still relevant tomorrow.

With that in mind, here is my definition of *management*:

> *The systematic pursuit of desired conditions by utilizing human capabilities in a concerted way.*

Since we cannot know the future, it is impossible to say what sort of management systems we will be using then. However, precisely because we cannot see ahead we can argue the following: that an effective management system will be one that keeps an organization adjusting to unpredictable, dynamic conditions and satisfying customers. Situations may always be different from place to place and time to time, so we cannot specify in advance what should be the content of people's actions. Leading people to implementing specific solutions such as assembly cells, Six Sigma tools, *kanban*, diesel or hybrid power trains, today's high-margin product, and so on will not make an organization adaptive and continuously improving. Of greater interest is how people can sense and understand a situation, and react to it in a way that moves the organization forward.

One of the best examples we currently have of an adaptive, continuously improving company is Toyota. Of course, Toyota makes mistakes too, but so far no other company seems to improve and adapt—every day in all processes—as systematically, effectively, and continuously. Few companies achieve so many ambitious objectives, usually on time and within budget.

How Does Toyota Do It?

We have known for a long while that Toyota does something that makes it more capable of continuously improving than other companies, and by now we have recognized that it lies in its management approach. But how Toyota manages from day to day and thereby embeds continuous improvement and adaptation into and across the organization has not yet been explained.

That is about to change.

In the ongoing effort to understand and describe what Toyota is doing, most books provide lists of the organization's practices or principles. The individual points may all be correct, yet making lists circumvents explaining how Toyota manages people, and as our now 20 years of unsuccessfully trying emulate Toyota's success shows, such lists are not actionable. This is because an organization's collection of practices and principles at any point in time is an *outcome* that springs from its members' routines of thinking and behavior. Any organization's competitiveness, ability to adapt, and culture arise from the routines and habits by which the people in the organization conduct themselves every day. It is an issue of human behavior.

The evidence of the last 20 years indicates that trying to copy or reproduce another company's tools, techniques, or principles does little to change an organization's culture, its way of doing things. For example, how do you get people to actually live principles? On the other hand, focusing on developing daily behavior patterns *is* a leverage point because, as the field of psychology shows us, with practice, behavior patterns are changeable, learnable, and reproducible.

What has been missing, and the gap that *Toyota Kata* fills, is a look inside the engine room, that is, a clear explanation of daily behavior patterns at Toyota and how they are taught. By describing these underlying thinking and behavior routines, *Toyota Kata* establishes the context within which the Toyota practices previously observed and written about are developed and function. This gives us new power.

This book describes two particular behavior routines, habits or patterns of thinking and conducting oneself, that are practiced over and over every day at Toyota. In Japan such routines are called *kata.* These behavior patterns are not visible, are not described in Toyota documents, and it takes a long time to recognize them. Yet they are how Toyota leads and manages its people. These two kata are taught to all Toyota employees and are a big part of what propels that company as an adaptive and continuously improving organization. If you want to understand Toyota and emulate its success, then these kata, more than the company's techniques or principles, are what you should be studying. Toward that end, they are presented here for you.

Toyota's intention in using these kata is different enough from our management style that, from the perspective of our way of doing things, we do not immediately understand or see it. However, I think we are now close to a eureka or "lightbulb" moment, a different way of viewing, interpreting, and understanding what Toyota is doing. Once we understand how Toyota uses the two kata described in this book, there can be a shift in our perception that will enable us to progress further, because once we recognize the underlying pattern in how something works, the subject becomes easier to grasp. "The penny finally dropped and now I understand it." The kata presented here cannot be explained in just one chapter, but the penny eventually drops, and once you get it they are not so difficult to comprehend. This makes sense too, since Toyota would like everyone in the organization to practice and utilize them.

This Book Will Help You Get It

The new information that is presented here does not supplant what has already been written about Toyota, although it will require some adjustment in how we have thus far approached adopting "lean manufacturing." The objective is that you will gain a much more useful understanding of how Toyota manages to achieve continuous improvement and adaptiveness, which will tell you a lot about Toyota as a whole, and a clearer view of what it will take to develop such behavior patterns in a non-Toyota organization. To do that, we'll tackle two overarching questions:

1. What are the unseen managerial routines and thinking that lie behind Toyota's success with continuous improvement and adaptation?
2. How can other companies develop similar routines and thinking in their organizations?

This book presents behavior patterns at Toyota at a level where we are talking about psychology in organizations rather than just Toyota. Although the behavior routines presented here were discovered through research in production settings, they are universal and applicable in many different organizations, old or new, manufacturing or otherwise, from top to bottom. This is about a different and more effective way of managing people.

How I Learned

I have never been a Toyota employee and I have not worked in a Toyota facility. In retrospect this handicap turned out to be an advantage for two reasons:

1. I had to figure things out myself by trying them, by experimenting, in real factory and managerial settings.
2. After numerous iterations of experimentation I began to notice patterns of thinking and behavior that are different from our prevailing managerial routines. These are the differences that Toyota insiders tend to overlook because they lack points of comparison, and that Toyota visitors, observers, benchmarkers, and interviewers will not see at the surface.

Most of the findings in this book are based on hands-on experimentation and firsthand observation working with a great many organizations. This iterative "test it yourself" approach takes a lot of time but provides considerably deeper understanding and insight than can be gained through benchmarking or interviewing alone. The lessons here come from several years of:

- Applying certain technical and managerial Toyota practices in non-Toyota factory settings. This involved iterative trials, with particular attention paid to what did *not* work as intended, investigating why, adjusting accordingly, and trying again. This experimentation approach is referred to as Plan-Do-Check-Act (PDCA).
- Periodically visiting Toyota group sites and suppliers, and meeting with a variety of Toyota employees and former employees, in order to make observations and discuss recent findings.

The work involved a regular interplay between these two aspects of the research, with one potentially influencing the direction of the other as I went back and forth between them. To facilitate and support this reciprocation, I maintain and regularly update a written document, to reflect on what is being learned and what the next questions are. This document not only captures learning, it also ensures that communication is focused on facts and data as much as possible. You are, essentially, holding the current, civilian version (as of this writing) of that document in your hands. This is how I have been distilling out fundamental but not immediately visible aspects of Toyota's approach, what is behind the curtain, so to speak.

Note that Toyota does not utilize some of the terminology that is introduced here. To help us understand the way that Toyota people think and operate, I had to create some new terms. A Toyota employee may respond to a particular terminology with, "I don't know what that is," but they will work and behave as described here.

The five parts of this book mirror how the research unfolded.

- Part I sets the challenge of long-term organizational survival.
- In Part II we use that lens to examine how we are currently managing our organizations. This is important as preparation, because to comprehend what is different about Toyota's thinking and behavior routines, we first have to understand our own.
- This then leads to the next question: How should people in an organization act so that it will thrive long term? A big part of Toyota's answer to that question is what I call the "improvement kata," which is examined in detail and is the heart of the book. The penny should drop for you in Part III.
- But the improvement kata does not come to life in an organization simply because it is a good idea. The next logical question was: How does Toyota teach people improvement kata behavior? The answer is what I call Toyota's "coaching kata," which is described in Part IV.
- Finally, after presenting these two Toyota kata the question becomes: How do we develop improvement kata behavior in non-Toyota organizations? That is the subject of Part V, how other companies can develop their own kata to suit their own organizations, and of most of my current research.

The research cycle never ends, of course, which means this book reflects a level of understanding at a point in time. There is more to learn and there are undoubtedly some mistakes here. It is an interim report, as is any book, because nothing is the last word.

A final comment: The way of thinking and acting described here has a potential beyond the business world. It shows us a scientifically systematic and constructive way of dealing with problems, uncertainty, and change, in other words, how we can work together and achieve beyond what we can see. The more I studied Toyota, the more I became intrigued by the broader possibility of such life lessons, and I invite you to think about them too as you go through this book.

M.R.
Spring 2009
Ann Arbor, USA/Cologne, Germany

TOYOTA
KATA

Part I

The Situation

Chapter 1

What Defines a Company That Thrives Long Term?

The applause dies down as the next conference speaker approaches the podium. The presentation is going to be about Toyota, and in his first slide the speaker presents some impressive statistics that demonstrate Toyota's superior performance. The audience is nodding appreciatively.

For about two decades now this scene has been repeated countless times. So many books, articles, presentations, seminars, and workshops have begun with statistics about Toyota just like these:

- Toyota has shown *sales growth* for over 40 years, at the same time that U.S automakers' sales reached a plateau or decreased.
- Toyota's *profit* exceeds that of other automakers.
- Toyota's *market capitalization* has for years exceeded that of GM, Ford, and Chrysler; and in recent years exceeded that of all three combined.
- In *sales rank,* Toyota has become the world leader and risen to the number two position in the United States.

Of course, such statistics are interesting and useful in only one respect: they tell us that something different is happening at Toyota. The question then becomes: What is it?

How have we been doing at answering that second question? Not so well, it seems. Books and articles about Toyota-style practices started appearing in the mid 1980s. Learning from such writings, manufacturers have certainly made many improvements in quality and productivity. There is no question that our factories are better than they were 20 years ago. But after 15 to 20 years of trying to copy Toyota, we are unable to find *any* company outside of the Toyota group of companies that has been able to keep adapting and improving its quality and cost competitiveness as systematically, as effectively, and as continuously as Toyota. That is an interesting statistic too, and it represents a consensus among both Toyota insiders and Toyota observers.

Looking back, we naturally put Toyota's visible tools in focus first. That is where we started—the "door" through which we entered the Toyota topic. It was a step in the learning process (which will also, of course, continue after this book). Since then I went back to the research lab—several factories—to experiment further, and present what I learned in this book. The visible elements, tools, techniques, and even the principles of Toyota's production system have been benchmarked and described many times in great detail. But just copying these visible elements does not seem to work. Why? What is missing? Let's go into it.

We Have Been Trying to Copy the Wrong Things

What we have been doing is observing Toyota's current visible practices, classifying them into lists of elements and principles and then trying to adopt them. This is *reverse engineering*—taking an object apart to see how it works in order to replicate it—and it is not working so well. Here are three reasons.

1. Critical Aspects of Toyota Are Not Visible

Toyota's tools and techniques, the things you see, are built upon invisible routines of thinking and acting (Figure 1-1), particularly in management, that differ significantly from those found in most

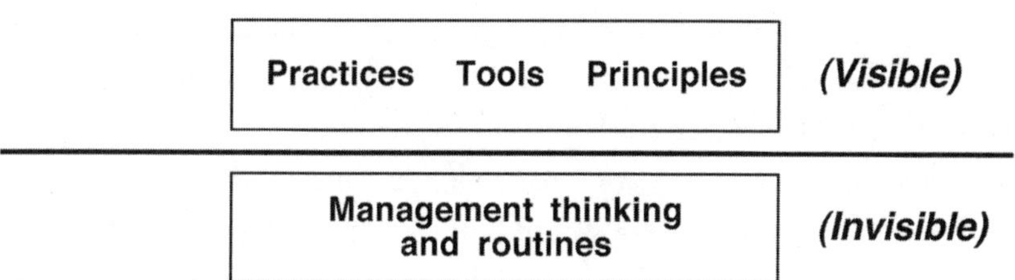

Figure 1-1. Toyota's visible tools and techniques are built upon invisible management thinking and routines

companies. We have been trying to add Toyota Production System practices and principles on top of our existing management thinking and practice without adjusting that thinking and practice. Toyota's techniques will not work properly, will not generate continuous improvement and adaptation, without Toyota's underlying logic, which lies beyond our view.

Interestingly, Toyota people themselves have had difficulty articulating and explaining to us their unique thinking and routines. In hindsight this seems to be because these are the customary, pervasive way of operating there, and many Toyota people—who are traditionally promoted from within—have few points of comparison. For example, if I ask you what you did today, you would tell me many things, but you would probably not mention "breathing." As a consequence, we cannot interview people at Toyota and expect to gain, from that alone, the deeper understanding we seek.

2. Reverse Engineering Does Not Make an Organization Adaptive and Continuously Improving

Toyota opens its factory doors to us again and again, but I imagine Toyota's leaders may also be shaking their heads and thinking, "Sure, come have a look. But why are you so interested in the solutions we develop for our specific problems? Why do you never study how we go about developing those solutions?" Since the future lies beyond what we can see, the solutions we employ today may not continue to be effective. The competitive advantage of an organization lies not so much in the solutions themselves—whether lean techniques, today's profitable product, or any other—but in the ability of the organization to understand conditions and create fitting, smart solutions.

Focusing on solutions does not make an organization adaptive. For example, several years ago a friend of mine visited a Toyota factory in Japan and observed that parts were presented to production-line operators in "flow racks." Wherever possible the different part configurations for different vehicle types were all in the flow racks. This way an operator could simply pick the appropriate part to fit the particular vehicle passing down the assembly line in front of him or her, which allows mixed-model assembly without the necessity of changing parts in the racks. Many of us have been copying this idea for several years now.

When my friend recently returned to the same factory, he found that many of the flow racks along that Toyota assembly line were gone and had been replaced with a different approach. Many of the parts for a vehicle are now put into a "kit" that travels along with the vehicle as it moves down the assembly line. When the vehicle is in an operator's workstation, the operator only sees those parts, and she always reaches to the same position to get the part.

My friend was a little upset and asked his Toyota hosts, "So tell me, what is the right approach? Which is better, flow racks or kitting?" The Toyota hosts did not understand his question, and their response was, "When you were in our factory a few years ago we produced four different models on this assembly line. Today we produce eight different models on the same line, and keeping all those different part variations in the flow racks was no longer workable. Besides, we try to keep moving closer to a one-by-one flow. Whenever you visit us, you are simply looking at a solution we developed for a particular situation at a particular point in time."

As we conducted benchmarking studies in the 1980's and 90's and tried to explain the reasons for the manufacturing performance gap between Toyota and other automobile companies, we saw at Toyota the now familiar "lean" techniques such as kanban, cellular manufacturing, short changeovers, andon lights, and so on. Many concluded—and

I initially did too—that these new production techniques and the fact that Western industry was still relying on old techniques were the primary reasons for Toyota's superior performance.

However, inferring that there has been a technological inflection point is a kind of "benchmarking trap," which arises because benchmarking studies are done at a point in time. Our benchmarking did not scrutinize Toyota's admittedly less visible inner workings, nor the long and gradual slope of its productivity improvement over the prior decades. As a result, those studies did not establish cause and effect. The key point was not the new production techniques themselves, but rather that Toyota changes over time, that it develops new production techniques while many other manufacturers do not. As Michael Cusumano showed in his 1985 book, *The Japanese Automobile Industry,* Toyota's assembly plant productivity had already begun to inch ahead of U.S. vehicle assembly plant productivity as far back as the early 1960s! And it kept growing.

Beyond benchmarking, a deeper look inside Toyota did not take place until Steven Spear conducted research at Toyota for his Harvard Business School doctoral dissertation, which was published in 1999. It describes how Toyota's superior results spring more from routines of continuous improvement via experimentation than from the tools and practices that benchmarkers had seen. Spear pointed out that many of those tools and practices are, in fact, countermeasures developed out of Toyota's continuous improvement routines, which was one of the impulses for the research that led to this book.

3. Trying to Reverse Engineer Puts Us in an Implementing Mode

Implementing is a word we often use in a positive sense, but—believe it or not—having an implementation orientation actually impedes our organization's progress and the development of people's capabilities. We will not be successful in the Toyota style until we adopt more of a do-it-yourself problem-solving mode. Let me use an example to explain what I mean by an implementation versus a problem-solving mode.

During a three-day workshop at a factory in Germany, we spent the first two days learning about what Toyota is doing. On the third day we then turned our attention to the subject of how do we wish to proceed? During that part of the workshop, a participant raised her hand and spoke up. "During the last two days you painted a clear picture of what Toyota is doing. However, now that we are trying to figure out what we want to do, the way ahead is unclear. I am very dissatisfied with this."

My response was, "That is exactly how it is supposed to be." But this answer did not make the workshop participant happy, which led me to drawing the diagram in Figure 1-2.

There are perhaps only three things we can and need to know with certainty: where we are, where we want to be, and by what *means* we should maneuver the unclear territory between here and there. And the rest is supposed to be somewhat unclear, because we cannot see into the future! The way from where we are to where we want to be next is a gray zone full of unforeseeable obstacles, problems, and issues that we can only discover along the way. The best we can do is to know the approach, the means, we can utilize for dealing with the unclear path to a new desired condition, not what the content and steps of our actions—the solutions—will be.

That is what I mean in this book when I say *continuous improvement and adaptation*: the ability to move toward a new desired state

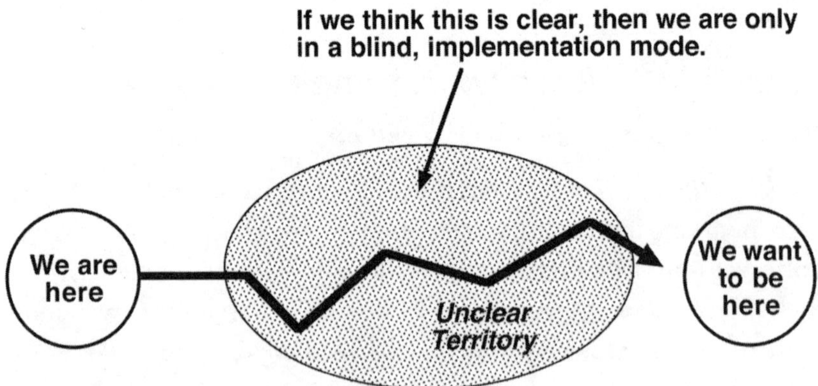

Figure 1-2. The implementation mode is unrealistic

through an unclear and unpredictable territory by being sensitive to and responding to actual conditions on the ground.

Like the workshop participant in Germany, humans have a tendency to want certainty, and even to artificially create it, based on beliefs, when there is none. This is a point where we often get into trouble. If we believe the way ahead is set and clear, then we tend to blindly carry out a preconceived implementation plan rather than being sensitive to, learning from, and dealing adequately with what arises along the way. As a result, we do not reach the desired destination at all, despite our best intentions.

If someone claims certainty about the steps that will be implemented to reach a desired destination, that should be a red flag to us. Uncertainty is normal—the path cannot be accurately predicted—and so how we deal with that is of paramount importance, and where we can derive our certainty and confidence. I can give you a preview of the rest of this book by pointing out that true certainty and confidence do not lie in preconceived implementation steps or solutions, which may or may not work as intended, but in understanding the logic and method for how to proceed through unclear territory.

How do we get through that territory? By what means can we go beyond what we can see? What is management's role in this?

What Is the Situation?

As most of us know, the following describes the environment in which many of our organizations find themselves.

- *Although they may seem steady state, conditions both outside and inside the organization are always changing.* The process of evolution and change is always going on in your environment, whether you notice it or not. The shift may at times be so slow or subtle that your way of doing things does not show up as a problem until it is late. Try looking at it this way: if your working life was suddenly 100 years long instead of 35, would you still expect conditions to remain unchanged all that time?
- *It is impossible for us to predict how those conditions will develop.* Try as we might, humans do not have the capability to see the future.

The future is fundamentally different than it appears through the prospectiscope.

—Daniel Gilbert, *Stumbling on Happiness*

- *If you fall behind your competitors, it is generally not possible to catch up quickly or in a few leaps.* If there was something we could do, or implement, to get caught up again quickly, then our competitors will be doing that too.

The implication is that if we want our organization to thrive for a long time, then how it interacts with conditions inside and outside the company is important. There is no "finish line" mentality. The objective is not to win, but to develop the capability of the organization to keep improving, adapting, and satisfying dynamic customer requirements. This capability for continuous, incremental evolution and improvement represents perhaps the best assurance of durable competitive advantage and company survival. Why?

Small, incremental steps let us learn along the way, make adjustments, and discover the path to where we want to be. Since we cannot see very far ahead, we cannot rely on up front planning alone. Improvement, adaptation, and even innovation result to a great extent from the accumulation of small steps; each lesson learned helps us recognize the next step and adds to our knowledge and capability.

Relying on technical innovation alone often provides only temporary competitive advantage. Technological innovations are important and offer competitive advantage, but they come infrequently and can often be copied by competitors. In many cases we cannot expect to enjoy more than a brief technological advantage over competitors. Technological innovation is also arguably less the product of revolutionary breakthroughs by single individuals than the cumulative result of many incremental adaptations that have been pointed in a particular direction and conducted with special focus and energy.

Cost and quality competitiveness tend to result from accumulation of many small steps over time. Again, if one could simply implement some measures to achieve cost and quality competitiveness, then every company would do it. Cost and quality improvements are actually made in small steps and take considerable time to achieve and accumulate. The results of continual cost reduction and quality improvement are therefore difficult to copy, and thus offer a special competitive advantage. It is highly advantageous for a company in a competitive environment to combine efforts at innovation with unending continuous improvement of cost and quality competitiveness, even in the case of mature products.

Relying on periodic improvements and innovations alone—only improving when we make a special effort or campaign—conceals a system that is static and vulnerable. Here is an interesting point to consider about your own organization: in many cases the normal operating condition of an organization—its nature—is *not improving*.

Many of us think of improvement as something that happens periodically, like a project or campaign: we make a special effort to improve or change when the need becomes urgent. But this is not how continuous improvement, adaptation, and sustained competitive advantage actually come about. Relying on periodic improvement or change efforts should be seen for what it is: only an occasional add-on to a system that by its nature tends to stand still.

The president of a well-known company once told me, "We are continuously improving, because in every one of our factories there is a *kaizen* workshop occurring every week." When I asked how many processes there are in each of those factories he said, "Forty to fifty." This means that each process gets focused improvement attention approximately once a year. This is not bad, and Toyota utilizes kaizen workshops too, but it is not the same thing as continuous improvement. Many companies say, "We are continually improving," but mean that every week some process somewhere in the company is being improved in some way. We should be clear:

Projects and workshops ≠ continuous improvement

Let's agree on a definition of continuous improvement: it means that you are improving all processes every day. At Toyota the improvement process occurs in every process (activity) and at every level of the company every day. And this improvement continues even if the

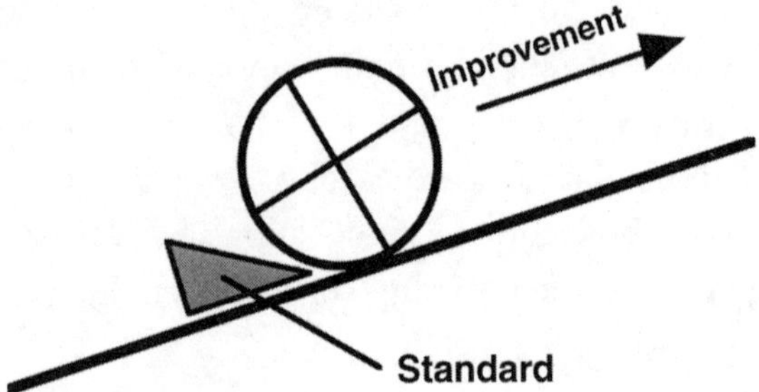

Figure 1-3. Standards depicted as a wedge that prevent backsliding. It doesn't work this way.

numbers have already been met. Of course, from day to day improvement may involve small steps.

We cannot leave a process alone and expect high quality, low cost, and stability. A popular concept is that we can utilize standards to maintain a process condition (Figure 1-3).

However, it is generally not possible simply to *maintain* a level of process performance. A process will tend to erode no matter what, even if a standard is defined, explained to everyone, and posted. This is not because of poor discipline by workers (as many of us may believe), but due to interaction effects and entropy, which says than any organized process naturally tends to decline to a chaotic state if we leave it alone (I am indebted to Mr. Ralph Winkler for pointing out to me the second law of thermodynamics). Here is what happens.

In every factory, small problems naturally occur every day in each production process—the test machine requires a retest, there is some machine downtime, bad parts, a sticky fixture, and so on—and the operators must find ways to deal with these problems and still make the required production quantity. The operators only have time to quickly fix or work around the problems, not to dig into, understand, and eliminate causes. Soon extra inventory buffers, work-arounds, and even extra people naturally creep into the process, which, although introduced with good intention, generates even more variables, fluctuation, and problems. In many factories management has grown accustomed to this situation, and it has become the accepted mode of operating. Yet we accuse the operators of a lack of discipline. In fact, the operators are doing their best and the problem lies in the system—for which management is responsible.

The point is that a process is either slipping back or being improved, and the best and perhaps only way to prevent slipping back is to keep trying to move forward, even if only in small steps. Furthermore, in competitive markets treading water would mean falling behind if competitors are improving. Just sustaining, if it were possible, would in that case still equal slipping.

> *Quality of a product does not necessarily mean high quality. It means continual improvement of the process, so that the consumer may depend on the uniformity of a product and purchase it at a low cost.*
>
> —W. Edwards Deming, 1980

Finding Our Way into the Future

By What Means Can Organizations Be Adaptive?

While nonhuman species are subject to natural selection—that is, natural selection acts upon them—humans and human organizations have at least the potential to adapt consciously. All organizations are probably to some degree adaptive, but their improvement and adaptation are typically only periodic and conducted by specialists. In other words, such organizations are not by their nature adaptive. As a consequence, many organizations leave a considerable amount of inherent human potential untapped.

How do we achieve adaptiveness? What do we need to focus on?

Although we have tended to believe that production techniques like cellular manufacturing and kanban, or some special principles, are the source of Toyota's competitive advantage, the most important factor that makes Toyota successful is the skill and actions of all the people in the organization. As I see it now, this is the primary differentiator between Toyota and other companies. It is an issue of human behavior.

So now we arrive at the subject of managing people.

Humans possess an astounding capability to learn, create, and solve problems. Toyota's ability to continuously improve and adapt lies in the actions and reactions of the people in the firm, in their ability to effectively understand situations and develop smart solutions. Toyota considers the improvement capability of all the people in an organization the "strength" of a company.

From this perspective, then, it is better for an organization's adaptiveness, competitiveness, and survival to have a large group of people systematically, methodically, making many small steps of improvement every day rather than a small group doing periodic big projects and events.

> *Toyota has long considered its ability to permanently resolve problems and then improve stable processes as one of the company's competitive advantages. With an entire workforce charged with solving their workplace problems the power of the intellectual capital of the company is tremendous.*
>
> —Kathi Hanley, statement as a group leader at TMMK

How Can We Utilize People's Capabilities?

Ideally we would utilize the human intellect of everyone in the organization to move it beyond forces of natural selection and make it consciously adaptive. However, our human instincts and judgment are highly variable, subjective, and even irrational. If you ask five people, "What do we need to do here?" you will get six different answers. Furthermore, the environment is too dynamic, complex, and nonlinear for anyone to accurately predict more than just a short while ahead. How, then, can we utilize the capability of people for our organization's improvement and evolution if we cannot rely on human judgment?

If an organization wants to thrive by continually improving and evolving, then it needs systematic procedures and routines—methods—that channel our human capabilities and achieve the potential. Such routines would guide and support everyone in the organization by giving them a specific pattern for how they should go about sensing, adapting, and improving.

Toyota has a method, or means, to do exactly that. At Toyota, improvement and adaptation *are* systematic and the method is a fundamental component of every task performed, not an add-on or a special initiative. Everyone at Toyota is taught to operate in this standard way, and it is applied to almost every situation. This goes well beyond just problem-solving techniques, to encompass a firm-specific behavior routine. Developing and maintaining this behavior in the organization, then, is what defines the task of management.

My definition of *management:*

The systematic pursuit of desired conditions by utilizing human capabilities in a concerted way.

Upon closer inspection, Toyota's way, as it is sometimes called, is characterized less by its tools or principles than by sets of procedural sequences—thinking and behavior patterns—that when repeated over and over in daily work lead to the desired outcome. These patterns are the context within which Toyota's tools and principles are developed and function. If there is one thing to look at in trying to understand and perhaps emulate Toyota's success, then these behavior patterns and how they are taught may well be it.

Kata

In Japan such patterns or routines are called *kata* (noun). The word stems from basic forms of movement in martial arts, which are handed down from master to student over generations. Some common translations or definitions are:

- A way of doing something; a method or routine
- A pattern
- A standard form of movement
- A predefined, or choreographed, sequence of movements

- The customary procedure
- A training method or drill

Digging deeper, there is a further definition and translation for the word:

- A way of keeping two things in alignment or synchronization with one another

Eureka! This last definition is of particular interest with regard to the dynamic conditions that exist outside and inside a company (Figure 1-4). It suggests that although conditions are always changing in unpredictable ways, an organization can have a method, a kata, for dealing with that. This is an interesting prospect. Such a method would connect the organization to current circumstances in the world, inside the organization, and in its work processes, and help it stay in sync—in harmony—with those circumstances. A key concept underlying kata is that while we often cannot exercise much control over the realities around us, we can exercise control over—manage—how we deal with them.

Kata are different from production techniques in that they pertain specifically to the behavior of people and are much more universally applicable. The kata described in this book are not limited to manufacturing or even to business organizations.

Kata are also different from principles. The purpose of a principle is to help us make a choice, a decision, when we are confronted with

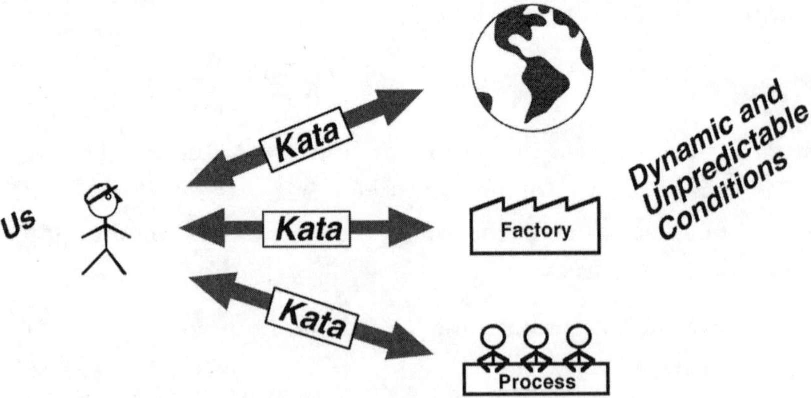

Figure 1-4. A kata is a means for keeping your thoughts and actions in sync with dynamic, unpredictable conditions

options, like *customer first,* or *pull, don't push.* However, a principle does not tell us how to do something; how to proceed, and what steps to take. That is what a kata does. Principles are developed out of repeated action, and concerted repeated action is what a kata guides you into. Toyota's kata are at a deeper level and precede principles.

What, then, might be some attributes of a behavior form, a kata, that is utilized for continuous improvement and adaptation?

- The method would operate, in particular, at the process level. Whether in nature or in a human organization, improvement and adaptation seem to take place at the detail or process level. We can and need to think and plan on higher levels, like about eliminating hunger or developing a profitable small car, but the changes that ultimately lead to improvement or adaptation are often detail changes based on lessons learned in processes.

> It is finally becoming apparent to historians that important changes in manufacturing often take place gradually as the result of many small improvements.
>
> Historians of technology and industrial archeologists must look beyond the great inventors and the few revolutionary developments in manufacturing; they must look at the incremental innovations created year after year not only in the drafting room and the mind of the engineer but also on the shop floor and in "the heart of the machinist." Maybe then we will begin to learn about the normal process of technological change.
>
> —Patrick M. Malone, Ph.D., Brown University[1]

- If the objective is to improve in every process every day, then the kata would be embedded in and made inseparable from the daily work in those processes. The kata would become how we work through our day.
- Since humans do not possess the ability to predict what is coming, the method that generates improvement and adaptation

Figure 1-5. Two fundamental Toyota kata

would be content neutral; that is, it would be applicable in any situation. The method, the procedure, is prescribed, but the content is not.

- Since human judgment is not accurate or impartial, the method would, wherever possible, rely on facts rather than opinions or judgments. In other words it would be depersonalized.
- The method for improvement would continue beyond the tenure of any one leader. Everyone in the organization would operate according to the method, regardless of who is in charge at the moment.

In this book we will examine in detail what are perhaps Toyota's two most fundamental kata (Figure 1-5). One I call the *improvement kata* (Part III), which is the repeating routine by which Toyota improves, adapts, and evolves. The improvement kata exactly fits the attributes spelled out above and provides a highly effective model for how people can work together; that is, how to manage an organization. The second I call the *coaching kata* (Part IV), which is the repeating routine by which Toyota leaders and managers teach the improvement kata to everyone in the organization.

The Management Challenge

Based on what I have been learning, the challenge we face is not to turn the heads of executives and managers toward implementing new production or management techniques or adopting new principles, but to achieving systematic continuous evolution and improvement across the organization by developing repeatedly and consistently applied behavioral routines: kata. Note that this challenge is significantly different than what we have been working on so far in our lean implementation efforts, and is primarily an issue of how we manage and lead people. Some adjustment in how we have been trying to adopt "lean manufacturing" will be necessary.

Before we go on I should mention that the idea of standardized behavioral routines often generates a prognosis that they will disable our creativity and limit our potential. What if, however, we can be even more creative, competitive, smart, out-of-the-box, and successful precisely *because* we have a routine that does a better job of tapping and channeling our human capabilities? A difference lies in what we define as the routine. Notably, Toyota's improvement kata does not specify a content—it cannot—since that varies from time to time and situation to situation, but instead only the form that our thinking and behavior should take as we react to a situation.

Humans derive a lot of their sense of security and confidence—what psychologist Albert Bandura calls "self-efficacy," from predictable routines: from doing things the same way again and again. However, it's not possible for the content of what we do to stay the same, and if we try to artificially maintain it, it causes problems, because we are then adjusting to reality far too late and in a jerky manner. Any organization whose members can face unpredictable and uncertain situations (which are the norm) with confidence and effective action, because they have learned a behavioral routine for doing that, can enjoy a competitive advantage.

Toyota's improvement kata is an excellent example of this second kind of routine. It tells us how to proceed, but not the content, and thus gives members of the organization an approach, a means, for handling an infinite variety of situations and being successful. We may be standing before a different way of operating our organizations, which can take us toward nearly any achievement we might envision.

But to see that, we have to grasp the current situation: how we are managing our organizations today.

Notes

1. Patrick M. Malone, Ph.D. (Associate Professor, American Civilization and Urban Studies, Brown University), "Little Kinks and Devices at Springfield Armory, 1982–1918," *Journal of the Society for Industrial Archeology*, vol. 14, no. 1, 1988.

Part II

Know Yourself

Introduction to Part II

One of the most difficult things to see is our presuppositions, our instincts and reflexes, and the contexts within which we operate that create them. What is our current thinking? Where does it come from? How do we tend to act as a result? What are the effects?

Understanding this gives us a point of comparison, a contrast, that puts us in a better position to perceive what Toyota is doing and to be more conscious designers of how we want our organizations to function. That is the purpose of Part II.

Chapter 2

How Are We Approaching Process Improvement?

As mentioned near the end of the last chapter, improvement and adaptation are critical success factors and tend to take place at the process level. How, then, are we currently trying to improve our processes? Based on observations in many factories, I currently find these main approaches: workshops, value-stream mapping, and, above all, action-item lists.

Workshops

Improvement workshops are special improvement efforts that temporarily bring together a team of people to focus on a particular process. The duration of a workshop is typically one to five days. Workshops are used extensively and do have their place. Toyota utilizes workshops too, for example, but not as its primary means of improving and adapting.

As discussed in Chapter 1, project-style improvement efforts only occur at any one process occasionally, not continuously, and involve a specially formed team. Thus, by definition, workshops are not at all the same as continuous improvement. In regard to workshops, it is also interesting to note that:

- Conducting a one- to five-day improvement workshop does not require any particular managerial approach. You can easily run a kaizen workshop without having to adjust the prevailing custom. This may explain some of the popularity of workshops.
- Since the workshop team moves on or is disbanded after a workshop ends, we have to expect that entropy will naturally begin eroding the gains that have been made.

Value-Stream Mapping

This highly useful tool looks at the flow of material and information, and the associated lead time, across multiple processes. However, the lead time through a value stream is an *outcome* that is correlated with inventory, and inventory in turn is an *outcome* that results from performance attributes of the individual processes in the value stream. Therefore, if you want to reduce lead time, you should improve processes.

As mentioned in the previous chapter, much of the mechanism of continuous improvement and adaptation takes place at individual processes. For example, applying the improvement kata at the process level—one level deeper than the value stream—is something you would do after drawing a value-stream map (see Figure 2-1).

Value-stream mapping is not intended to be a method for process improvement, but rather a method to help ensure that process-level improvement efforts:

- Fit together from process to process so that a flowing value stream is developed
- Match with the organization's targets
- Serve the requirements of external customers

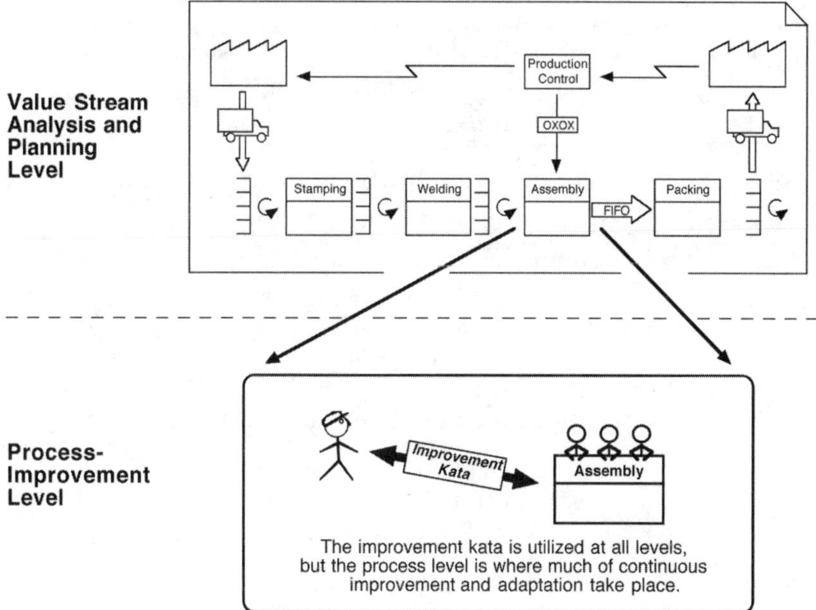

Figure 2-1. Value stream and process levels

If we try to rely on value-stream mapping as a method for process improvement, then the following negative effects may arise:

- A value-stream map can reveal so many improvement potentials at so many places that it is hard to know what needs to be done. Attacking problems here and there in the value stream, rather than focusing on and pursuing specific process-level target conditions, dilutes our improvement capacity by scattering it piecemeal across the value stream.
- As useful and necessary as value-stream maps are, they still focus more on the surface and thus do not develop our capability to see deeply into the real situation at the processes.

It is more effective to use value-stream mapping for keeping an eye on the overall picture, and to step into the process level with the improvement kata as described in Part III.

What happened to suggestion systems? Enthusiasm around suggestion systems seems to have died down. I currently do not find much going on with them at manufacturing facilities.

We often hear about the relatively high number of suggestions per employee and high number of implemented suggestions at Toyota, but we are not comparing apples to apples. Toyota production operators work with a team leader who follows the improvement kata. Within that framework, team leaders are also expected to actively obtain a certain number of suggestions from their team members. Furthermore, the team leader also helps team members fine-tune their suggestions, via mentoring, before they are submitted. This is very different from simply installing a suggestion box, so to speak, and actually has a different purpose. More on this in Chapter 7.

The Action-Item List

Based on my observations, the action-item list is currently *by far* our most widely used approach for process improvement. You find managers and engineers relying on them in nearly every factory. The approach is so widespread that it needs almost no explaining, although many of us have probably not yet realized that we are using such lists as an *approach*.

An action-item list is a listing of multiple improvement ideas and action items to be implemented at a process. The lists are sometimes called "open points lists" and appear in various forms, such as on flip-chart sheets, cards, or on whiteboards (see Figure 2-2). The action items on the lists originate from recording process problems, brainstorming, problem-solving activities, waste walks, value-stream mapping, and so on. Although we may believe that those uptake activities—like waste walks or problem-solving activities—constitute our improvement approach, all of them merge into the same thing: a list of action items. And it is with those lists that we actually try to manage the improvement process.

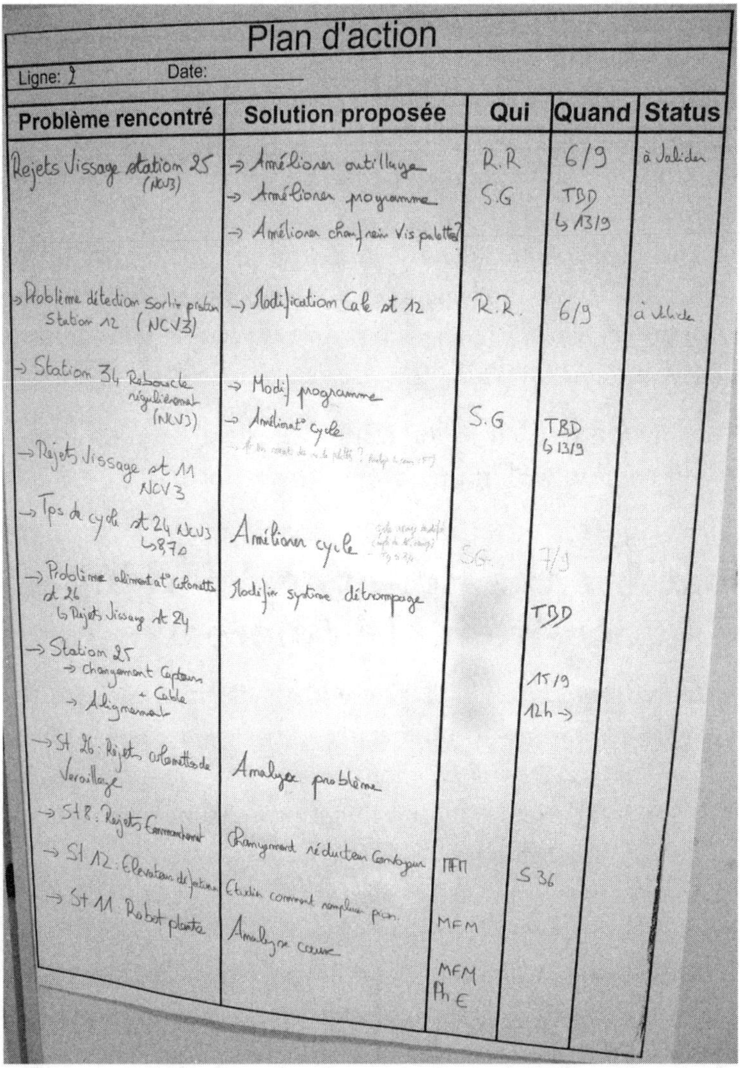

Figure 2-2. An action-item list on a factory floor in France

In short, the list approach is done as follows:

1. When people visit a production process, they make good point observations. We have clearly internalized what is waste and are able to spot plenty of problems, wastes, and opportunities for improvement.

2. With few exceptions we turn such observations into lists of several action items.
3. There may be a prioritizing or ranking of items by, for example, voting or estimating benefits.
4. Action items are assigned to persons or teams, and due dates are established.
5. The manager then focuses on who is to do what by when. Regular review meetings are scheduled, for example on a weekly or biweekly basis, to check if people are carrying out on time the action items for which they are responsible.

To convince yourself of the truth of these observations, this may be a good point to walk through your own factory.

What Are the Results of Working with the Action-Item List Approach?

1. *It doesn't work very well.* The underlying thinking with the list approach appears to be that *the more action items we have, the more the process will be improved.* The longer the lists of action items and the more improvement projects under way, the more we feel like something positive is happening. In many cases, however, the opposite is true. There may appear to be a lot of motion, but there is little progress.

   Once you finish Part III of this book you will be able to see that the list approach is an unscientific and ineffective method for process improvement. It is in actuality a scattershot approach: multiple action items are initiated in the hope of hitting something. Although few people admit it, surprisingly little cost and quality improvement is generated via the list approach. The negligible results it produces can be observed in the lack of progress—in the wasteful and unstable processes that persist on factory floors everywhere. In many cases the scattershot list approach creates even more, not less, variability and instability in a process.

Upon closer inspection, many of the cost reductions companies talk about come from cutting resources or moving production to low-wage locations rather than truly improving the way a process operates; that is, improving how things are done. And many of the quality improvements people talk about are improvements in *delivered* quality, achieved by increasing inspection and sorting out more defects rather than improving the process to reduce the number of defects created.

2. *We are in the dark.* Defining and introducing several action items simultaneously, and sometimes even voting to prioritize them, indicates that we don't know what we need to do to improve. It would be better to simply stop and say *we don't yet know what exactly to do.* "I don't know" is a completely acceptable answer and much preferable to pretending we do know, but this seems to be one of the hardest things to say.
3. *We are asking ourselves the wrong question.* When we hunt for wastes or opportunities to improve and make a list of action items, we are focusing on the question, "What *can* we do to improve?" That question is actually too easy, and it automatically leads us to lists and a scattershot approach. The more focused question is, "What do we *need* to do to improve this process?" Admittedly, this is a more difficult question.

   Here's an example of what I mean. A large auto-parts manufacturer was training four young engineers to begin work in the company's supplier development department. As part of this training, each engineer was sent to a different supplier factory to conduct an analysis and make a report.

   Three of the engineers returned with lists of 30 to 40 improvement ideas to implement at the factory they visited. The fourth engineer, however, returned with only 8 suggestions for improvement. The head of the supplier development department was angry with the fourth engineer, saying, "Your colleagues found 30 to 40 opportunities for improvement and you only have 8? I think you need to go back and look again."

Interestingly, the better response by the boss would have been exactly the opposite. He would say to the three engineers: "Anyone can make a long list of things we can improve and hope that something in that list will work. Please go back, look again, and tell me just the one, two, or three things that we need to do now to begin the improvement process at the supplier site."

It is much more difficult to see deeply and understand what we *need* to do.

4. *We are jumping to countermeasures too soon.* A weakness in the list approach is a tendency to jump to countermeasures before we understand a situation (Figure 2-3). Generating a list of action items and implementing several countermeasures, often simultaneously, reflects an unspoken goal of, essentially, *just shut off the problem!* People are rewarded for fixing a problem, for firefighting, not for analyzing, even though the problem may recur later because it was not yet sufficiently understood.

   In contrast, Toyota's goal in process improvement is to learn; to develop an ever deeper understanding of the work process and to improve the process from that basis.

   When you throw several countermeasures at a process, the problem sometimes does go away. This is often not because the causes have been discovered and eliminated, but because of the extra attention the process has received. Sometime later the same problem returns—well after the improvement success was celebrated.

5. *We are not developing our people's capabilities.* The list approach does not harness or grow our problem solving and improvement capability in a very effective manner.

Figure 2-3. The tendency is to jump right from a problem to possible solutions

Why Does the List Approach Persist?

The bottom line is that we are wasting a lot of time with the action-item list approach. Yet if it is not very effective as a method for managing process improvement, why does it persist? Why do we tend to create such lists again and again?

One probable reason, already mentioned, is the erroneous feeling that the more action items we have, the more improvement we have. Another reason may be that managers find it convenient to fit the list approach and regularly scheduled reviews of action-item assignments into existing work schedules. For everyone involved, the list approach provides a way to feel engaged in improvement activity without having to alter their current work routines very much.

The list approach also provides a way to avoid receiving blame. We can say, "I completed my action items on time," and thereby fulfill our obligations without necessarily having to generate real process improvement. The objective becomes to carry out the action items for which I am responsible, not the improvement itself. If the desired results do not come, it is not my fault, because I did what I agreed to do.

It has also been suggested to me that long lists of opportunities or action items may be regarded as a reflection of how observant or smart we are.

There Is a More Effective Way to Improve

Not only is the list-oriented improvement approach not very effective, it also makes improvement too complicated and difficult.

To see what I mean, consider that Toyota teaches people to try to change only one thing at a time, and then to check the result against the expected result. You may work on several things simultaneously, but if possible do not change more than one thing at any one time in a process. Such "single-factor experiments" are preferred because Toyota wants its people to see and understand cause and effect, which helps to develop a deeper understanding of the work processes. Studying this Toyota improvement tactic leads to some interesting discoveries:

- Whenever we alter any one thing in a process, we create, in effect, a new process with possibly new and different characteristics. This means that once we have implemented one or two items from an action-item list, then the rest of the items on that predefined list *may no longer suit the new situation and new priorities at the process*. Are you beginning to see how making scattershot lists of action items is a waste of time?
- Multifactor experiments (known as Design of Experiments, or DOE) where multiple variables are changed at once are sometimes necessary, but only a small group of specialists is qualified to conduct them. Ideally we want everyone in the organization involved in continuous improvement, and single-factor experiments are something that anyone can understand and carry out.
- If I tell you that you should, if possible, only change one thing at a time in a process, how does that make you feel?
    - Yes, it seems way too slow.

    Yet we know that Toyota is improving faster than other companies. So what does this mean for our cycles in an only-change-one-thing-at-a-time approach?
    - They must be fast!

    In other words, with Toyota's approach, we cannot wait for the next scheduled weekly or biweekly review cycle to come around. If we wait that long to check, then our progress will be too slow. By the time we do check the process, the parameters may have shifted. We should check the results of a change as soon as possible and then, based on what we learn, consider the next steps. Unlike our current workshop and list-oriented approach to process improvement, this one does have implications for how managers, engineers, and executives slice up their work days.

Improvement is hard work, but it doesn't have to be too complicated. After studying Toyota's improvement kata in Part III, you are likely to call a stop to and reorient any improvement effort that relies on the list approach. Instead you will know that there is a better way to proceed and lead.

Chapter 3

Philosophy and Direction

To understand Toyota's improvement kata and coaching kata we need to consider two aspects of the context within which they operate: the business philosophy, or purpose, of the company; and its overall sense of direction.

The Company's Business Philosophy

The business philosophy of a company does much to define the thoughts and actions of everyone in the organization. However, by "business philosophy" I do not mean those nice, generic statements printed on the poster in the lobby. I mean if you stood in the factory for a day and observed what people do—what is important to them, what gets measured—then what would you conclude is important to this company? As they say at Toyota, "The shop floor is a reflection of management."

For many manufacturers the company philosophy or purpose would boil down to something like the statement in Figure 3-1.

Many manufacturers:

"Make good products for the customer."

Figure 3-1. A typical company philosophy

Toyota:

"Survive long term as a company by improving and evolving how we make good products for the customer."

Figure 3-2. Toyota philosophy

And this is not bad by any means. But consider Toyota's philosophy in comparison (Figure 3-2).

While this sounds similar to the first philosophy, there is a significant difference. Notice the position of improvement and adaptation in each case. In the first philosophy, improvement and adaptation are an add-on; something we do when there is time or a special need. In the second philosophy, improvement and adaptation move to the center. They are what we do.

Along these lines, here are a few questions to help you think about the position of improvement in your organization. Only you can answer them for yourself:

- Do I view improvement as legitimate work, or as an add-on to my real job?
- Is improvement a periodic, add-on project (a campaign), or the core activity?
- Is it acceptable in our company to work on improvement occasionally?

The last question, in particular, can make things clear. Imagine you were to walk into a manager's office and say, "We made a nice improvement in process X . . . and next month we will take another look at improving that process further." That would probably be acceptable. Now imagine that you said, "We produced 400 pieces of product at process X today . . . and next month we will take a look at producing some more product at that process." That would not be acceptable at all! And so we can see the relative position that improvement has in our company. If your business philosophy is to improve, then periodic improvement projects or kaizen workshops are okay but not enough. You would only be working on your organization's core objective occasionally, during periodic events.

At Toyota, improving and managing are one and the same. The improvement kata in Part III is to a considerable degree how Toyota manages its processes and people from day to day. In comparison, non-Toyota companies tend to see managing as a unique and separate activity. Improvement is something extra, added on to managing.

Non-Toyota thinking:	normal daily management + improvement
Toyota thinking:	normal daily management = process improvement

An interesting point is that many of us would probably be afraid to focus so heavily on the second philosophy, improvement, at the expense of the first philosophy, make production. We would feel we were letting go of something we currently try very hard to control, because we're accustomed to focusing on outcomes, not process details. In our current management approach we concentrate on outcome targets and consequences. In contrast, as depicted in Figure 3-3, Toyota puts considerable emphasis on how people tackle the details of a process, which is what generates the outcomes.

Outcome targets, such as the desired production quantity, are of course necessary. But if you focus on continuously improving the process—systematically, through the improvement kata, rather than

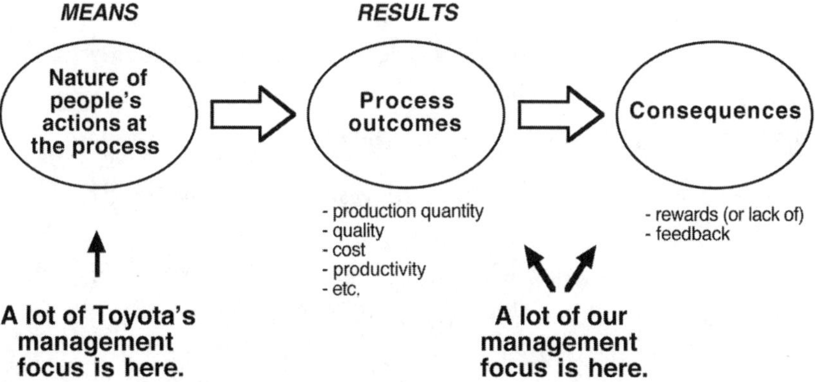

Figure 3-3. Focusing on means in order to achieve desired results

just random improvement—then the desired outcomes will come. Making the desired production quantity, for example, will happen automatically when you focus on the details of a process through correct application of the improvement kata.

The following story from before the Second World War, when Toyota made weaving looms, provides an example of this way of thinking. It comes from a Toyota booklet about the spirit and ideas that created the company, and relates how Kiichiro Toyoda (1894–1952), founder of the Toyota Motor Corporation and son of Toyoda Automatic Loom Works founder Sakichi Toyoda, supposedly responded when someone once stole the design plans for a loom from the Toyoda loom works:

> *Certainly the thieves may be able to follow the design plans and produce a loom. But we are modifying and improving our looms every day. So by the time the thieves have produced a loom from the plans they stole, we will have already advanced well beyond that point. And because they do not have the expertise gained from the failures it took to produce the original, they will waste a great deal more time than us as they move to improve their loom. We need not be concerned about what happened. We need only continue as always, making our improvements.*[1]

Does a lean value stream equal lean manufacturing?

Many years ago I visited a small automobile-component factory that ostensibly operated with a lean strategy. And, in fact, the plant sported a fairly short lead time through its value stream. Its strategy involved the following elements:

- Hire recent high school graduates. The turnover rate was high, but the labor was young and inexpensive.
- Staff processes with about 40 percent extra operators, which was possible because of the low hourly wage. This was done so that despite problems and stoppages, each process could still produce the required quantity every day

with little or no help from indirect staff or management. With extra operators in the line, the operators could dispense with problems themselves (but not eliminate the causes) and still achieve the target output. Autonomous teams, if you will.

- A flat organization, that is, one with few levels of management.
- Inventory levels were kept low, since each process was generally able to produce the required quantity, which is why the lead time through the value stream was short. Only a little over one day of finished goods, for example, was kept on hand.

The low inventory levels, flat organization, and short value stream, sound "lean," but here's the problem: from day to day and week to week the same problems would arise and the operators would simply work around them. This meant that the plant was standing still—not continuously making progress or improving—and that is quite possibly what Toyota fears most of all.

Honesty Required

We are considering business purpose or philosophy early in this book because this is where many companies trying to copy Toyota are, from the start, already on a different path. At this point some honesty is required from you. *What is the true business philosophy of your company?*

While we talk about the importance of providing value for the customer and continuous improvement, more than a few of us are, in truth, focused narrowly on short-term profit margin. The unspoken business philosophy at some companies is simply to produce and sell more. Or it is about exercising rank and privilege, and thus avoiding mistakes, hiding problems, and getting promoted, which become more important than performance, achievement, and continuous improvement.

Direction

Having an improvement philosophy and an improvement kata is important, but not quite enough. Ideally, action would have both form (a routine or kata) and direction. For example, many of us would say that improvement—or "lean"—equals "eliminating waste." Although this popular statement is basically correct, it is by itself too simple. The negative result of "improvement equals eliminate waste" thinking is twofold: we cannot discern what is important to improve, and we tend to maximize the efficiency of one area at the expense of another, shifting wastes from one to another rather than optimizing and synchronizing the whole.

A classic example of this involves material handling. In the quest to eliminate waste, we often come upon the idea of presenting parts and components to production operators in small containers. The small containers reduce waste at the process because they can be placed close to the operator's fingertips (less reaching and walking to get parts), and more part varieties can be kept within the operator's reach (no changeover is necessary for producing different products). Of course, those parts currently arrive from the supplier in large containers on pallets, which are dropped off in the general vicinity of the production operators with a fork truck.

At this point a logistics manager will usually speak up and say, "Wait a minute, let me get this straight. My department is evaluated on its productivity, and you want my people to take parts out of the large containers and repack them into small containers. Then you want my people to get off the fork truck and place those containers near the operator's fingertips. And since the quantity of delivered parts will now be smaller—because fewer parts can be stored so close to the operator—my people will have to deliver several times a shift, rather than only once or twice per shift. Now we all know that 'lean' means eliminating waste. All those extra non-value-added activities would obviously be waste, so this cannot be the right solution."

I have observed this type of debate many times, and it always goes around and around the same way. Whoever is most persuasive wins and sets the direction *for a while*, until someone else brings up a different persuasive argument or idea. Or we use a voting technique to make it seem that we're being systematic and scientific about choosing the direction. What in fact is happening is that the organization is essentially flailing about and frequently shifting direction as it hunts for the "right" solution to implement, and jumps from one potential solution to another. Sometimes an external consultant will be brought in to provide a seemingly clear answer and be the tie breaker, or to be the person to blame in case the choice does not work out.

So who is correct in this situation: the production manager who wants small containers, or the logistics manager who wants to avoid extra handling? Under the simple concept of lean equals eliminate waste, everyone is. What is missing here is a sense of direction. Although we may think of adaptation as essentially a reactive activity, it is actually what happens on the way to somewhere. Evolution in nature may not be heading in any particular predefined direction or have any particular boundaries, but for a human organization to be consciously adaptive, it helps to have a long-range vision of where we want to be. That is something we can choose or define, while the adaptation that will take place between here and there is not. By long range I mean a vision that may extend beyond one working lifetime, perhaps even to 50 years or more (Figure 3-4).

Note that a vision, or direction giver, is not simply a quantitative target. It is a broad description of a condition we would like to have achieved in the future. To repeat, the definition of continuous improvement and adaptation I am using in this book is: *moving toward a desired state through an unclear territory by being sensitive to and responding to actual conditions on the ground.*

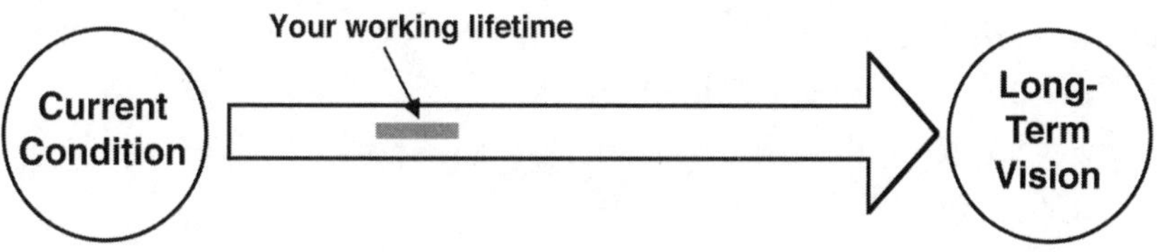

Figure 3-4. A vision is a direction-giver

You've got to think about big things while you're doing small things, so that all the small things go in the right direction.

—Alvin Toffler

A long-term vision or direction helps focus our thinking and doing, because without it proposals are evaluated independently, instead of as part of striving toward something.

Defining longer-term direction/vision can be tricky, and even dangerous, however. For example:

- Although we cannot see what is coming, a vision based exclusively on current paradigms, competencies, products, or technologies can limit the future range of our adaptation too much. Toward that end, a vision should probably focus more on the customer, and broad-scale customer needs, than on ourselves.
- Visions developed in a way that seeks to protect current sacred cows are often so watered down that they are essentially useless for providing direction.

An example of a useful but not overly confining long-term vision is Toyota Motor Corporation's early vision of "Better cars for more people."[2] What would this vision, this direction, lead an automobile manufacturer to do? Consider Toyota's current market position, global presence, and product mix with this old vision statement in mind.

Toyota's Vision for Its Production Operations

As depicted in Figure 3-5, in its production operations, Toyota has for several decades been pursuing a long-term vision that consists of:[3]

- Zero defects
- 100 percent value added
- One-piece flow, in sequence, on demand
- Security for people

Toyota sees this particular ideal-state condition—if it were achieved through an entire value stream—as the way of manufacturing with the

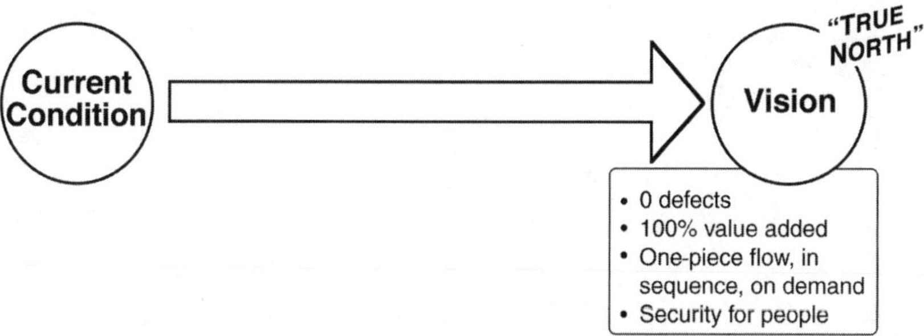

Figure 3-5. Toyota's vision for production operations

highest quality, at the lowest cost, with the shortest lead time. In recent years Toyota began referring to this as its "true north" for production. You can think of this production vision as "a synchronized one-by-one (1x1) flow from A to Z at the lowest possible cost" or as "one contiguous flow." Note that Toyota's production vision also describes a condition, not just a financial or accounting number.

What is a one-piece flow? In its ideal, one-piece flow means that parts move from one value-adding processing step directly to the next value-adding processing step, and then to the customer, without any waiting time or batching between those steps. For many years we called this "continuous flow production." Toyota now refers to it as "one-by-one production," perhaps because many manufacturers will point to a moving production line with parts in queue between the value-adding steps and erroneously say, "We have continuous flow, because everything is moving." Such a misinterpretation is more difficult to make when we use the phrase "one-by-one production."

Toyota's production vision, which will be the example of a vision that we use throughout this book, is actually an old concept and it does not come from Toyota or Japan. The advantages of sequential and 1x1 flows have been known for a long time, and in one form or another the flow ideal has been pursued on and off again for centuries. Some examples:

- During the mid-1500s the Venetian arsenal developed a system for mass production of warships, and could produce nearly one ship a day with standardized parts on a sequential, production-line basis.
- In the late 1700s Oliver Evans developed a sequence of machines and conveyance devices that connected all parts of the flour milling process into one continuous system. Grain was poured in at one end of the mill and flour came out the other, without sacks of material (batches) being moved around between the processing steps inside the mill.
- In the 1820s at the Springfield Armory in Massachusetts, Thomas Blanchard developed a sequence of 13 or 14 machines to process gun stocks.

My colleague Gerd Aulinger takes a perhaps even more insightful and universal view on the quest to move closer to 1x1 flow, with examples such as the following:

- In the nineteenth century if you wanted to hear Strauss play a waltz, you had to invite him to your court. Later we could go to the store to buy records and CDs. Today, music plays on your mp3 player, downloaded from the Internet. Payment for that music file is made without paper money through an automatic charge to your credit card.
- Prior to the fifteenth century if you wanted a book, someone had to write it out by hand. Then Gutenberg began printing them. Eventually publishing companies were born and you could buy a book at the store, during business hours. Now you order the book online anytime, and perhaps it is even downloaded to your reading device or printer.
- At one time we sent letters by horse rider. Then came mail coaches. Following that came once-daily delivery to your doorstep. Today we communicate at any time, via telephone, e-mail, and Skype.

Remarkably, we still find plenty of organizations that argue internally about whether to accept this endless trend toward 1x1 flow—as if it were something we have the power to control.

When I first came across Toyota's true north vision, I thought I had caught a mistake, and indicated as much to a Toyota person. "One hundred percent value added is probably not even achievable," I said. "If you just move the product from one spot to the next then there is waste!" The response was, "Well, it could be that our production true north is theoretical and not achievable, but that does not matter. For us it serves as a direction giver, and we do not spend any time discussing whether or not it is achievable. We do spend a lot of effort trying to move closer to it."

In other words, it is acceptable and perhaps even desirable for the vision to be a seeming dilemma and thus a challenge.

The Toyota person's comments reminded me of the story about two people being chased by a hungry tiger. When one of them stops to put on some running shoes, the other says, "What are you doing? Do you not see the tiger coming?" The first person replies, "Yes I do, but as long as I am ahead of you I'll be fine." In a way, this is part of Toyota's strategy. Toyota is by no means perfect and is still a long way from its ideal state condition. But as long as the product is what the customer wants, whoever is ahead on the way there will essentially get the money and survive. A trick for manufacturers is to stay ahead of your competitors in this direction.

The striving for improvement in this direction, in all work activity, is a guiding light in Toyota's manufacturing operations, and apparently does not change. Both the company's philosophy of survival through improvement plus this direction giver have remained consistent beyond the tenure of any one leader.

> *As production expanded during the 1950s, Toyota shifted its priorities from improving capacity and basic manufacturing technology to developing an integrated, mass-production system that was as continuous as possible from forging and casting through final assembly.*
>
> —Michael A. Cusumano, *The Japanese Automobile Industry*

Toyota's progress toward this true north condition is by no means linear, but due in part to this consistent focus for over 50 years, Toyota has achieved a lead in eliminating waste and improving the flow of value. And it continues to move forward.

Vision as an Overall Direction Giver, but Not Much More

Toyota's production system seeks to reduce cost and improve quality by moving ever closer to a total, synchronized, waste-free, one-by-one flow. But how do we get an organization of hundreds or thousands or tens of thousands of people to work continuously and effectively in the direction of a vision? We cannot simply move from where we are today to a low-cost, synchronized one-by-one flow from start to finish. In fact, it is dangerous to jump too far too fast; to cut too much inventory and closely couple processes too soon. A vision is far away, and the path to it is long, unclear, and unpredictable (Figure 3-6). How do we find and stay on that path?

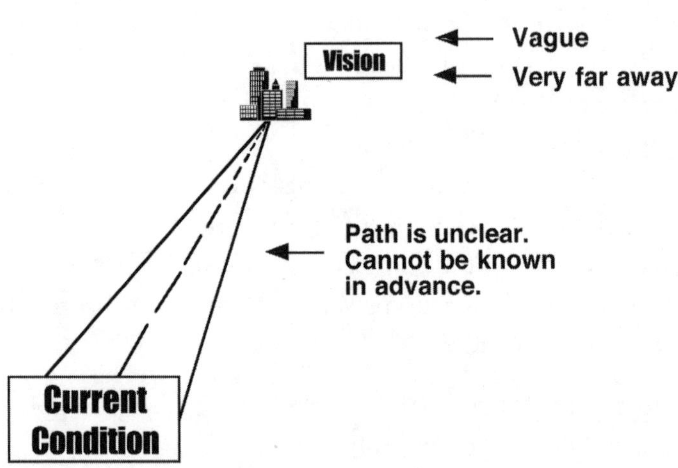

Figure 3-6. A vision serves primarily as a direction giver

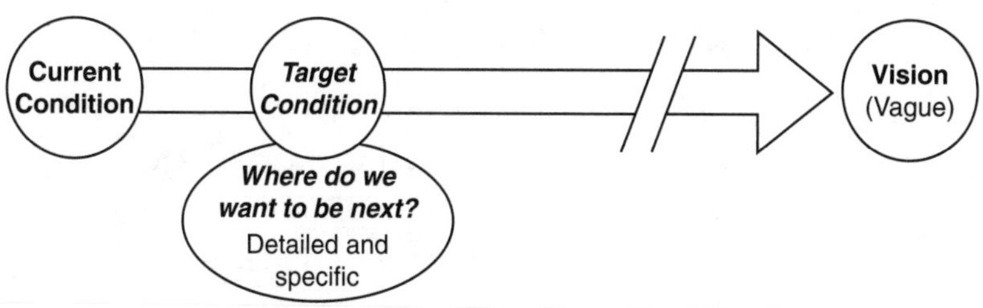

Figure 3-7. Target conditions are where the action is

Target Conditions

Toyota moves toward a vision by working with something I call "target conditions." Across the organization Toyota people learn to set and work toward successive target conditions in the direction of whatever vision is being pursued (Figure 3-7). This condition typically represents a step closer to the vision and a challenge that goes somewhat beyond current capability. You can think of a target condition like a much shorter-term desired state that is more clearly defined than the distant vision. Like the vision, an interim target condition is also not a financial or accounting target, but a description of a condition.

Once a target condition is defined, it is not optional nor easily changeable. It stands. *How* to achieve that target condition *is* optional and can tap into what humans are good at: roll-up-your-sleeves effort, resourcefulness, and creativity to achieve new levels of performance. That is, if they have a kata and are well-managed. Target conditions are a component of Toyota's improvement kata, and we will look at them closely in Chapter 5.

Utilizing the Sense of Direction to Manage People

How does Toyota utilize its production vision to help manage people? A couple of examples will clarify this.

Example 1: Sensor Cables

In visiting the assembly area of a factory that produces automotive ABS-sensor cables (wires with a connector at one end and a sensor at the other), we found that the batch size in the assembly processes was one week. That is, a five-day sales quantity of one sensor-cable type is produced, and then the assembly process is changed over to produce a five-day batch of a different type. A quick calculation showed, however, that there was enough free capacity to permit more changeovers and smaller assembly batch sizes. The assembly area could set a target condition of a one-day batch size, rather than the current five days, and achieve that without even having to reduce the already short changeover time.

In the conference room, we pointed out the potential for smaller batch sizes to the management team. The benefits of smaller lot sizes are well known and significant: closer to 1x1 flow, less inventory and waste, faster response to different customer requirements, less hidden defects and rework, kanban systems become workable, and so on.

Almost immediately the assembly manager responded and said, "We can't do that," and went on to explain why. "Our cable product is a component of an automobile safety system and because of that each time we change over to assembling a different cable we have to fill out lot-traceability paperwork. We also have to take to the quality department the first new piece produced and delay production until the quality department gives us an approval. If we were to reduce the assembly lot size from five days to one day we would increase that paperwork and those production delays by a factor of five. Those extra non-value-added activities would be waste and would increase our cost. We know that lean means eliminate waste, so reducing the lot size is not a good idea."

The plant manager concurred, and therein lies a significant difference from Toyota. A Toyota plant manager would likely say something like this to the assembly manager: "You are correct that the extra paperwork and first-piece inspection requirements are obstacles to achieving a smaller lot size. Thank you for pointing that out. However, the fact that we want to reduce lot sizes is not optional nor open for discussion, because it moves us closer to our vision of a one-by-one flow. Rather than losing time discussing whether or not we should reduce the lot size, please turn your attention to those two obstacles standing in the way of our progress. Please go observe the current paperwork and inspection processes and report back what you learn. After that I will ask you to make a proposal for how we can move to a one day lot size without increasing our cost."

Using Cost/Benefit Analysis in a Different Way

As the sensor cable example illustrates, without a direction we tend to evaluate proposals individually on their own merits, rather than as part of striving toward something. This creates that back-and-forth, hunting-for-a-solution, whoever-is-currently-most-persuasive effect in the organization.

Specifically, without a sense of direction we tend to use a short-term cost/benefit analysis to decide and choose on a case-by-case basis whether or not something should be done—in which direction to head and what to do—rather than working through challenging obstacles on the way to a new level of performance. How many times have you witnessed a potentially interesting though still unformed idea quickly torpedoed and killed with the question, "Is there a financial benefit to that?"

Toyota uses cost/benefit (CBA) analysis too, but differently than do we. While we have learned to utilize CBA to determine *what* to do, at Toyota one first determines where one wants or needs to be next—the target condition—and then cost/benefit analysis is utilized to help determine *how* to get there. At Toyota, CBA is used less for deciding whether something should be done, and more for deciding *how* to do it.

Traditional: CBA determines direction; that is, whether we do something or not. "This proposal is too costly? Then we must do something else."

Toyota: CBA helps define what we need to do to achieve a predefined target condition. "This proposal is too costly? Then we must develop a way to do it more cheaply."

Do not think, however, that Toyota's approach is about achieving target conditions at any cost. Toyota has strict budgets and target costs. The idea is to first determine where you want to go, and then how to get there within financial and other constraints. This is where the sense of direction from the vision plays its role. Do not let financial calculations alone determine your direction, because then the organization becomes inward-looking rather than adaptive, it oscillates on a case-by-case basis rather than striving toward something, and it seeks to find and implement ready solutions rather than developing new smart solutions. An economic break-even point is a dependent variable, not an independent constraint that determines direction.

Example 2: New Production Process

When a new assembly process is being designed, there are usually a few different process options from which to choose. For example, there may be a fully automated line concept, a partially automated version, as well as a manual line concept. When we run these options through a cost/benefit analysis—a return-on-investment, or ROI, calculation—more often than not the fully automated option wins and is what we select. Later, when the line is in place, there are complaints that the automated line does not fit well with the situation.

To follow Toyota-style thinking, we would take a different approach. First we would determine where we want to be. In this case that means determining what type of assembly process is most appropriate for the particular situation. Fully automated, partially automated, and manual lines all have their place, depending on the situation, and all of them can be a "lean line." In the early start-up phase of production for a new product, the product's configuration is still apt to change and the sales volume ramp-up may be different than expected. In this situation it can make sense to begin with a flexible, easily altered manual line and move to higher levels of automation when the product matures and sales volume increases.

Now comes the cost/benefit analysis, which, let's say, shows that the manual line design is too expensive. In the Toyota way of thinking, this does not mean that the manual line option is dropped. The target condition, a manual line, has already been defined and stands. What the negative outcome of the cost/benefit analysis tells a Toyota manager is that more work is needed on the design of the manual line, in order to bring it into the target cost objective. The manager will ask his engineers to sharpen their pencils and go over the design again, and this will continue iteratively until the target condition is reached within budget constraints. The sense of direction was used to manage people—in this case the engineers who were charged with developing a new production process.

Stay Home

One lesson implicit in this discussion is that we should not spend too much time benchmarking what others—including Toyota—are doing. *You yourself are the benchmark*:

- Where are you now?
- Where do you want to be next?
- What obstacles are preventing you from getting there?

For example, if you find that your technical support staff cannot respond quickly enough to machine problems, you might think, "I wonder how Toyota handles this?" Or you could stay home and ask, "How fast do we want our technical support to respond? What is preventing that from happening? What do we need to do to achieve the desired condition?"

Remember, the ability of your company to be competitive and survive lies not so much in solutions themselves, but in the capability of the people in your organization to understand a situation and develop solutions.

And you don't have to be perfect, just ahead of your competitors in aspects of your product or service.

Notes

1. "Open the Window. It's a Big World Out there! The Spirit and the Ideas That Created Toyota," pamphlet published by Toyota Kaikan, Toyota Motor Corporation, October 1993.
2. Note that this may no longer be an effective vision for an organization in the transportation business in the twenty-first century.
3. In early years this production vision was referred to as "Highest quality, lowest cost, shortest lead time."

Chapter 4

Origin and Effects of Our Current Management Approach

Much of our current managerial template comes out of the United States automobile industry of the 1920s, and a short, focused look back at the early history of its two giants, the Ford Motor Company and the General Motors Corporation, sheds light our current thinking.[1]

The Ford Motor Company Approach (1906–1927)

In regard to pursuing the 1x1 flow ideal state, Toyota was clearly preceded by the Ford Motor Company, which undertook, arguably, Western manufacturing's last focused and sustained pursuit of the contiguous flow vision early in the twentieth century. (Note that I am intentionally using the word *contiguous* rather than *continuous*.)

Flow Experiments in Fabrication Processes

Everyone has heard about Ford's 1913 moving-conveyor final assembly line for the Model T automobile at the Highland Park, Michigan, factory. But Ford's flow experiments had already begun before the Model T was introduced in 1908.

In 1906, to meet expanding sales of the Model N automobile, Ford engineers began arranging machine tools for the fabrication of engine and transmission parts in the sequence of processing steps, rather than grouping them by machine type, as was then common practice. For example, if a heat treatment was required, then the heat-treat oven would be located directly between the previous and next machining steps, rather than in a separate oven area. The result was considerably higher productivity. Over the next few years, Ford strove to apply this sequential processing concept to the production of many different fabricated parts.

At that time, Ford's various *assembly* processes (engine, transmission, axle, magneto, dashboard, final assembly, and so on) were still set up as stationary tables or stands on which a whole item was assembled, typically by a single person who fit all the parts together. Even when Ford moved its parts fabrication and assembly processes to the Highland Park factory in 1910, the primary assembly approach remained stationary tables and stands.

Sequential Flow Assembly Line

By 1913 the Highland Park factory still could not meet the runaway demand for the Model T; more orders were coming in than cars going out. Ford engineers, seeking ways to fill those orders, established their first sequential and moving assembly line for subassembly of the flywheel magneto. After a few weeks of experimentation and fine-tuning, the productivity of this process was increased fourfold.

You can imagine the enthusiasm with which Ford's engineers then worked to spread this sequential, flowing, and often moving-conveyor based assembly approach to the many other assembly processes at Highland Park, including the famous final vehicle assembly lines.

Putting It All Together

By the end of 1913, Ford had more or less the following situation in its Highland Park factory. The upstream parts-making processes (stamping, machining, etc.) had been arranged in the order of processing steps for some time. As indicated in Figure 4-1, the various downstream assembly

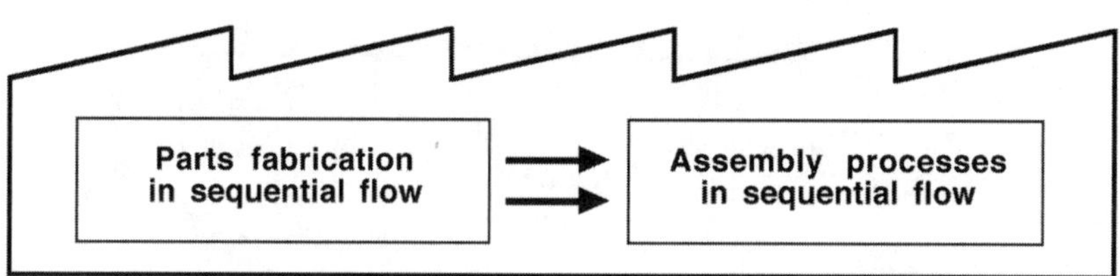

Figure 4-1. Fabrication and assembly

processes (engine, final, etc.) were now also being put into sequentially flowing line arrangements.

Furthermore, there was also only one product being produced, the Model T, which meant that no changeovers were required. Except for a few different body types, all other parts on every Model T in production were the same.

What would Ford's next step be in this situation?

With their successes in making both fabrication and assembly processes flow, and since they were only manufacturing one product, Ford engineers tried to take flowing production to its logical conclusion: Why not connect all processes in one contiguous flow from raw material to finished product (Figure 4-2)?

We were not there and we cannot interview the Model T era Ford engineers to ask them about this, but they did leave us an exoskeleton of their thinking with the unusual, still-standing six-story buildings at Highland Park. These buildings (one of which is depicted in Figure 4-3 in its original elevation drawing)[2] were added to the Highland Park factory complex in 1914, and Model T–related production took place there until 1919.

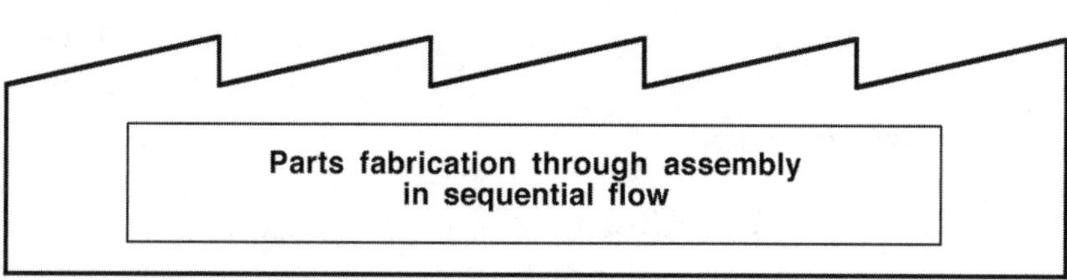

Figure 4-2. Connecting it all into a single flow

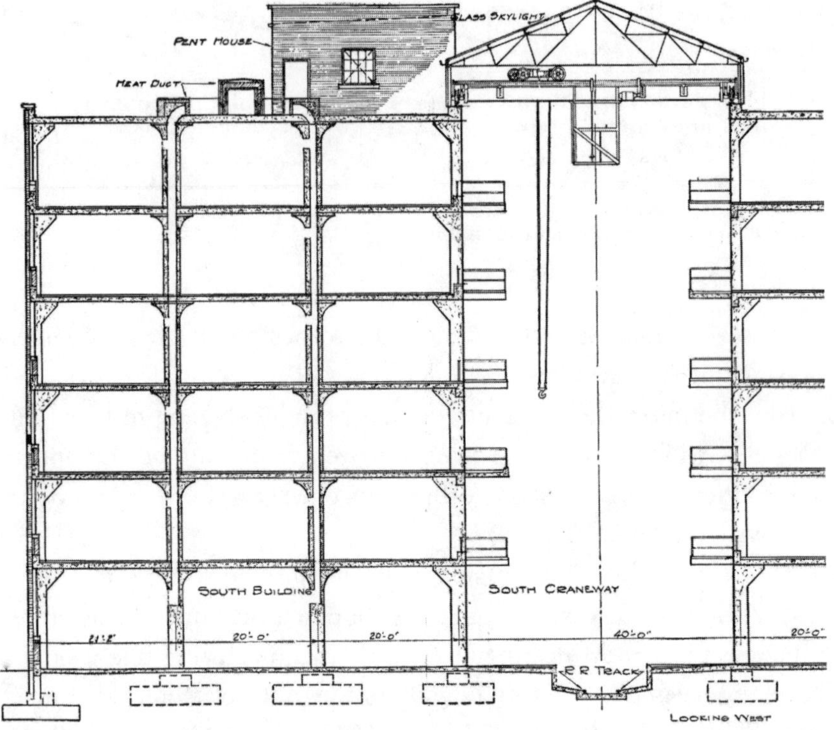

Figure 4-3. Cross section of Ford Highland Park six-story buildings, 1914

The concept behind these unique buildings was that final assembly is on the ground floor, and subassembly and parts fabrication processes are on the upper floors. In those days, materials were brought to factories by rail, and as you can see in the elevation drawing, railroad tracks went down the center craneway of the building. In the craneway, material would be hoisted from the railcars onto balconies that opened to the appropriate floors.

At this point I'll let Mr. Edward Gray, Ford's chief construction engineer at the time, describe the rest of the material flow in these buildings, which he designed:

> *There are thousands of holes cut through the various floors of those buildings, so that the parts that started in the rough on the top floor gravitated down, possibly through chutes or possibly through*

conveyors or tubes, and finally became a finished article, well down on the ground floor; landed on the conveyor at the ground floor.[3]

In doing some secondary research for this book, my colleague, Jim Huntzinger, and I became fascinated with Ford's six-story buildings at Highland Park, and this statement in particular. Once we had read Edward Gray's testimony in the Ford Tax Case files at the Detroit Public Library, it seemed that the assertion of Ford's Model T era engineers striving for one contiguous flow could only be confirmed by seeing for ourselves the holes in the floors of the six-story buildings.

Imagine how disappointed we were when we could not find even one hole in the floors as our Ford hosts kindly walked us through the now-unused six-story buildings. Fortunately, we had an astute University of Michigan Ph.D. student with us, Eduardo Lander, who suddenly realized, "These floors are 90 years old and have probably been resurfaced many times. We should be looking at the ceilings, not the floors." And as we looked up, there they were, plain as day, lots of patched holes.

Ford's six-story building experiment was ultimately not a success and the concept did not spread. We can speculate that the two cranes in each craneway—for unloading materials from the railcars—would have been a serious flow bottleneck. Transferring parts through holes in a reinforced concrete floor must also have been quite inflexible, since changing a machine layout could mean having to patch one hole and jackhammering open a new one.

There was also still plenty of work-in-process inventory in the Highland Park value streams; in all the different conveyors, chutes, slides, barrels, etc., transferring components between processes, and often between individual processing steps within one process too. Ford was still a long way from the ideal of a 1x1 flow from A to Z, but that misses this key point: *whether consciously or not, by striving to continuously improve the production flow toward an ideal of one connected flow, the early Ford Motor Company was utilizing a vision and interim target conditions in a way that highlights critical obstacles and makes them something to be worked through rather than circumvented.* This is surprisingly similar to how Toyota's improvement kata utilizes a long-term vision and interim target conditions to manage people and move the organization forward (Figure 4-4). Ford's story has been told many times, but from a management and organization behavior perspective, we have missed this point.

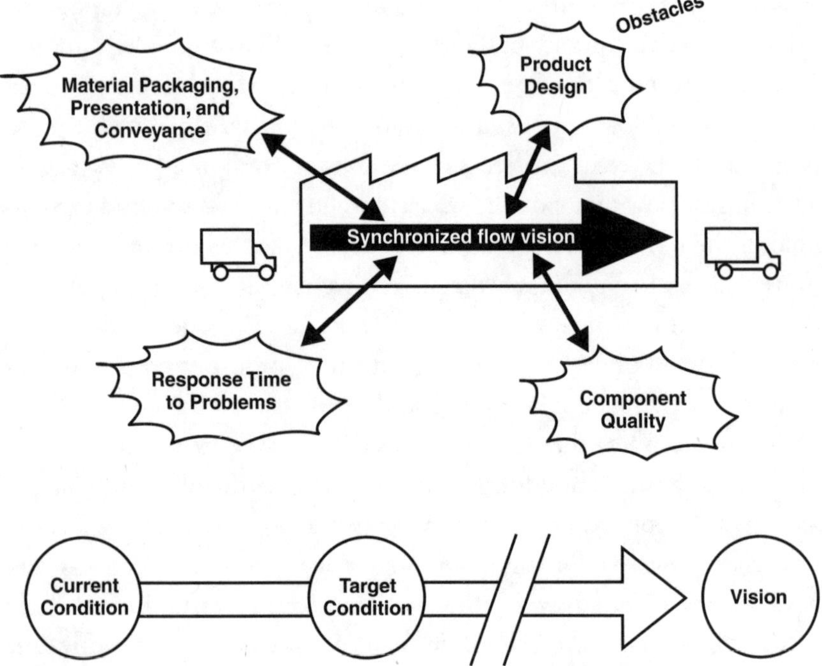

Figure 4-4. Early Ford utilized a vision and target conditions similar to the way that Toyota does

End of the Flow Experiments

After the six-story buildings Ford made one more big attempt to connect all processes from raw material to finished product, at the integrated, horizontal layout River Rouge factory complex. The Model T completed its production run there from 1919 to 1927. But by the mid 1920s customers were less willing to keep buying the same Model T. The number of different product variations began increasing, while the lifespan of any one model decreased.

These two new demands on the factories—higher variety and shorter product life span—made it much more difficult to try to synchronize the production flow compared to the one-product Model T days. Some processes in the value stream now had to produce different versions of an item and change over between them. Say, for example, a crankshaft machining process that had produced only one crankshaft for the Model T would now have to produce a few different crankshafts for a few different engine variants. Ideally this machining process would change over at the same time the engine assembly process changes over, in sync, but this is difficult because a machining area often feeds more than one assembly process and has significantly longer changeover times.

In this situation there are two basic options. The challenging option is to continue pursuing the "one contiguous flow" vision. This requires tackling and working through the admittedly difficult obstacles to a connected, synchronized flow and developing new solutions. The easier and quicker option, on the other hand, is to move away from the synchronized flow ideal, decouple the processes in the value stream from one another and operate them as islands.

Generally speaking, after the Model T, manufacturers increasingly chose the decoupling option. Besides the increasing product variety, another reason for the move away from pursuing the flow ideal may have been that, around 1924, the production capacity of the U.S. automobile companies finally began to match the demand level. Orders were no longer outpacing capacity, and this conceivably reduced the urgency to keep striving for further flow and productivity improvements.

Another reason was that General Motors struck out in a new direction with its new management approach, and it, no longer Ford, became the company to emulate. As the Model T era came to a close, it seems that so did focused experiments to keep improving factory flow, and the associated improvement kata style behavior. Pursuit of the one contiguous flow ideal went dormant again, until Toyota took up the mantle in the 1950s.

The General Motors Approach (1920s to Present)

A New Direction in Management

Early Ford put emphasis on and effort toward a vision that described a condition—the production flow ideal—but ultimately focused too little on product development and on organizing and managing the company in systematic ways. In contrast, General Motors (GM) put a lot of attention on developing systematic management and structuring the organization. Three concepts from GM's then new management approach pertain in particular to our discussion here. They should look familiar to anyone who has worked in a medium- or large-sized company.

Rate-of-Return for Decision Making

The GM financial committee relied on a rate-of-return analysis (cost-benefit analysis or return-on-investment calculation) for decision making on investments. The predicted return determined the choices that were made, as opposed to early Ford's idea to do what is necessary to pursue an ideal.

In other words, *make money* became the guiding vision or overall direction for further development of the business or the factory. We were now not moving in a particular direction (aiming at successive target conditions on the way to a vision) but rather judging and selecting options independently based on their rate of return.

> *No other financial principle with which I am acquainted serves better than rate of return as an objective aid to business judgment. . . .*
>
> *We are not in the business of making cars, we are in the business of making money.*
>
> —Alfred P. Sloan, Jr., President of General Motors, 1923–37; Chief Executive, 1937–46; Chairman of the Board, 1937–56[4]

Maximizing the Output of Individual Processes

Early GM seems to have concluded that low costs are achieved when large quantities are produced with high machine utilization. Management began to think of the production value stream in terms of separate segments or departments, viewing each as an island, and created incentives that led those departments to produce as much as possible as fast as possible in order to reduce cost according to managerial accounting calculations (pieces per man hour per department or segment of the value stream).

Centralized Planning and Control Based on Managerial Accounting Data

GM introduced a decentralized divisional operating organization, but, increasingly, with centralized operational decision making and control. That control was based on setting quantitative targets for the divisions and reporting back performance metrics from the divisions. Decision making was based heavily on analysis of reported managerial accounting data.

> Of course, GM also introduced well-known practices to influence the consumption side of the equation. These included segmenting the consumer market and providing each segment with a product line, an annual model change, segment-specific marketing, and providing credit to consumers. Since this book is about organization management, I will concentrate on changes GM introduced inside the company, on the management side of the equation.

Intended and Unintended Effects

The results of General Motors' new approach and practices were dramatic and positive. GM achieved phenomenal success, grew to be the world's largest corporation, and greatly influenced the nature of business management. Over the following decades GM's management approach was widely publicized and was adopted by countless other companies. By the 1950s it had become general practice at U.S. corporations and at companies around the world. Today it is so pervasive that it is essentially invisible. It is simply how things are done.

I should add one qualification to the above paragraph however: GM's managerial approach achieved great success *in the market conditions that prevailed through the 1960s*. In later years, under different conditions, the same management approach no longer worked as successfully.

Let's take a look at some of the effects that those three GM concepts had on how companies are managed. Again, the following should look familiar to anyone who has worked in a manufacturing company.

Effect of Rate-of-Return for Decision Making

GM's formula-based rate-of-return decision-making approach is effective enough in a growing market when there are business opportunities from which to choose, but it becomes less so in the crowded or low-growth marketplaces we have today.

GM's approach involved, to a degree, selecting between options in the early days of the U.S. automobile industry, when there were multiple options from which to choose. But in a lower-growth market with many competitors, the immediately profitable opportunities—the low hanging fruit—will have been picked. In this situation, management's task becomes more one of nurturing promising processes, products, and situations into profitability than selecting ones that would be directly profitable.

The ROI approach of General Motors is more about making choices than about improving and adapting. For example, in the second half of the twentieth century, Detroit automakers opted repeatedly to not significantly enter the market for small cars, even as that market grew noteworthy, because from an ROI-selection perspective it was not profitable. The media has often criticized these decisions, but that denunciation is at least partially misplaced. Executives were making those decisions rationally and correctly, in accordance with the management system within which they worked.

In contrast, Toyota's approach is about getting people to work systematically and creatively at the detail level to do what is necessary to achieve ambitious target conditions, which at first pass may not make it through a rate-of-return calculation. As shown in the previous chapter, Toyota utilizes cost benefit analysis less as a means for determining direction or what to do, and more as a means for figuring out how to cost-effectively achieve a desired condition.

If we go even further with our ROI thinking and use it to evaluate individual decisions or steps, then the result is likely to be suboptimization. According to systems theory, trying to maximize the individual parts of something reduces the effectiveness of the whole.

As we make these comparisons between GM and Toyota, we should keep in mind that it is not a judgment. The two approaches represent reactions to different conditions at different points in time in the history of the automobile industry. What's most important is that we understand their long-term effects on an organization.

Effect of Maximizing the Output of Individual Processes

Seeking to maximize individual process output—for example, by measuring each process separately with a pieces per man hour calculation—generates the following effects on a value stream:

- A process or department becomes even more decoupled from the next process as it strives to produce as much as possible as fast as possible.
- Since changeovers interrupt production, there is a natural tendency to avoid them and produce large lots.
- The next process in the value stream does not yet need all those parts that were produced too soon, so the parts must be stored as in-process inventory. (Inventory which is, by the way, counted as an asset by the managerial accounting system.)
- When the next process finally does use the parts, it will discover defects among them. However, it is impossible to trace the root

causes of those defects because the parts were produced some time ago, and the conditions in the preceding process that caused the defects have long since changed.

This situation repeats over and over all the way through the value stream and results in a total lead time through the factory that is measured in days or weeks, whereas the total value added time is actually only minutes. Interestingly, when we speed up a process to improve its pieces-per-man-hour numbers, we only reduce the minutes of value-adding time and do nothing to reduce the days and weeks of lead time. You can observe these effects in factories around the world.

To keep inventory from swelling too much in this situation, we started placing limits on inventory buffers and set targets for inventory levels, without necessarily understanding the actual situation in the factory processes. The goal then became trying to schedule each individual segment of the value stream so accurately that items would be made not long before the next segment actually needs them. But this holy grail is not consistently attainable in the real world, even with sophisticated software, because process conditions up and down the value stream are constantly changing.

It takes a certain amount of inventory to hold a value stream together, and the quantity of inventory required depends on the current performance characteristics of the processes in that value stream. If we reduce inventory targets to below this level, then shortages, expediting, and emergency freight will increase. Every day's work in the factory then involves adjusting schedules and expediting. Such daily adjustments in turn cause even more volatility in the value streams, and soon everyone in the factory becomes almost completely occupied with trying to make the production quantities and shipments.

People in an organization act rationally in a way that maximizes their success. Putting the emphasis on departmental output maximization, rather than on optimizing the overall flow for the customer, means that the natural interests of the departmental manager may come into conflict with the long-term survival interests of the company. In the long run, overall cost will be higher and the organization will become so involved in firefighting that it is standing still, even though the departmental manager is meeting and even exceeding his or her objectives.

Again, systems theory tells us that we cannot optimize a system by trying to maximize its individual parts.

Effect of Centralized Planning and Control Based on Managerial Accounting Data

As the above description of everyday life in a factory illustrates, with centralized decision making from a distance based on accounting data, management tends to lose connection with, and understanding of, the actual situation on the work floor. Trying to manage from a distance through data abstractions often results in managers making incorrect assumptions and inappropriate decisions, and trying to make adjustments and adaptations too long after the fact. In addition, on-site managers naturally try to make the numbers upon which they are evaluated look good, which means that even less accurate information is reaching the decision makers in the levels above.

Not only are the centrally controlled divisions unable to adapt autonomously and quickly, but the decision makers in the central office are basing their decisions on inaccurate, after-the-fact quantitative abstractions.

What Happened to Management By Objectives?

The original thinking behind management by objectives (MBO), as outlined by Peter Drucker in his 1954 book *The Practice of Management*, is not too distant from how Toyota is managing. Drucker even mentions, in a short case example, how what he calls "some of the most effective managers I know" go beyond only deploying quantitative targets downward. He briefly describes how these managers engage in a two-way dialogue with the level below them in order to develop written plans for the activities that will be undertaken to reach the targets. In other words, paying attention to the means that are utilized to achieve the results.[5]

It appears, however, that in subsequent actual business practice and education, MBO became something more like planning and control from above executed to a large degree by setting quantitative targets and assessing reports of metrics. Some call this "management by results." Unfortunately, there are plenty of different ways to achieve a quantitative outcome target, many of which have nothing to do with making real process improvement and moving the pieces of an organization in a common direction.

So why did a watered-down version of MBO work so well for us for so long? Here are some possible reasons:

- In the period of limited international competition and continued growth, which ran until the 1970s, occasional improvement was good enough. In such market conditions it is possible to make a good profit even if there is considerable waste in the system and we are not continually improving.
- In those market conditions, there were still some profitable choices available, and thus less need for nurturing products and situations into profitability.
- As the need for improvement and evolution became apparent in the mid- to late 1970s, it may have been possible to stay ahead for a while by simply cutting inventories and head count, which might have been bloated. Today, however, we might well be reaching the limits of improving by simply cutting.
- The competition was ramping up only slowly, which made it seem as if conditions were not changing all that much.

Interestingly, moving production to lower-cost countries in order to reduce cost—another form of cutting—does not change the underlying system or improve the production process. Some have called this "making waste cheaper," because it does not actually change the underlying way of doing things.

What Are the Lessons from This History?

Lesson 1

Simply put, after the Model T era the basic attributes of factory flow in the West barely changed during the rest of the twentieth century, as a consequence of the management system. There were, of course, many technological developments since the end of the Model T days, but as Michael Cusumano, in his early 1980s Ph.D. research, and the famous late 1980s IMVP study, both asserted, from 1930 to the 1980s there was little further development in productivity and factory flow (inventory turns) in Western automobile factories. The basic production techniques stayed about the same.

Toyota's way of moving forward, in contrast, is very much one of adaptation and continuous improvement; of nurturing processes, products, and businesses into profitability by doing what is necessary to achieve target conditions (Figure 4-5).

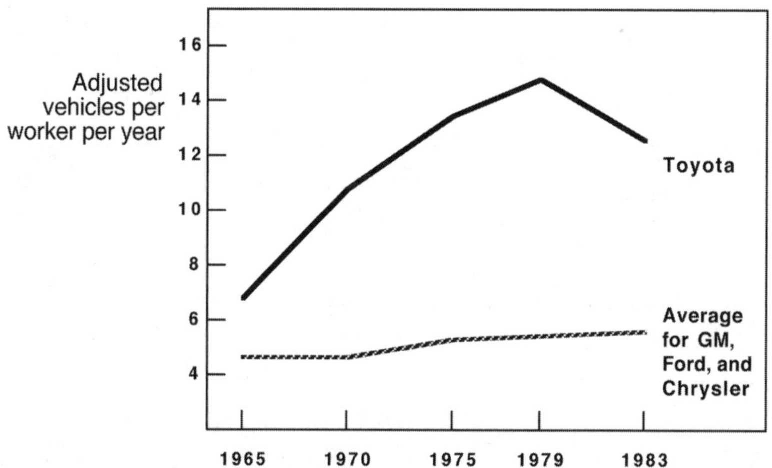

Figure 4-5. Productivity trends, Toyota and the Detroit Big Three
Source: Michael A. Cusumano, *The Japanese Automobile Industry: Technology & Management at Nissan & Toyota* (Cambridge, Massachasetts: The Harvard University Press, 1985).

Lesson 2

In the early 1950s the baton of continuous process improvement toward the ideal flow vision was picked up again, and this time by Toyota. In production, for example, Toyota decided to keep working step by step toward something like the early Ford Motor Company vision: a connected and synchronized flow with ever shorter lead time. In fact, both early Ford and Toyota have referred to the production ideal as "one long conveyor."

Toyota recognized that a main source of low cost is not high machine utilization by itself, but rather when parts flow uninterrupted from one process to the next with little waste in between. For Toyota, striving toward this kind of a synchronized flow meant taking on the challenge of eliminating or reducing the time required to change over between the different items required by the customer.

Lesson 3

The most important lesson to derive from this chapter is that many of us are managing our companies with a logic that originated in the 1920s and 1930s, a logic that might not be appropriate to the situation in which your company finds itself today.

GM's approach proved highly lucrative during the period of growth and oligopolistic isolation from global competition that extended until the 1970s. It became our model and accepted management practice, and is still taught in business schools today. That means, for many of us the way we currently manage our companies is built on logic that originated in the conditions faced by companies in the U.S. automobile industry during the late 1920s. The problem is not that the logic is old, but that it does not incorporate continuous improvement and adaptation. If our business philosophy and management approach do not include constant adaptiveness and improvement, then companies and their leaders can get stuck in patterns that grow less and less applicable in changing circumstances.

The solution is not to periodically change your management system or to reorganize, but to have a management system that can effectively handle whatever unforeseeable circumstances come your way. The fact that Toyota has maintained much of its same management thinking for the past 60 years is a testament to this. Several of us are curious to see how Toyota's management system will maneuver and weather the next few decades.

Let us now take a look at that management system.

Notes

1. Keep in mind as you go through this chapter that in retrospect all history is revisionist, and despite my best efforts to dig deep and be impartial, that undoubtedly holds true for this history as well.
2. The elevation drawing is found in: Horace Lucien Arnold and Fay Leone Farote, *Ford Methods and the Ford Shops* (New York: The Engineering Magazine Company, 1915).
3. Testimony of Edward Gray, Ford Tax Cases, 1927, page 1241.
4. Alfred P. Sloan, Jr., *My Years with General Motors* (New York: McFadden-Bartell, 1965).
5. Peter Drucker, *The Practice of Management* (New York: HarperBusiness, 1993). Originally published in 1954.

Part III

The Improvement Kata: How Toyota Continuously Improves

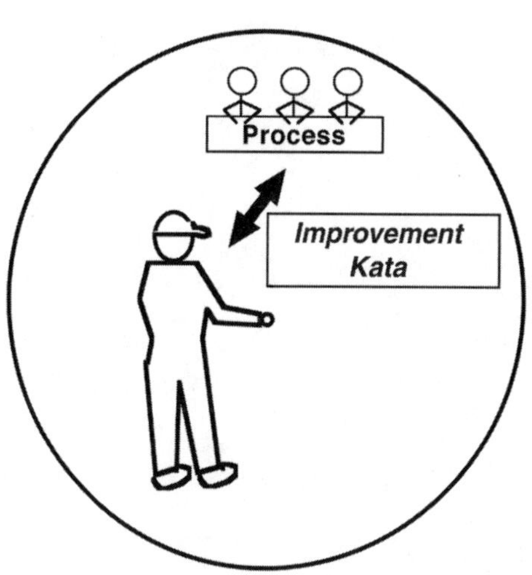

Introduction to Part III

In Chapter 2 we saw that the question "What can we do?" often results in scattershot improvement attempts. The more difficult and focused question is, "What do we need to do?"

How does Toyota determine the answer to that question?

Briefly put, the continuously repeating routine of Toyota's improvement kata goes like this: (1) in consideration of a vision, direction, or target, and (2) with a firsthand grasp of the current condition, (3) a next target condition on the way to the vision is defined. When we then (4) strive to move step by step toward that target condition, we encounter obstacles that define what we *need* to work on, and from which we learn (Figure P3-1).

Chapters 5 and 6 together comprise a description of the improvement kata. Chapter 5 explains target conditions, and Chapter 6 explains how to go about moving toward a target condition.

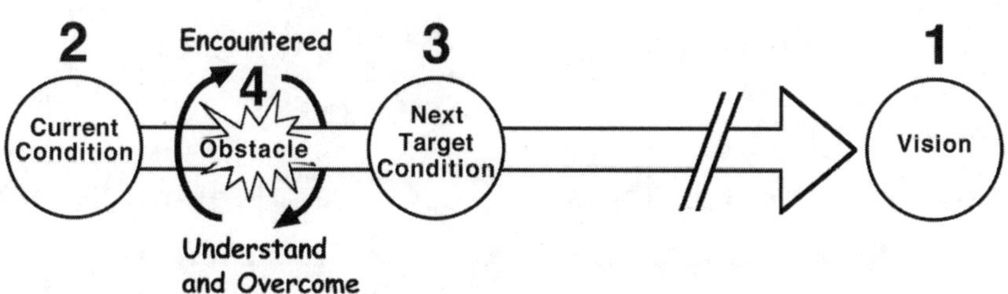

Figure P3-1. The improvement kata in brief

Although the improvement kata describes a routine for continuous improvement, keep in mind that this kata is also part of Toyota's way of managing people every day. The psychology of the improvement kata is universal, and at Toyota everyone is taught to operate along the lines of this systematic approach. You will find it applied to many different situations, not just in manufacturing. The content varies, but the approach is the same.

You will also find the improvement kata is practiced at all levels at Toyota, like fractals. The same kata is utilized on both the operative and strategic levels. The scope of the issues addressed with the improvement kata gets broader the higher in the organization you go, but the approach at all levels is basically the same.

The examples in Part III of this book are at the process level in production operations, where I first learned about the improvement kata. The process level is a good place to first focus our attention and learn, since this, along with product development, is where value is added in a manufacturing company. To distinguish between target conditions at the process level and those at higher levels I will sometimes use the phrase "process target condition."

In production, processes are the individual chain links of a value stream (Figure P3-2), and the word *process* refers to several different kinds of activity, not just material-conversion activities such as stamping, welding, painting, or assembly. Material handling and scheduling, for example, though not value adding (NVA) in themselves, are nonetheless processes in a production value stream. Such necessary NVA processes should be continuously improved too, in a way that moves the value stream toward the 1x1 flow ideal state.

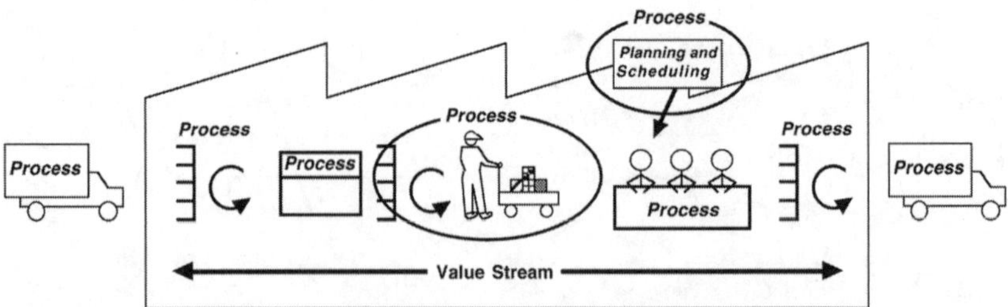

Figure P3-2. Some examples of processes in a manufacturing value stream

Chapter 5

Planning: Establishing a Target Condition

Once you have experienced the role a target condition plays in Toyota's improvement kata, you will find it difficult to work without one. You will also discover how difficult it is to explain what a target condition is and its importance to any manager, engineer, or executive who has not experienced it for themselves. That is a Catch–22 we will deal with in Chapter 9. Over the course of this chapter the target condition idea should become clearer to you, but in the end there is no substitute for learning by doing.

Having a target condition is so important for effective process improvement and management that Toyota will usually not start trying to improve or move forward before a target condition has been defined. This ensures that people's efforts will be focused on actual needs rather than on various ideas and opinions about what we *can* do.

A target condition describes a desired future state. It answers questions like:

- How should this process operate?
- What is the intended normal pattern?
- What situation do we want to have in place at a specific point in time in the future?
- Where do we want to be next?

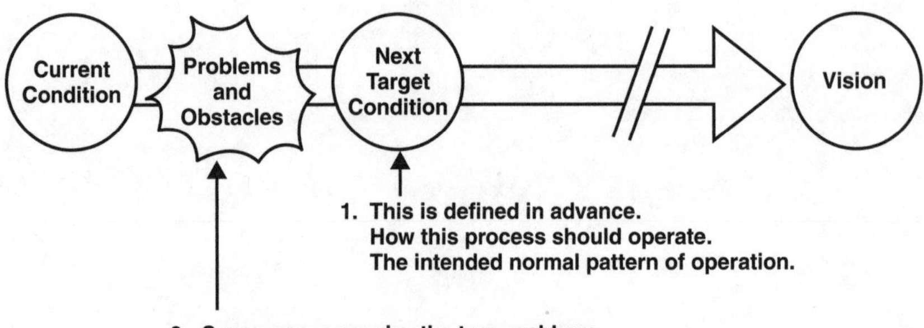

Figure 5-1. The role of a target condition

A target condition works like a pair of eyeglasses that helps you focus and see what you need to do. You will discover problems and obstacles any time you establish a target condition and then try to move toward it (Figure 5-1). This is completely normal, and you have two choices:

1. Avoid the obstacle(s) and move off in a direction other than the vision.
2. Work through the obstacle(s) by understanding and eliminating its causes.

For example, the employees at the sensor cable company in Chapter 3, who pointed out the problems associated with reducing the lot size from one week to one day, were correct, but what they were pointing out were obstacles, not reasons to change direction.

Seeing Lean Techniques in a New Light

A good way to begin our discussion of target conditions, or *target-condition thinking*, is to look at some lean techniques we may think we already understand. For each of the four techniques below I will briefly review the technique and then discuss its less apparent but more important intention from the perspective of target conditions.

- Takt time
- 1x1 production (continuous flow)

- *Heijunka* (leveling production)
- Kanban (pull systems)

After using these techniques as examples to get us started in understanding the idea of a target condition, I will broaden the discussion to describe important characteristics of target conditions overall.

Takt Time

Takt time is the rate of customer demand for the group, or family, of products produced by one process. Takt time is used most often at assembly-type processes that serve external customers.

Takt time is calculated by dividing the effective operating time of a process (for example, per shift or day) by the quantity of items customers require from the process in that time period (Figures 5-2 and 5-3). "Effective operating time" is the available time minus planned downtimes such as lunches, breaks, team meetings, cleanup, and planned maintenance. Note that unplanned downtimes and changeover times are not subtracted at this point, because they are variables you want to reduce.

Say an assembly process has 26,100 seconds effective operating time per shift, and over some period of time the customer requires an average of 450 pieces per shift:

The quotient of 58 seconds means that, based on our available time, on average the customer is currently buying one unit every 58 seconds.[1]

$$\text{takt time} = \frac{\text{your effective operating time per shift}}{\text{quantity customer requires per shift}}$$

Figure 5-2. The takt time calculation

$$\frac{\text{26,100 seconds available time}}{\text{450 pieces required}} = \text{58 seconds takt time}$$

Figure 5-3. Calculating takt time

How is this number used?

It does not automatically mean you should produce at a rate of one piece every 58 seconds. The actual intended cycle time of an assembly process, called *planned cycle time*, is usually less (faster) than the takt time. For example, if there is a changeover time between different part types, we have to cycle the process faster than takt in order to compensate for time lost during changeovers. So in a sense takt time represents an ideal repetitive cycle for an assembly process, a cycle at which we would be producing in sync with the customer demand rate—sell one, make one.

The Intention Behind Takt Time

Takt time becomes interesting in our discussion of target conditions when we use it as something to strive for. Two ways to do this are trying to produce consistently to planned cycle time, and trying to move the planned cycle time closer to the takt time.

Trying to produce consistently to planned cycle time means striving to develop a stable process. Many of us track pieces produced per hour or per shift and therefore are unable to answer the question: "At how many seconds per piece should this process be cycling?" We have an aggregate outcome target, but not a target condition, and we get trapped by such outcome metrics because they prevent us from seeing the actual condition of the process. The result is that an astonishing number of processes come close to making their numbers on average, but their output cycles actually fluctuate excessively from cycle to cycle (Figure 5-4). This condition is not only expensive

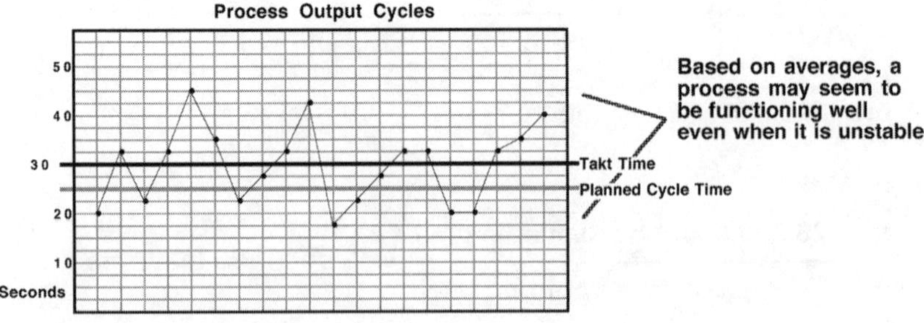

Figure 5-4. An unstable process

(requiring extra resources) and adversely affects quality, but many process improvement efforts will simply not stick when the process fluctuates too much.

When you have identified the degree of fluctuation from cycle to cycle in a process, the next question becomes: "What should the range of fluctuation be?" With that desired condition in mind, you can then observe the process with an eye to identifying, understanding, and eliminating obstacles to that condition.

Once a process cycles relatively consistently within the desired range, you have a basis to possibly go further by striving to reduce the gap between takt time and planned cycle time. For example, we might establish a process target condition that includes a planned cycle only 15 percent less (faster) than takt time. As you try to achieve this condition you will again discover obstacles (changeovers, machine downtime, scrap, absenteeism, etc.) you need to work on (Figure 5-5).

Takt time and planned cycle time are only one part of a target condition for a production process, and I am not suggesting that utilizing takt time in this way is the priority improvement for every situation. The point is, we have missed the target-condition intention behind it. Most factories I have visited know about takt time and even calculate

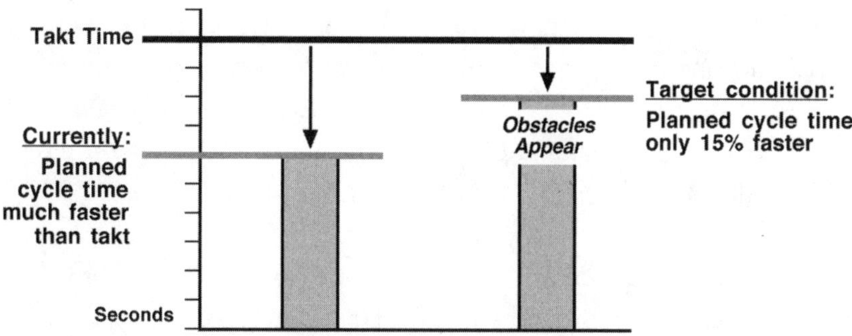

Figure 5-5. Reducing the gap between takt time and planned cycle time

Note: Toyota subtracts changeover time in calculating the planned cycle time of a process, but not unplanned downtime, which is made up with overtime, as necessary, at the end of each shift, rather than by further speeding up the planned cycle time to compensate for it in advance. This is done to keep problems visible. Of course, to take this approach you need a time gap between shifts that can accommodate such overtime.

it, but so far I've found few factories outside of the Toyota group that use takt time as something to strive for in the manner described here. Only then does it become useful.

> I once mentioned to one of Toyota's supplier support specialists that I'd figured out how to see what one needs to work on at a process. My idea was to ask the supervisor what would happen if we were to slow his process cycle down so it was only 15 percent faster than the customer takt time. The obstacles and objections that the supervisor mentioned would be what we needed to work on!
>
> "Well," the specialist replied, "the supervisor will be telling you her opinion. To understand the true obstacles, maybe you should build up a little safety stock and temporarily run the process at the slower cycle time. The obstacles that then actually arise are the true ones you need to work on next."

1x1 Flow

Let us begin by looking at two processes: one without 1x1 flow and one with 1x1 flow. The assembly process depicted below has four workstations, and one operator at each one. There are small quantities of in-process "buffer" inventory between the workstations, as indicated by the inventory triangles (Figure 5-6). The work content each operator has per cycle is shown by the black bars of the operator balance chart.[2]

Is there a 1x1 flow in this process?

No. Work pieces do not move from one processing step directly to the next. They pass through small buffer inventories.

Is the number of operators correct here?

No. The four operators are not fully loaded up to the planned cycle time. There are extra operators in this process.

What happens if one operator experiences a problem?

Not much. The other operators can keep working because of the buffers between the processing steps.

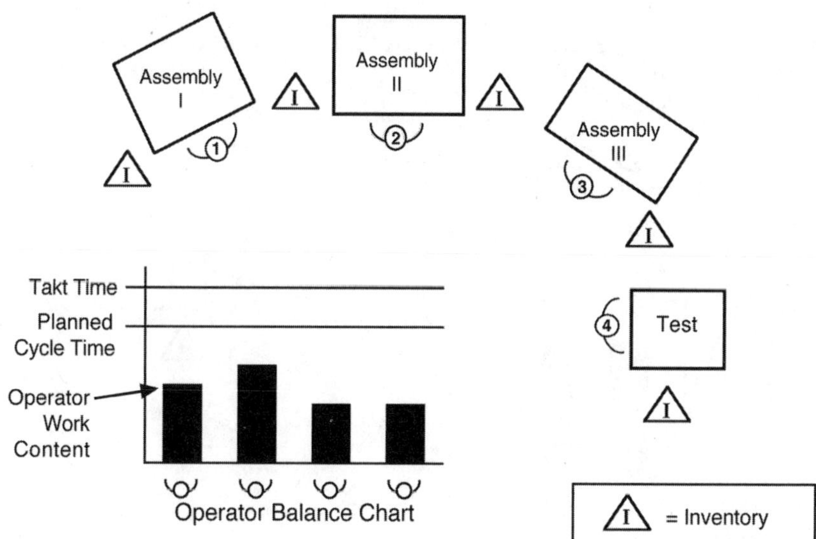

Figure 5-6. Assembly process with four workstations

Is this process flexible?

Many of us would say yes, this process is flexible, because despite small process problems and stoppages, it can still produce the required quantity every day. With extra operators in the line, the process has the "flexibility" to work around problems and still make the target output.

Now here is the same process, but with the workstations moved a little closer together and the work content distributed in a different manner. There are now two operators who move across the workstations, as shown in Figure 5-7, and no buffers between the processing steps. Takt time and planned cycle time are the same as in the previous diagram.

Is there a 1x1 flow in this process?

Yes. Work pieces move directly from one processing step to the next, rather than passing through buffer inventories between the processing steps.

Is the number of operators correct here?

Yes. The two operators are fully loaded up to the planned cycle time. This process is operating with the correct number of operators for the current planned cycle time.

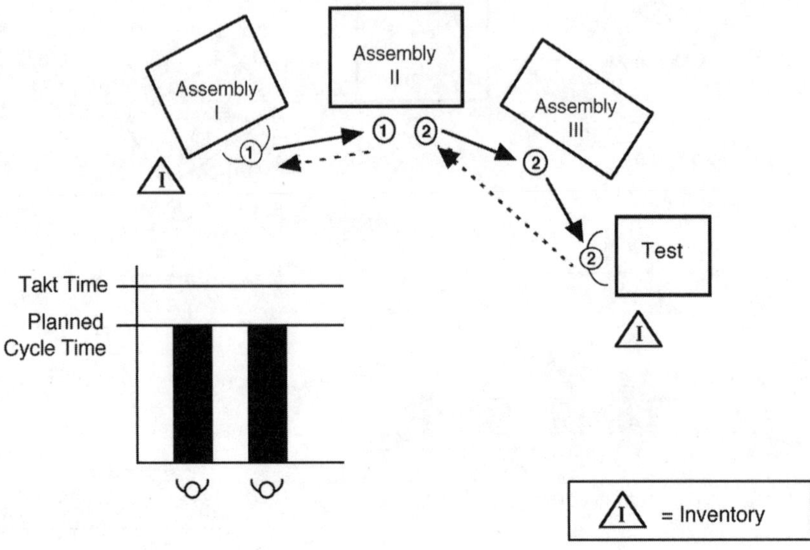

Figure 5-7. Assembly process operated in a different manner

What happens if one operator experiences a problem?

The entire process will come to a stop. The other operator cannot continue working because there are no buffers between the processing steps.

The Intention Behind a 1x1 Flow

Here is a key point: of these two process configurations, the one that looks better depends upon your philosophy. If the prevailing philosophy is to "make production," then the first process with four operators seems preferable. This process can work around problems and still make the target output, which is why you find this kind of arrangement on so many shop floors. On the other hand, at Toyota this sort of flexibility is considered negative, since problems go unresolved and the process gets into a nonimproving, firefighting cycle.

With Toyota's philosophy of surviving by continuously improving, striving for the second configuration, a 1x1 flow, is preferable because both that striving and the 1x1 flow itself reveal obstacles and show us what to focus our attention on. A 1x1 flow is not just part of the ideal state condition, it is also a means for helping to get there.

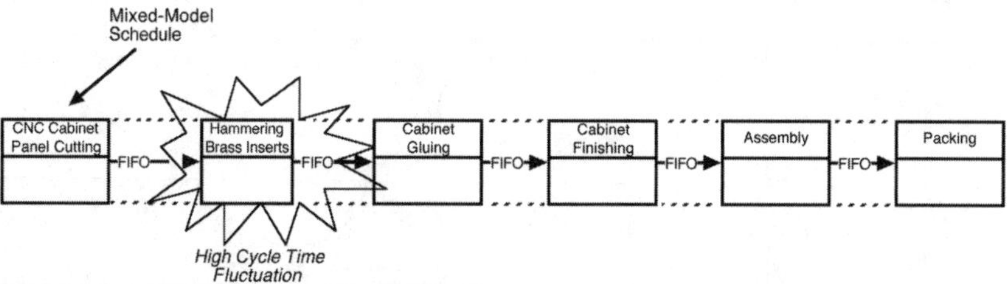

Figure 5-8. The speaker value stream

Figure 5-8 depicts an example from a factory that makes a variety of stereo loudspeakers. The factory has three nearly identical neighboring production value streams, whose individual processes are operated in a connected FIFO fashion (FIFO = first in, first out), as shown in the simplified value stream map. Speakers are built to order, so different size speakers go through the value stream one after another. A small speaker may be followed by a large speaker, and so on.

The leadoff process involves cutting the wood panels for a speaker cabinet, one speaker at a time, on an automatic CNC machine. This process has a consistent cycle time regardless of speaker cabinet size. In the next process (Figure 5-9) an operator manually hammers threaded brass inserts into predrilled holes in the cabinet face panel. The cycle time for this process varies greatly. A large cabinet with 18 brass inserts requires much more operator hammering time than a small cabinet that gets just eight inserts. As a result of this fluctuation, the rest of the downstream processes and operators often receive work at an uneven rate.

To compensate for this fluctuation, the downstream operators naturally walk from one value stream to assist in another, rather than idly waiting. When a set of large loudspeaker cabinet panels takes a long time to get through the brass insert process, operators step over to a neighboring value stream to assist there. Of course, this workaround is not a process improvement, and although it is done with good intention, it introduces even more fluctuation into the value streams.

What is happening here is that there is no process target condition other than "make production" or "keep the operators working," and as a result, problems push factory operations in different directions on an

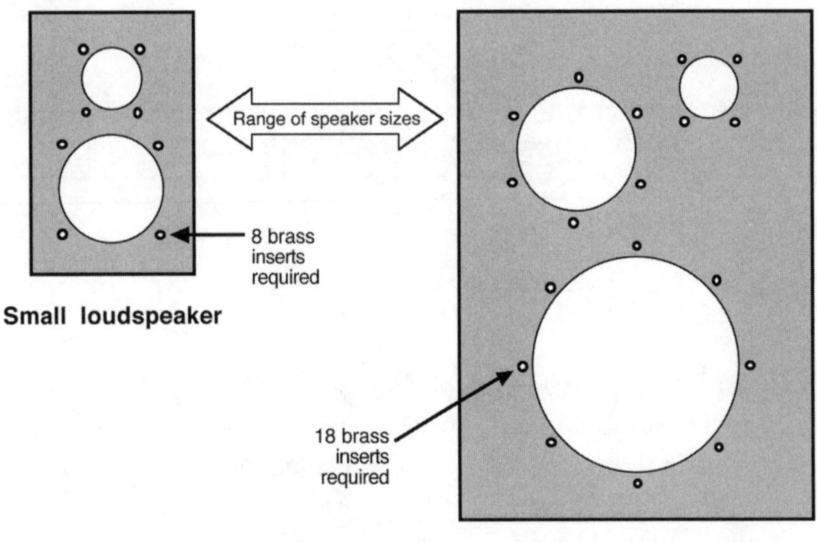

Figure 5-9. The number of brass inserts varies with loudspeaker size

ad hoc basis. What would happen instead if the process target condition included a 1x1 flow with the right number of operators at a consistent cycle time from speaker to speaker? Now there is only one choice: be creative and develop a way to install the brass inserts with the same cycle time no matter what size cabinet is being processed. If this is done resourcefully, at low cost and complexity, it would be a true process improvement, and progress for the company.

As this example illustrates, a target condition is a challenge. We do not know up front how we will achieve a consistent cycle in the brass-insert process, and that is how it should be. If we knew the answer up front, we would only be in the implementation mode, as discussed in Chapter 1.

A similar and common example is assembly cells that have been designed with the intention that the cell operators will help one another when a problem occurs, rather than having a firm target condition. Say Operator A normally performs assembly steps one, two, and three, and Operator B normally performs steps four, five, and six. If Operator A gets stuck at step two, then Operator B will also pick up step three on that cycle. This self-adjusting mechanism is often considered positive, but it is actually a work-around that reveals a "make production" rather than an improvement mind-set.

At Toyota, such self-compensating flexibility in processes would strike fear in the hearts of managers because of all the problems that go unnoticed and unaddressed. Such a mode of operation would not be allowed, and would be viewed as a failure to manage the process. This does not mean, however, that Toyota would just enforce work standards and prohibit the cell operators from assisting one another. The problems the operators are experiencing are real, and we must deal with them in some way. If we're going to strive for a consistent 1x1 flow target condition and expose problems, then we need to have a way of responding to and dealing with those problems. More on this in Chapter 7.

For a long time I misunderstood Toyota's desire to staff processes with the correct number of operators as simply a productivity goal. Higher productivity, higher quality, and lower cost may indeed be the overall objectives. But today I see that Toyota sets target conditions that include a 1x1 flow with the correct number of operators as a means to find out what needs to be worked on step by step to achieve those objectives.

In a processing area at a Nippondenso factory in Japan (part of the Toyota group of companies), aluminum parts go directly from hot die casting to machining in a 1x1 flow—that is, with no buffer in between. This is a great achievement and a true improvement. But the important point for us to learn is not the solution, but how it was developed. Imagine the factory establishing this particular 1x1 flow as a challenging target condition and then working through the obstacles one by one for months, and perhaps even years, until they achieved it.

Heijunka (Leveling Production)

It is a misconception, perhaps stemming from the pull system idea, that Toyota assembles vehicles in the same order in which customers buy them. Someday Toyota would like to have achieved that kind of 1x1 flexibility in its production operations (and also to have smoothened customer demand in the market). Today, however, Toyota is at the point that it strives to run an intentionally levelized schedule in many of its assembly processes. The diagram in Figure 5-10 illustrates, in a simplified fashion, the basic mechanics of *heijunka*, or leveling an assembly process.

The schedule for the assembly process—in this case kanban cards that circulate when customers pull corresponding items from the finished goods inventory—is not sent directly to the assembly process. Instead, the cards are routed through a kind of sorter, depicted in the diagram as a box.

This sorter typically levels two things, the mix and the quantity:

1. *Leveling the mix.* The sorter rearranges customer orders (the kanban cards) into a predefined sequence by item type. The sequence could be selected, for example, to minimize total changeover time or to break up large batches of demand and spread them across the day. In the example, the predefined sequence is A→B→Z→E→D→F→G→H. Two additional slots in the example sequence box are left open for various low-volume items, which are ordered only occasionally.[3]

   The assembly process will try to produce items in this predefined sequence. The intended time to get through the entire sequence depends on the lot size. If, for example, the process can change over often enough in one day to make every type, called "every part every day," then the lot size for any item is one day's worth. In this case the process would try to get through the entire sequence each day, and begin again at the front of the sequence the next day.
2. *Leveling the quantity.* The sorter also defines for each item the maximum quantity of that item that should be produced on one pass through the sequence. This is based on the production lot size and the current customer demand rate for each item. If the lot size is one day, then on any one pass through the sequence the maximum quantity that the process should produce of any item is the average one day demand for that item. In the example, the average one-day quantity of item A = eight boxes, item B = seven boxes, item Z = nine boxes, and so on.

In the diagram, you can see that a customer has purchased eight boxes of Item B, pulling them out of inventory, which puts eight kanban cards for B in circulation. However, according to the leveling pattern (the sorter), the current average demand for item B is seven boxes and the assembly process should only produce a maximum of seven boxes of B before changing to item Z. The eighth kanban card for item B should be filled on the next pass through the sequence.

This is where Toyota's leveling efforts get counterintuitive from the process perspective. Imagine the assembly supervisor having eight kanban cards for item B in hand, the assembly process is currently making item B, all is running well, and now we are telling the supervisor that he should only produce seven boxes of item B and go on to item Z.

Why do this?

Two already well-known reasons for leveling production in an assembly process are to be able to serve a variety of customers in a short lead time, and to limit the bullwhip effect, aka the "Forrester effect." The latter states that any unevenness in assembly is increasingly amplified as the demand is transmitted to upstream processes. Since upstream processes must hold enough inventory to meet demand spikes, the amount of inventory—that is, lead time—in a value stream will be lower when the downstream assembly process operates in a level

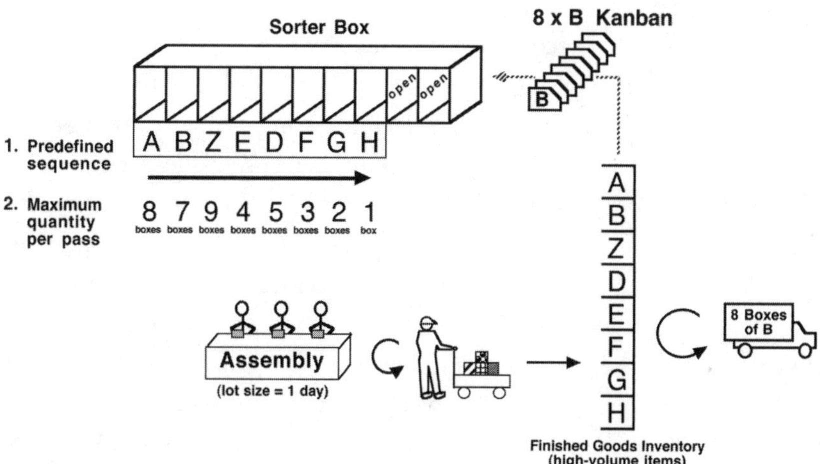

Figure 5-10. Example of a leveling scheme

fashion. For this reason, leveling in assembly is often a prerequisite for introducing kanban to upstream processes, since without it the upstream kanban-system stores ("supermarkets") may have to hold an unacceptably large amount of inventory.

In the example, a customer has ordered eight boxes of item B, which is one box more than his current average daily demand rate. The assumptions are that over a period of time the customer will be buying the average quantity, and if the customer buys one extra box today, he will buy one less box in the near future.[4] If the assembly process were to produce that extra box right away, it would send a demand spike upstream, which will be amplified and generate waste and extra cost the farther upstream it goes.

Smoothing production activities is the prevailing rationale behind leveling, or heijunka, but despite many attempts, I was never able to make heijunka work for very long. And neither can a lot of factories that I visit. I understood how to lay out the leveling sequence and lot sizes just like Toyota, but within a very short time we would have to deviate from the intended sequence because of problems, and we would quickly be back to frequent schedule changes, expediting, and firefighting. It seemed that Toyota must be experiencing fewer problems and practicing more stick-to-the-leveled-schedule discipline. But how?

The answer came to me because of two events.

When I paid my second visit to a factory in southern Germany, the production control manager met me with an angry face and the exclamation, "Please go away with that leveling concept!" On my first visit we had established a leveling sequence for one assembly process, but it did not last long, as usual. "We constantly experience part shortages," the manager told me, "so if we try to stick to a predefined assembly sequence, we would lose valuable production capacity." I had to agree.

The manager went on to show me the scheduling software program they had developed and were using instead. Every day, customer orders, inventory quantities, and parts availability are entered into the program, and from that information the next day's assembly schedule is generated. "See," the manager explained, "this is an assembly schedule that we know we can run." Of course, the assembly schedule was different every day.

The second event came later that same week. I was having dinner with a Toyota person, and at one point in our conversation he said, "Well, so many of the things we do at Toyota we do so there is a pattern." The penny finally dropped for me at that moment.

The Intention Behind Heijunka

What the heijunka leveling sequence provides is a pattern, or in other words, a target condition. It is something to strive for; something that helps us see what we need to work on, and to focus our improvement efforts where they are needed. Here is how it works:

1. Load the leveling device, the sorter, with kanban according to the intended sequence and maximum lot size specification.
2. Ask, "Can we run this way today?"
3. If yes, do so. If no, ask, "What is preventing us?" Pursue one problem, and meanwhile temporarily go off the intended sequence. Strive to get back on the intended sequence as quickly as possible.

At the beginning, the answer to the question, "Can we run this way?" will be no more than yes. But if you do this over and over and tackle the obstacles one by one, the yeses will increase. What you are doing is improving the associated processes step by step in a systematic way—by leading people in a direction.

Now we can see that while the scheduling software at the German factory does ensure a feasible schedule every day, in doing so it works around problems and leaves the factory standing still rather than improving its processes.

"Ah, I see," the German production control manager said when I explained what I had learned. "Toyota is trying to get to the point where the answer to the question, 'Can we run this way?' is always yes."

In fact, that is not the case. At that point we will not yet have reached the ideal state, and there must still be waste in the system. If the answer to the question, "Can we run this leveling pattern?" is almost always yes, then Toyota might, for example, reduce the lot size further in order to get back to a situation where the answer is no occasionally. Otherwise we are likely to stop improving.

One way to assess your efforts in leveling an assembly process is to measure sequence attainment per day. At one factory in the United States we set up a leveling sequence, and after one month the team proudly reported a sequence attainment of 73 percent. But I have never seen sequence attainment get so high so fast. We took a closer look and realized that the team was not measuring sequence attainment, but rather the old outcome metric—schedule attainment. That is, no matter how you did it, if today's shipments went out on time, you have schedule attainment for that day. Sequence attainment is a tighter process metric, which means if the assembly process has to deviate from the intended leveling sequence, then even if shipments are still made on time, you do not have sequence attainment for that day.

The team recalculated and was crestfallen to find that their sequence attainment after one month was actually only 13 percent. But this is not a reason to be sad. It is simply the current situation, nothing more and nothing less. The only thing to think about is, "Okay, what is the first obstacle that we need to tackle?" By thinking this way, the team began to go after the obstacles to achieving a level pattern one at a time, with considerable enthusiasm and on their own initiative. It became a challenge. After one year the sequence attainment for this assembly process was in the 60 percent range and the team continued to work. Each step forward represented a true improvement for the factory, and people were adopting a new way of thinking. Not bad.

After almost 20 years of benchmarking Toyota, we have set up a lot of leveling boxes and schemes at various production processes in factories all over the world. It is revealing, however, to observe what happens when a senior manager visits the factory. The leveling boxes are cleaned up beforehand and put in perfect order. All the right kanban cards are in the proper slots, and someone explains to the guest how the leveling system works. The visitor asks a few probing questions about the mechanics of the leveling scheme, eventually nods in approval, and then everyone moves on to the next stop on the facility tour.

What is happening here is a bit of a charade. Many leveling schemes are not working (which is, in fact, what one would expect, at least at the start) and are not actually in use, because we have misunderstood what they are for. The reality in many cases is that the assembly process still decides what to produce based on a schedule prepared anew every day. What the senior manager or executive who is being shown a leveling scheme should be asking is, "Okay, and what is currently your biggest obstacle to being able to run in this fashion?" There are a lot of heijunka boxes in our factories, but for the most part we are not yet using them as target conditions.

Contrary to what we might have thought, the heijunka pattern itself is not why production processes at Toyota factories run more level and more on time than in our factories. Establishing the heijunka pattern changes little in most cases. The point is how Toyota utilizes the heijunka pattern as a target condition to drive process improvement (Figure 5-11). It is the process improvement—the striving toward the target condition—that makes the difference.

Heijunka is one of the most far-reaching techniques in the Toyota toolkit, and a particularly useful target condition because pursuing it sheds light on so many elements of an assembly process and its associated value stream. Once we understand that heijunka, or leveling, is not a straitjacket, but a target condition, we can better reap the benefits of pursuing it.

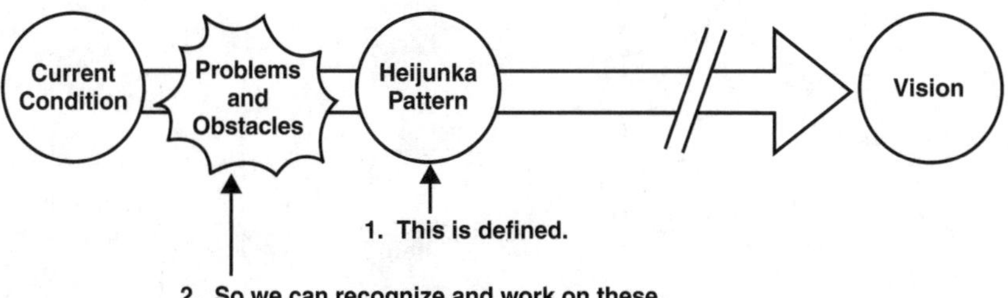

Figure 5-11. The heijunka pattern as a target condition

Pull Systems (Kanban)

The traditional approach for regulating production, which is still in wide use, is that each process in a value stream gets a schedule. These schedules are based on predictions of what the downstream processes will need in the future. Since humans, even with the help of computer software, cannot accurately predict the future, this approach is called a "push system." That is, each process produces what we believe the next process will need and pushes that material on toward the next process.

The alternative approach for regulating production—Toyota's "pull," or kanban, system—is by now also well known, and its basic mechanics are summarized in Figure 5-12.

1. The customer process, here assembly, receives some form of production instruction. Perhaps this is a leveled production instruction as described on the previous pages under *heijunka*.
2. The material handler serving this assembly process regularly goes to the upstream store and withdraws the parts that the assembly process needs in order to fulfill the production instruction.
3. The supplying process then produces to replenish what was withdrawn from its store.

The difference with the pull approach is that production at the supplying process is regulated by the customer process's withdrawals from the supplying process's store, rather than by a schedule. In this manner the supplying process only produces what the customer process has

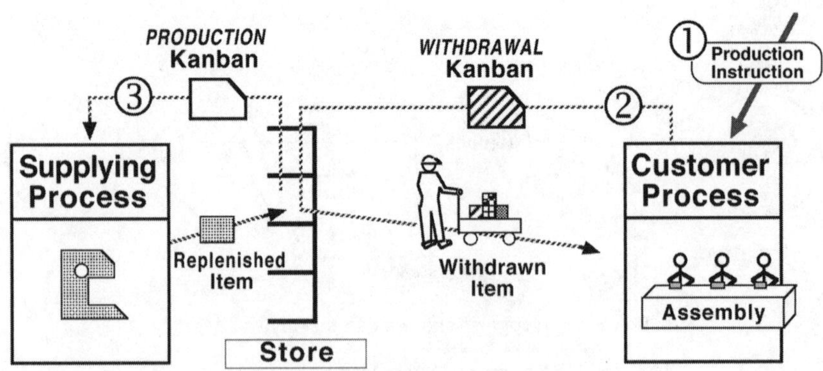

Figure 5-12. Basic kanban, or pull-system, mechanics

actually used, and the two processes become linked in a customer/supplier relationship.

These *mechanics* of the kanban system are what we benchmarked at Toyota, and those mechanics are what we have been trying to implement in our factories for many years. However, as with leveling, our success with pull systems has not been so good. In many cases what begins as an effort to introduce a pull system devolves into just better-organized inventory, and the supplying process continues to produce to some kind of a schedule.

Let us use the depiction in Figure 5-13 of a material flow between two production departments to take a deeper look at Toyota's kanban

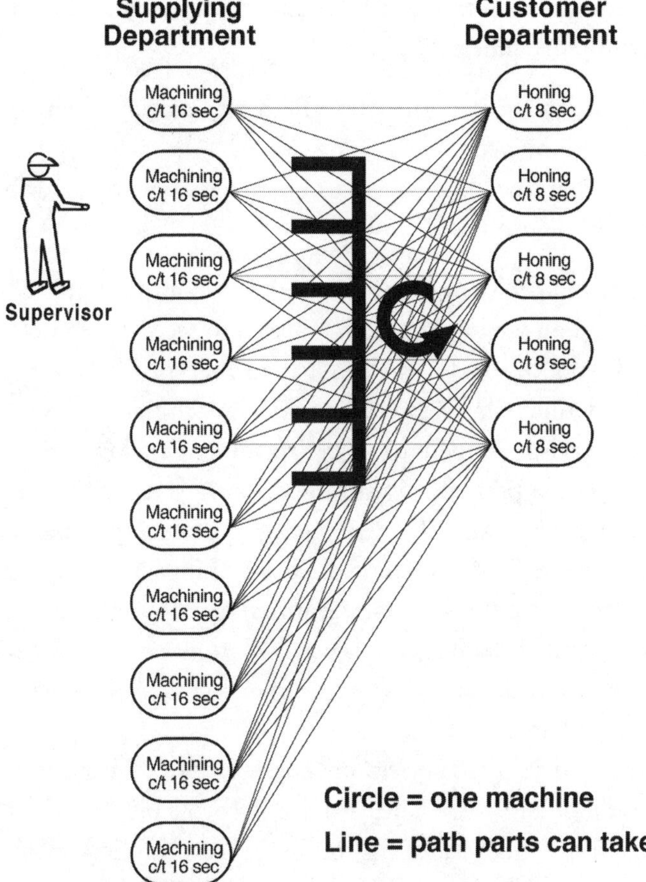

Figure 5-13. Material flow between two production departments

system. Each circle in the diagram represents one machine, and there are multiples of the same machine in each department. Each line in the diagram represents a path that parts may take, and any part number can be run on any machine. As is suggested by all the lines, currently the supplying department runs parts on whatever machine is available at the time. Also shown is the supervisor of the supplying department.

Now assume that we would like to insert a supermarket (kanban system) between these two departments, as shown. Perhaps we are doing this because the departments are located far apart, or maybe the machines in the supplying department have vastly different changeover times than those in the customer department.

To set up this pull system, we will need some information, which includes, among other things, part numbers, quantity, and the following two locations, or "addresses":

1. Where, in the supermarket, the parts associated with a kanban card will be kept
2. On what machine the parts associated with a kanban card should be produced

The act of specifying the second address—of defining what parts should be run on what machine—helps us to see what kanban is really about at Toyota. How do you think the supervisor will respond if we ask him to define what parts run on what machine?

The supervisor is likely to object to someone taking away his flexibility to run the parts on whatever machine is available. Perhaps he will say something like, "If we are going to define what parts will run on what machine, and thereby reduce my ability to run items on any machine, then we better start improving the reliability of these machines." And so kanban has already started working for us. It has shown us an obstacle, and now we need to roll up our sleeves and look into that problem.

I have heard many managers and engineers say, "We tried the kanban system, but it doesn't work here." To this, a Toyota person might well say, "Ah, kanban is actually already working. It has revealed an obstacle to your progress, which you now need to work on and then try again." We gave up at the place where Toyota rolls up its sleeves and gets going.

Flexible

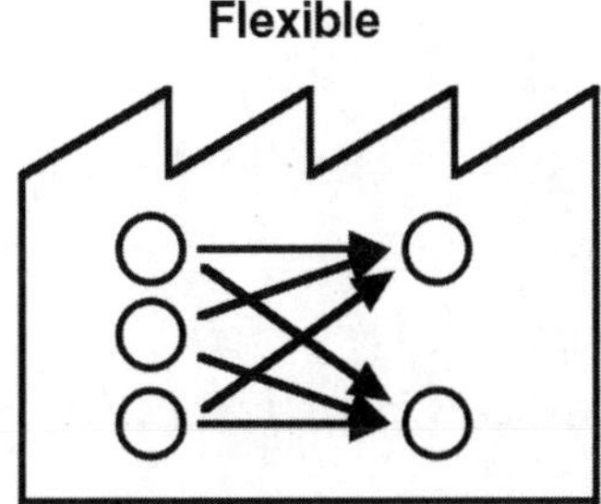

- *Can run any part on any process*
- *Many variables*
- *Difficult-to-understand causes of problems*

Pattern

- *Striving to dedicate part numbers to processes*
- *Easier-to-understand causes of problems*

Figure 5-14. Two different approaches

It is the same point again. Whether all those crossing lines—the flexibility to run parts on any available machine—look good or bad to you depends on your purpose (Figure 5-14):

- If your purpose is "make production," then the flexible system looks good because despite the existence of problems you can work around them and still make the numbers.
- If your purpose is "survive by continuously improving," then the flexible system looks bad. In fact, operating this way is not permitted at Toyota.[5] Working around problems by making the same part here and there increases the number of variables and makes understanding the cause of problems considerably more difficult. Flexible systems that autonomously bypass problems are by their nature nonimproving. You may make production today, but will you still beat the competition tomorrow?

The Intention Behind Kanban

The overt, visible purpose of kanban is to provide a way of regulating production between processes that results in producing only what is needed when it is needed. The invisible purpose of kanban is to support process improvement; to provide a target condition by defining a desired systematic relationship between processes, which exposes needs for improvement. In a push system, processes are disconnected from one another and routings are too flexible. There is no target condition to strive for.

> *. . . according to Ohno, the kanban controlled inventories . . . served as a mechanism to make any problems in the production system highly conspicuous . . .*
>
> —Michael Cusumano, *The Japanese Automobile Industry*

The difference between the visible and invisible purposes of kanban is very much the difference between the *implementation* and *problem solving* orientations I described in Chapter 1. We have been trying to implement the visible purpose of kanban without the invisible problem-solving effort, but one does not work without the other. No matter how carefully you calculate and plan the details of a pull system, when you start up that system it will not work as intended. This is completely normal, and we are setting ourselves an impossible target if we think we can achieve otherwise. What we are actually doing with all our careful preparation for a pull system—as with so many Toyota techniques—is defining a target condition to strive for.

My colleague Joachim Klesius and I once visited a large, 6,000-person factory that had decided to get into lean manufacturing. When we asked the plant's management what their first step would be, the answer was, "We will be introducing the pull system across the entire factory." This not only reveals our flawed thinking about pull systems, it also simply cannot work:

- Anytime you start up a pull system, it will crash and burn within a short time. There will be glowing and charred pieces, so to speak. But it is precisely these charred and glowing pieces that tell you what you need to work on, step by step, in order to make the pull system function as intended. Your second attempt to make that pull system work may then last a bit longer than the first, but it too will soon fail. And again you will learn what you need to work on. This cycle will actually repeat, albeit with longer intervals between the problems, until someday you have a 1x1 flow and no longer need the pull system. Keep in mind, by the way, that the kanban system does not cause problems, it only reveals them.

- Pull systems are rarely the first step in adopting lean manufacturing. Many production processes are currently unstable, and the amount of inventory you would need in order to have a functioning pull system between unstable processes would be unacceptably high. That much inventory would be detrimental anyway, since you would be covering up instability rather than first setting other process target conditions that help you understand and eliminate that instability.

If kanban is a tool for process improvement, then it makes sense to introduce pull systems on a small scale first and expand step by step as we learn more about and improve the relevant processes. If we try to introduce kanban quickly across an entire factory, an unmanageable number of problems will surface. Toyota's organization could not handle that either.

All this means that just introducing a kanban system by itself will improve very little; the system only mirrors and sheds light on the current situation. It does not, for example, by itself reduce inventory. It just organizes and utilizes inventory.

This in turn means it is impossible to implement a pull system. We should think of and use the pull system as a tool to establish target conditions in our effort to keep improving toward the ideal state condition. Each state we achieve is simply the prelude to another.

This last point was made clear by remarks from two Toyota people. The first was: "The purpose of kanban is to eliminate the kanban." While I was still pondering that one, I heard another Toyota person say: "We don't know how you make progress without kanban."

Ah-ha! Kanban is a tool to help us shrink the supermarket (inventory) over time and move progressively closer to 1x1 flow. That is why when a kanban loop at Toyota has been running trouble-free for some time, a manager might remove a kanban card from the loop. In this manner inventory is reduced, in a controlled fashion, and problems can begin surfacing again. Kanban is used to define successive target conditions, on the way to a 1x1 flow (Figure 5-15).

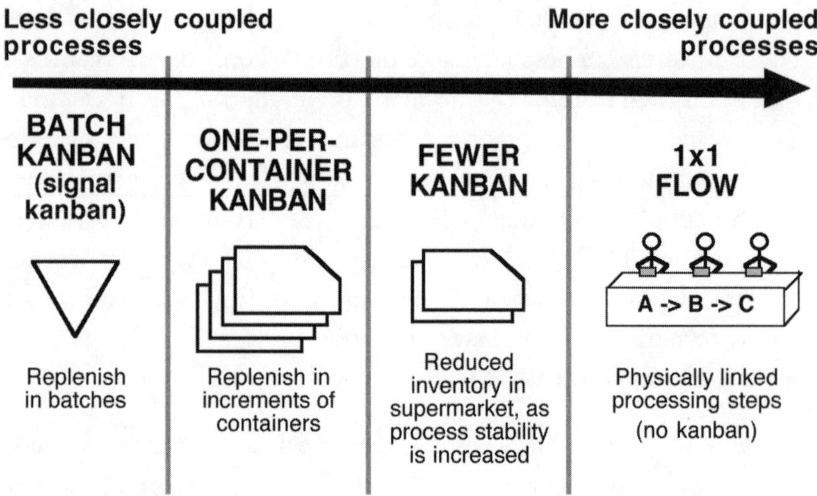

Figure 5-15. Kanban allows us to define challenging target conditions on the way to a 1x1 flow

Now Toyota's Tools Make More Sense

Toyota's tools and techniques become more understandable, and effective, when we view them in the context of striving to achieve a target condition by working step by step through obstacles. These tools and techniques are subordinate to the routine of Toyota's improvement kata, not independent of that routine, and our failure to see this perhaps explains some of the limited success we have had in trying to copy them.

> *Simply introducing kanban cards or andon boards doesn't mean you've implemented the Toyota Production System, for they remain nothing more then mere tools.*
>
> —Teruyuki Minoura, President and CEO 1998–2002,
> Toyota Motor Manufacturing North America

If your primary objective is to "make products," then many of Toyota's techniques—which by their nature limit your ability to work around problems—actually make little sense. To "make products" you want to be able to jump quickly to another machine if one breaks down (kanban makes this more difficult), to change to a different production schedule when there is a parts shortage (heijunka makes this more difficult), and so on.

Toyota uses many of its tools, such as takt time, 1x1 flow, heijunka (leveling), and kanban, as target conditions in order to better see problems and obstacles. There is possibly an even more deep-seated and subtle reason for our missing this intention and for our limited success, so far, in utilizing those tools.

Take the example where we monitor process output per shift or day, and thereby fail to recognize how much a process's individual output cycles fluctuate. Perhaps we tend not to think about individual process cycles because we have learned to manage by outcomes and feel we do not have the time to observe such detail. However, with many processes it only takes 20 minutes or so with a stopwatch to see if the process is fluctuating in or out of control. Despite such ease of analysis, I find very few companies where this is done. Why?

As discussed in Chapter 1, there is a human tendency to desire and even artificially create a sense of certainty. It is conceivable that the point here is not that we do not see the problems in our processes, but rather that we do not *want* to see them because that would undermine the sense of certainty we have about how our factory is working. It would mean that some of our assumptions, some things we have worked for and are attached to, may not be true.

In hindsight it seems somewhat foolish to have thought that simply implementing a kanban system or leveling scheme, for example, would result in significant and continuous improvement. The production processes themselves are still performing with essentially the same attributes as before. (There may be small, onetime improvements due to better organizing or paying closer attention.) We can now see that it is not actually the leveling pattern or kanban routine by itself that generates the improvement, but the step by step pursuit of conditions required to make those techniques work as intended. It is the striving for target conditions via the routine of the improvement kata that characterizes what we have been calling "lean manufacturing."

An interesting side note is that since Toyota is pursuing the one contiguous flow ideal, then any solution, tool, or practice that does not yet equal that ideal can be thought of as a temporary countermeasure. For example, I am sometimes asked for a formula to calculate how many kanban cards one needs in a pull system loop. Viewed in the light of moving toward the ideal state, having exactly the right number of kanban is not important at the start. You just need enough inventory, or kanban, to hold the system together while striving to continually improve processes and reduce the necessary number of kanban over time. To want to know the precisely correct number of kanban at the start suggests that we are thinking in static rather than continuous improvement terms.

Mobilizing Our Improvement Capability

Putting our capability for improvement, resourcefulness, and creativity to use takes managing ourselves in a way that marshals that capability. If people act before having a target condition, they will tend to produce a variety of ideas and opinions about where to go and what to do. At each juncture they often end up shifting direction or simply selecting the path of least resistance.

> *Success depends on your challenge.*
>
> —Shinichi Sasaki, former TME President and CEO

In contrast, a target condition—that is, a target pattern—creates a challenge that depersonalizes a situation (not your idea versus my idea about what we *could* do) and brings people's efforts into alignment. The diagram in Figure 5-16 based on an insightful sketch by my colleague Bernd Mittelhuber, depicts this well.

Of course, it is not enough to simply set a challenging target condition and hope people will find a way to achieve it. Toyota's improvement kata requires more than just that, and in the next chapter we will look at Toyota's routine for how to move toward a target condition.

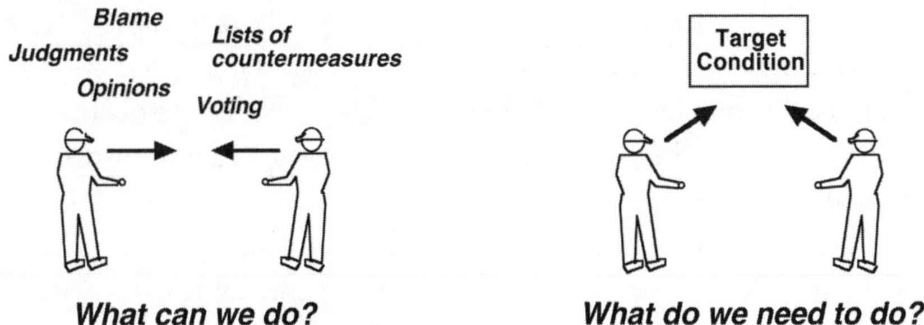

Figure 5-16. What a difference a target condition makes

Target Condition ≠ Target

It is important to recognize the difference between a target and a target condition. A *target* is an outcome, and a *target condition* is a description of a process operating in a way—in a pattern—required to achieve the desired outcome (Figure 5-17). It may take some practice before this distinction becomes instinctively clear to you.

Unfortunately, when they are speaking English, Toyota people from Japan still often use the word *target* when they mean a target condition. This has led to misinterpretations by westerners who are accustomed to

Target Condition	Target An outcome, result, or goal
Process A description of how the process should operate in order to achieve the target.	Inventory level Inventory turns Lead time Output per hour Cost, Labor cost Quality level Productivity etc.
Actionable These conditions will generate...	Cannot be achieved directly ...these outcomes and results

Figure 5-17. Difference between a target condition and a target

managing by setting quantitative outcome targets and focusing less on process details. When a Toyota person asks, "What is the target?" we naturally assume they are referring to a quantitative outcome metric. In actuality, a target condition as defined here is a good description of what Toyota people often mean when they say *target*.

The danger in not being clear about this distinction is that there are many different ways to achieve target outcome numbers, many of which have little to do with actually improving how processes are operating. Having numerical outcome targets is important, but even more important are the means by which we achieve those targets.[6] This is where the improvement kata, including target conditions, comes into play.

For example, a quantitative cost reduction target by itself is not descriptive enough to be actionable by people in the organization. The overall goal may be to improve cost competitiveness, but having that alone will tend to make people simply cut inventory and people.

Inventory-reduction targets are also very common, and when utilized without associated process target conditions, cause a lot of problems. For instance, I have a nice award on my office wall that was given to me for *increasing* inventory. The plant manager at this particular factory had decreed a target of no more than one day of finished goods inventory, and people complied with this by reducing inventory. The result was a tremendous increase in expensive expedited shipping, because one day of inventory was too low for the current lot-size performance of the assembly processes. What I did was point out that the process, not the inventory, should be the focus of our attention.

I once ran into this while touring a Detroit factory with a group that included a mostly Japanese speaking former Toyota executive. At one point on the tour the Toyota person pointed and said, "More inventory here." We chuckled and said, "Oh, your English is a little difficult to understand, but we know Toyota's system and of course you mean less inventory here." To which the former executive exclaimed, "No, no, no! More inventory here! This process is not yet capable of supporting such a low inventory level."

It is easy to say "reduce inventory" and much harder to understand the appropriate and reasonably challenging next target condition for the processes causing that inventory. The inventory around and in a process is an outcome, and there are reasons it is there. We need to dig into the related processes themselves, set the next process target condition, and then tackle the obstacles that arise on the way to achieving that target condition. Then we will learn what it is that requires us to have so much inventory.

The Psychology of Challenge

An interesting question that is still debated is whether Toyota's approach for continuous, incremental improvement would be appropriate for crisis and innovation situations, since in such situations we need to be more aggressive and fast in our efforts to improve. Interestingly, Toyota's improvement kata—including the use of target conditions—resembles how we tend to manage and behave in crisis situations. At such times, it's even more important to focus hard and resourcefully on what you need to do to achieve a challenging condition within the time, budget, and other constraints. You work in rapid cycles, adjust based on what you are learning along the way (see Chapter 6), and concentrate only on what you need to do. To some degree, Toyota is using its improvement kata to make a way of managing and working that we normally reserve for crisis situations an everyday way of working.

For example, the following may be difficult for many of us to accept and adopt, but it is one key to effectively utilizing our improvement capability: only work on what you need to work on. As people make suggestions for what to do, a reasonable question to ask is: "Do we expect this particular action to help us move toward the current target condition at this process?" If the action does not relate to a target condition, then it may be a good idea to stop spending time and resources on that action for now.

You may be thinking that, yes, some have proposed that we should create a crisis, but that's not what I mean. It is easy to create a crisis situation and hope people will then work appropriately. That, by itself, is still too much on the periphery and is not enough. What I mean is teaching people across the organization a behavior routine, a way to proceed, that mirrors good crisis behavior—behavior that aligns people and functions in accordance with the organization's philosophy and vision. Then if you want to create a crisis, okay, because people will have an effective means for reacting to and proceeding through it.

I can illustrate this with an experiment I have conducted many times. At a factory in Germany I took a group of engineers and managers to a shop-floor assembly process, equipped them with pencil, paper, clipboard, and stopwatches, and gave them, in writing, the following assignment:

Please observe this process.

- *Do not conduct interviews, but observe for yourself.*
- *Make a written report on a flip chart answering the following question:*

What do you propose for improvement?

In this case, I had the participants work in pairs and asked each pair to observe a particular segment of the assembly process. One team focused on a particular line segment with one operator and generated the following broad brush list of proposals, which was not very useful. Their list was similar to what most of the other participants produced:

- Reduce setup time
- Clean up and organize the area
- Hunt for waste
- Several suggestions regarding workstation layout
- Apply kanban
- Make a U-shaped line so the operators are not isolated

After this first round of the experiment we went back and carefully analyzed the assembly process and defined a target condition that describes how the process should be operating. (In Appendix 2, I show you a process analysis procedure.) Armed with that process target condition, the teams were given exactly the same assignment and sent to observe the same line segments as before. The results are diagrammed in Figure 5-18.

In this second round of the experiment, the team that focused on the one-operator line segment made completely different and considerably more useful observations. Part of the process target condition was a planned cycle time of 16 seconds, which is to say that the line should be producing a part every 16 seconds. This team watched its line segment and timed for several successive cycles how often a part moved past a specific point. The cycle times they observed fluctuated widely; this line segment was not producing a part every 16 seconds. Then the team asked itself the following question:

"What is preventing us from having a part come by this point every 16 seconds?"

In trying to answer that question, the team observed that the operator had to periodically walk away from the line to get new trays of parts. Of course, this had an impact on the stability of the line cycle time. Can you see the entirely different nature of this team's observations and thoughts before and after a process target condition was defined?

Another example, this one from several years ago. At a factory in Michigan that makes file cabinets, product development was once

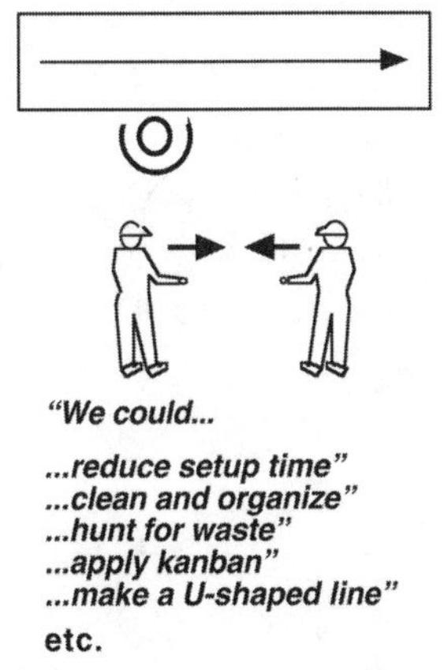

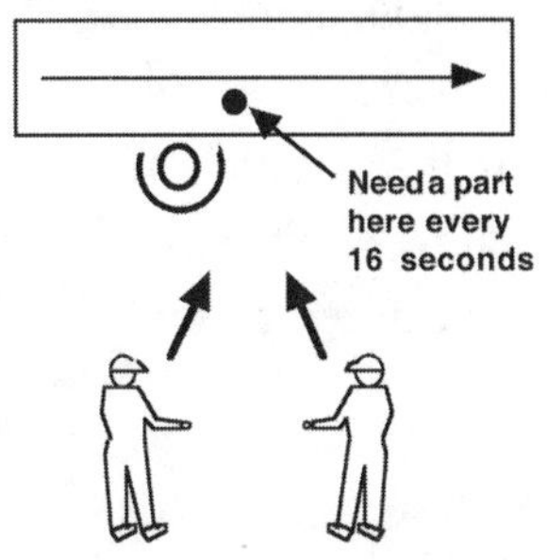

Figure 5-18. What a difference a target condition makes

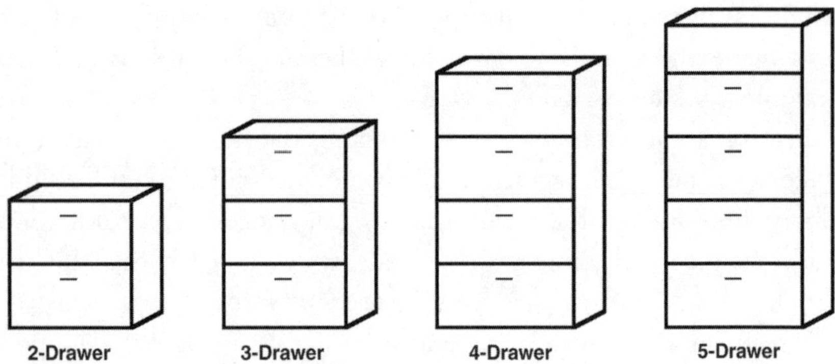

Figure 5-19. The four file cabinet sizes

designing a new line of cabinets that were to be produced in an already existing file cabinet value stream. The production value stream would have to be reconfigured somewhat, and some capacity added, to accommodate the new products.

File cabinets produced in this value stream came in four sizes, as shown in Figure 5-19.

The three main processes for producing all files cabinets were: bending and welding sheet steel→painting→assembly. The current production flow is shown in Figure 5-20.

There was one bending/welding process, consisting of expensive, automated equipment. This process was, in particular, where additional capacity would be needed. Then there were two chain-conveyor paint lines, which already had sufficient capacity to handle the additional new cabinets. These paint lines and their conveyor systems were so monumental that no change was currently feasible here, which is

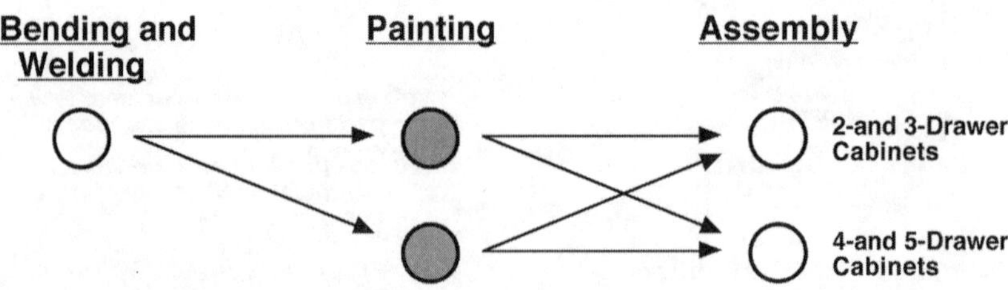

Figure 5-20. Current production flow

why they are shaded in the diagram. Finally, there were two assembly lines: one for the smaller two- and three-drawer file cabinets, and one for the larger four- and five-drawer cabinets. The arrows show the material flow.

The debate among the engineers about how to configure the value stream had gone on for several weeks. There was still no consensus, but it was time to specify and order any necessary equipment. At this point I was asked to spend a week working with the team.

The production design team consisted of about 10 people, and during my first day with them our discussion went in circles. Someone would make a suggestion, such as having two bending/welding lines so there could be more dedicated flows, as in Figure 5-21.

The group would go in this direction for a while, until someone made the counterargument that a second bending/welding line would be too expensive for the budget.

Then we would switch to another suggestion, such as altering the two assembly lines so each one could assemble all four cabinet sizes (Figure 5-22). This would be an advantage because sometimes big

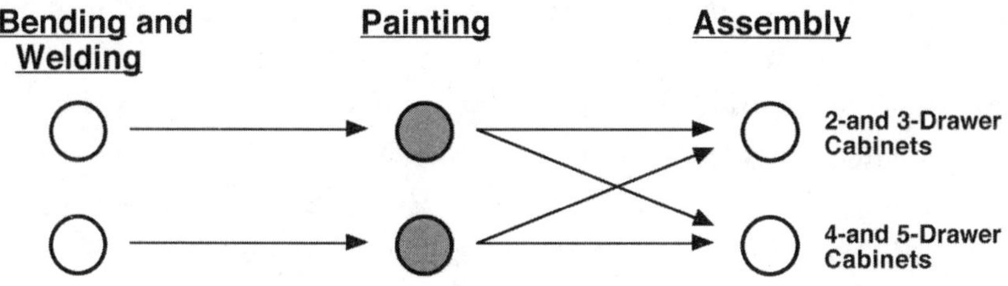

Figure 5-21. First proposal: adding a second bend/weld line

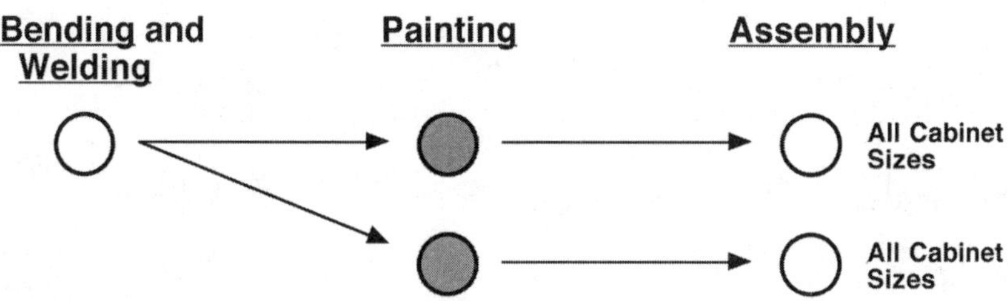

Figure 5-22. Another proposal: universal assembly lines

customers order predominantly the small or large sizes, which overwhelms one assembly line while the other sits idle.

This idea was pursued until someone pointed out that the operator work content and time was much higher for the larger cabinets than for the smaller cabinets, and that the line for small cabinets was elevated for better assembly ergonomics. Small and large cabinets were just too different from one another, and so again we switched to other ideas.

By the end of the first day we were no further along, and I sat in my hotel room thinking about what to do. As mentioned in Chapter 2, many group discussions and efforts go exactly this way. Whoever is most persuasive sets the tone and direction, until someone else has a convincing counterargument. In the worst cases, a voting technique is employed to give an artificial feeling that we know what to do.

Tuesday morning we began with a different approach. I asked the group what would be better, two bending/welding lines or one? Clearly two would be better because of the dedicated flows, but hands quickly went up in objection. "We have already been over that option several times. A second weld/bend line is too expensive." We left the idea on the board, however. Then I asked if it would be better if both assembly lines could process all sizes of cabinets? "Yes, of course, but we've been over that option several times too. The small and large sizes are too different from one another."

Then we drew the value stream shown in Figure 5-23 on the board.

Probably because I was an outsider, the group went along with me as I said, "Okay, no more discussion about where we want to go. This is our direction. Now let's instead put all our effort and discussion into how we can achieve this condition within the allotted budget and time." We had established a basic target condition.

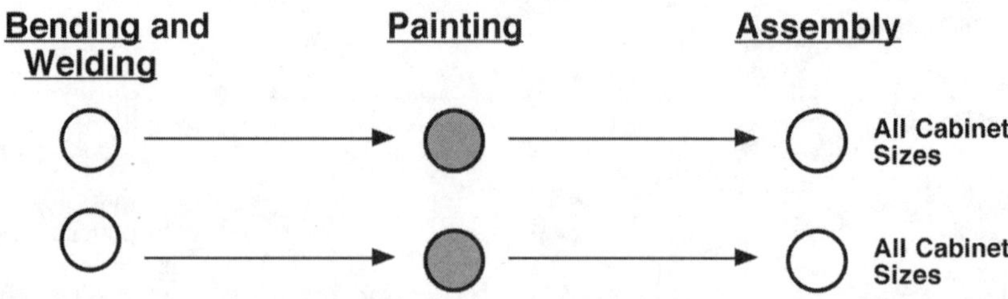

Figure 5-23. A target condition

The change in the group dynamic was striking. We put one team of engineers on the challenge of adding a second bend/weld process within the budget constraints, and it was remarkable how creative and resourceful they were. Here are just a few excerpts from that team's work during the rest of the week:

"We looked at an old unused weld line we have in the back of the plant, and there are several parts of that equipment we can reuse."

"Maybe we can do without the expensive automatic transfer of steel sheets between the steps of the bending process."

"We could utilize simple switches to enable or disable individual spot-weld tips depending on the size of the cabinet being welded, without using a numeric controller."

The team assigned to modifying the two assembly lines so that each could handle all sizes was equally creative:

"How can we make a simple lift system for good ergonomics when a short cabinet comes down the line?"

"If we have a high-assembly-content cabinet coming down the line, let's leave one pitch empty behind it so the operators have twice as long to work on it as on a small cabinet."

Not all ideas could be implemented, and in the end the target condition we set for ourselves was not fully achieved this time, but the progress made was a great example of human capabilities … if we channel them.

Target Condition = Challenge

A target condition normally includes stretch aspects that go beyond current process capability. We want to get there, but we cannot yet see how.

An interesting perspective on this was provided by Toshio Horikiri, the CEO of Toyota Engineering Company Ltd., in a presentation he made at the Production Systems conference in Munich on May 27, 2008. Mr. Horikiri linked the degree of learning, fulfillment, and motivation to the level of challenge posed by a target condition. He proposed that both "easy" target conditions—ones that from the start we can already see how to achieve—and "impossible" target conditions, do not provide us with much sense of motivation and fulfillment (Figure 5-24). It is when a target condition lies between these extremes and is achieved that an adrenalinelike feeling of breakthrough and accomplishment is

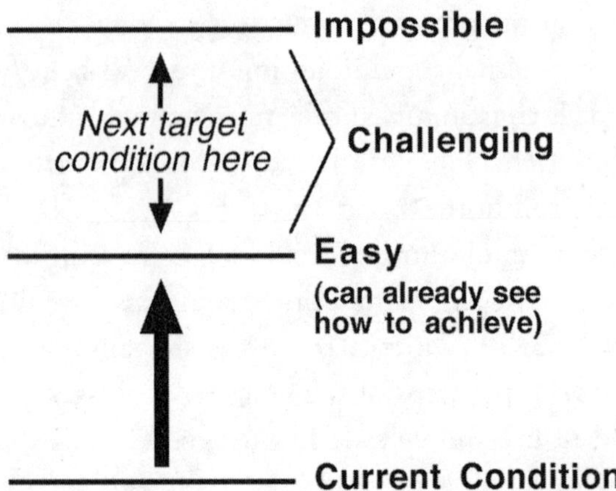

Figure 5-24. Target conditions as a challenging but achievable stretch

generated ("We did it!"), which increases motivation and the desire to take on more challenges.

A simple example: An operator at a metal-forming press fabricates small parts, which will later be painted and then used at an assembly process. The press operator carefully stacks the formed parts into their storage container, which makes it easier for the paint line operators to pick them up one by one. But the stacking takes too much time, and a suggestion is made to reduce time by having the press operator just drop these unsensitive metal parts into the container.

Right from the start we can see how to achieve this suggestion, which means there is probably no real improvement in the work system. It is a reshuffling of already existing ways of doing things or a shift of waste from one area to another. On the other hand, if we set a process target condition that includes stacking the parts in *x* time—*x* being less than the current time—we cannot immediately see how to achieve that. And when we do achieve it, then a true, creative process improvement will have been made.

As you define a target condition, you should not yet know exactly how you will achieve it. This is normal, for otherwise you would only be in the implementation mode. Having to say, "I don't know," often means that you are on the right path. If you want true process improvement, there often needs to be some stretch.

With this in mind, do not utilize a cost/benefit analysis (ROI) to determine what a target condition should be. That is the error the Detroit automakers' managerial system led them to make whenever they tried to decide whether to also produce smaller cars. First define the next target condition—a condition that you need or want—then work to achieve it within budget and other constraints. A target condition must be achieved within budget, of course, but it normally takes resourcefulness to achieve the challenge within that constraint.

Target Condition Thinking

Over time and with practice you should be able to develop a kind of target condition thinking, and Toyota's concept of "standardized work" helps illustrate what I mean. A "standard" is a description of how a process should operate. It is the prespecified, intended, normal pattern (Figure 5-25).

On the other hand, at Toyota "standardized work" means, in essence, that a process is actually operating as specified by the standard (Figure 5-26). Standardized work is a condition, and you can look at a process and ask, "Does that condition exist or not?"

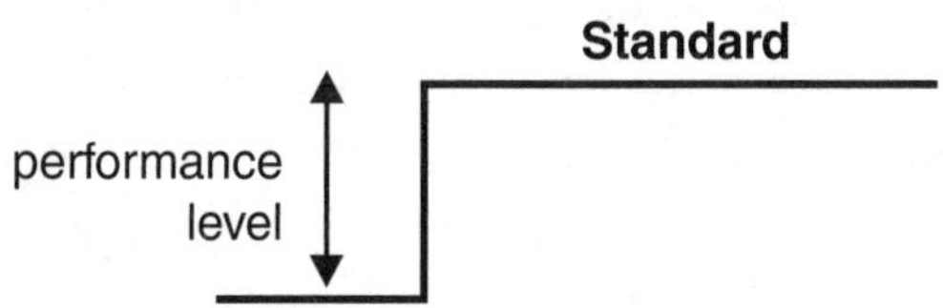

Figure 5-25. A "standard" = how a process should operate

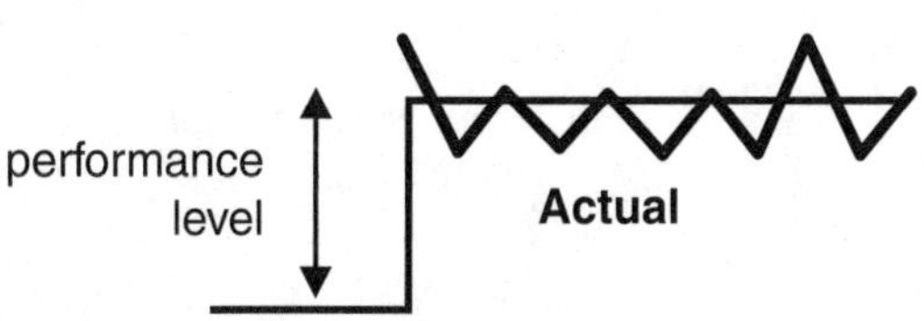

Figure 5-26. "Standardized work" = the process is actually operating as the standard specifies

At a manufacturing conference in Chicago a group of Toyota's production system specialists presented how they improved a production process at a supplier's facility. During the presentation someone in the audience asked the speakers, "Do you post standards in the production line?" In typical Toyota fashion (the student should learn for himself), the answer was brief, "Yes, we do." I noticed a lot of audience members writing this down, and envisioned them posting standards over the heads of their operators in the false assumption that this would improve something. So I asked a follow-up question: "Who are the work standards for?"

"Well," came the reply, "when it was time to post the standards in the line"—Toyota does not always post them in the line—"we had to decide whether to post them facing the operators or facing the aisle." The speaker paused for effect and said, "We posted them facing the aisle."

The aisle side is where the team leader is, and it is the team leader who primarily uses the work standard.

The key question is not, "Have we posted work standards?" but rather, "How do we achieve standardized work?" The primary intention of specifying standards at Toyota is not, by doing so, to establish discipline, accountability, or control the workers, but rather to have a reference point; to make plan-versus-actual comparison possible, in this case by the team leader, so that gaps between what is expected and what is actually occurring become apparent. In this way we can see what the true problems are and where improvement is needed.

When we are asked if we have standardized work, we usually point to a posted work standard as evidence and say, "Yes, see, we have standardized work." When a Toyota person is asked the same question, they also look for the standard, but then observe the process and compare it to the standard. If there is a difference between the two—and there often is, even at Toyota—they say, "Not yet." Toyota is achieving quality excellence, for example, not because a process is done the same way each time, *but because Toyota is striving to achieve the target condition of*

Figure 5-27. How do we think when an abnormality occurs?

the process being done the same way each time. The difference is subtle, but it's important if you want to understand and successfully emulate Toyota's success.

How we are thinking about standards is also revealed when there is an abnormality in a process (Figure 5-27). In the traditional way of looking at it, we think the abnormality means we are slipping back; that we need a corrective action and more discipline. My impression is that the Toyota way of thinking turns this around: the abnormality means we have not yet reached the target condition, and we need to keep applying the improvement kata.

So what is the difference between a standard and a target condition? In many cases not much. A good way to think of many standards is as something you are striving to achieve, and the main issue is: "How we will get this process to actually operate as described in the standard?" That is the hard work. (More on that in Chapter 6.)

So the following standards, and many others in a factory, can be seen as target conditions (Figure 5-28).

Consider what could be achieved if everyone in your company learned to think of such standards not as straitjackets, but as target conditions to strive for.

WORK STANDARDS	Takt time, correct number of operators, 1x1 flow, operator work elements, times for the elements, etc.
LEVELING	Planned sequence, maximum lot size, finished goods quantity, etc.
PULL SYSTEM	Location in supermarket, inventory quantity, kanban cards, etc.
LOGISTICS	Delivery route, stops, timing, etc.

Figure 5-28. These standards, and many others, can be viewed as target conditions

Establishing a Target Condition

A target condition is developed out of a detailed grasp of the current condition, through direct observation and analysis, coupled with an understanding of the direction, vision, target, or need. You need to adequately understand the current condition in order to define an appropriate target condition.

The first few target conditions for a production process often spring only from analyzing the process itself. Then, as you progress there, target conditions should be aligned with or based on departmental targets. However, even if departmental targets are met, you should continue defining further process target conditions, because if a process is not striving toward a challenge, it will tend to slip back. Ultimately you should be able to walk through the factory and at each process ask, "What challenge"—target condition—"are you currently trying to reach here?"

One of the most common early target conditions with production processes, as well as again and again after process changes are introduced, is to establish stability as measured by fluctuation in workstation cycles and output cycles. Most production processes I see are not operating in a stable condition yet.

With regard to production processes, Appendix 2, "Process Analysis," shows you a typical procedure for analyzing the current condition of a production process and obtaining the facts and data you need in order to establish an initial target condition for it.

What Information Is in a Target Condition?

A target condition describes a state that we want to have reached at some future point in time, on the way toward a longer-term vision. There are both technical and nontechnical target conditions, since the improvement kata has application in a wide range of situations. At least some aspects of any target condition should be measurable, however, so that you can tell if you have reached it or not.

A factor in establishing a target condition is to draw a line between the target condition and, in contrast, countermeasures or steps. A target condition should describe a desired condition, but not how you will get there (Figure 5-29). Trying to put countermeasures into a target condition is a common error that I still catch myself making. We like to jump to spelling out solutions, but this actually impedes the operation of the improvement kata. Engineers, for example, often try to define target conditions in terms of solutions because that is what they are accustomed to working with. You have to learn to hold yourself back and first define where you want to go before you get started on moving there. Countermeasures, then, are what you develop as

NOT A TARGET CONDITION	***WHY***
"Implement a pull (kanban) system" **"Introduce milk-run material delivery"**	**Too vague. A kanban or material-delivery system can in fact be a target condition, but you need to describe in detail how they should operate.**
"Apply 5S" (housekeeping and workplace organization) **"Install a barcode system"** **"Change the layout"**	**These are countermeasures, which should not be confused with a target condition. First describe how the process should operate. Countermeasures are then developed *as needed* on the way to that target conditon.**
"Minimize" "Reduce" **"Improve" "Increase"**	**Words like *minimize, reduce, improve, increase* do not belong in a target condition, because a target condition describes a desired condition *at a point in time*.**
"Two fewer operators" **"Reduce inventory by two days"**	**Reduced headcount or reduced inventory are outcomes, not target conditions. They do not describe how the process should operate in order to be able to meet customer demand with less people or less inventory.**

Figure 5-29. Examples of what is not a target condition

needed once the target condition has been defined and you are striving to move toward it, as described in Chapter 6.

As a guideline, the target condition for a manufacturing process tends to include the following four categories of information. The first three items are used in conducting process improvement day to day through the improvement kata. The fourth item is only used periodically to gauge the outcome of process improvement efforts.

1. *Process steps, sequence and times*
   What is the sequence of steps required to complete one cycle through the entire process, how long should each step take, and who is to perform that step?
2. *Process characteristics*
   Other attributes of the process:
   - Number of operators
   - Number of shifts
   - Where 1x1 flow is planned
   - Where buffers are to be held (including intended buffer quantity)
   - Lot size/EPEI/changeover times
   - Heijunka/leveling pattern
3. *Process metrics*
   These are metrics for checking the condition of the process in short time increments, in real time while the process is running, to help guide improvement efforts, such as:
   - Actual cycle time for each step, per piece, or per standard quantity of pieces (such as one tray or packing layer)
   - Amount of fluctuation from cycle to cycle
4. *Outcome metrics*
   - Number of pieces produced per (time increment)
   - Productivity
   - Quality indicators
   - Cost
   - Fluctuation in output from shift to shift

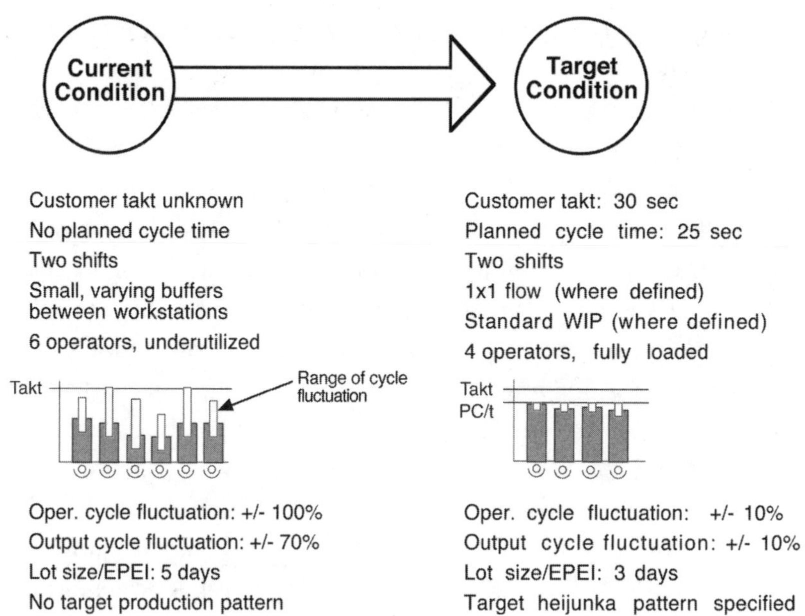

Figure 5-30. An example process target condition

In Figure 5-30 we see typical elements of a target condition for an assembly process. However, this target condition is only for illustration purposes and has too many elements that are a leap in comparison with the current condition. Moving from this current condition to this target condition would probably involve a series of target conditions.

As you can see, manufacturing target conditions tend to define how a process should be operating to a greater level of detail than is currently the practice in many factories. As we will see in the next chapter, this detail creates a condition in which learning can take place.

How Much Detail?

At production processes it is sometimes possible to define in advance a detailed target condition, because the current condition can be observed, analyzed, and understood in detail. In most situations, however, it is not possible to fully see and understand the true current condition right away, and thus not possible to define a target condition in full detail up front. For example, think of setting out to develop or market a new product. That is, you do not yet know the details about what customers want.

Caution is advised, for in situations where you cannot yet adequately discern the current condition—which is most situations—you may mistakenly feel confident that you do understand. We often don't realize what we do not know, and can thus easily slip into specifying target condition details that are actually based on conjecture.

So there is a dilemma. Before you get started, you need a target condition—but you cannot yet see a lot of target condition detail. The way out of this predicament is to begin with a well thought out but basic, less detailed definition of the target condition and add in detail as you move forward and learn about the obstacles (Figure 5-31). When in doubt, err on the side of being a little vague in defining the target condition, and narrow down and add detail as you move into the unclear territory. This leaves options open rather than specifying them too early based on suppositions.

For example, at production processes, I have had good results by making close observations, establishing an initial target condition that defines the following, and then getting going (as described in Chapter 6):

- Takt time and planned cycle time

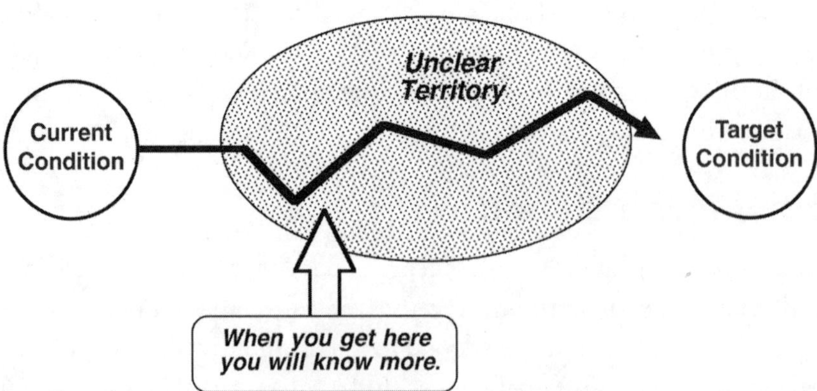

Figure 5-31. Once under way, more details become clear

- Where in the process a 1x1 flow should be achieved next (based on experienced judgment)
- The number of operators and shifts
- Process stability

For detailed guidance on defining these points see Appendix 2.

After a day or two of working at the process, we have usually learned enough about it to have defined a more detailed target condition. This frequently involves simply attempting to run the process as described in the initial target condition, as an experiment; that is, in order to see what happens. You might call this "further analyzing the current condition by getting going toward the target condition." The approach of defining initial target conditions vaguely is in widespread use at Toyota, where it is considered bad form to specify in detail something you do not yet understand.

Note that I do not mean changing the target condition as you move forward, but rather, fleshing it out. Once a target condition is established—even an initially vague one—its content and achieve-by date are not easily changed. This is done so we take time to analyze the current condition, think carefully about the target condition, and, when the going gets tough, work hard to understand and with creativity get through the obstacles that arise step by step. This way we achieve a new level of system performance, rather than simply altering the target condition.

Do or do not. There is no try.

—Yoda

Defining some terminology can be helpful here. I call an initial, vague target condition a *challenge*, and once sufficient detail has been added, I call it a *target condition*. For example, the manager of an assembly area *challenges* his team to bring the machining of some die cast components, which is currently done in batches elsewhere in the plant, into the 1x1 flow at an assembly process. As the team studies the situation, develops a concept and perhaps even experimentally moves the machining center into the assembly process, it defines the further details that characterize a *target condition*.

How Challenging Should a Target Condition Be?

Knowing what is an appropriate target condition—a challenging but achievable stretch—depends on the situation and is an acquired skill. As you gain experience in using the improvement kata, you will become a better judge of what a particular process and people are ready for next. As I began to learn about and work with the improvement kata, I thought we would tend to make our target conditions too easy. In fact, we tended to make them too difficult. Why? Because when we do not yet understand a situation firsthand and in detail, we overlook or underestimate obstacles and thus may develop target conditions that are too ambitious for the allotted time frame.

For example, sometimes we jump to introducing a FIFO (first in, first out) flow through long stretches of a value stream, with the idea that this must be good because it is much closer to the ideal state. However, if a FIFO flow has a beginning-to-end lead time of greater than, say, one day, it may generate chaos as process conditions change while parts work their way through the long FIFO route. What seemed like more flow becomes disorder, because we tried to leap ahead too quickly rather than proceeding step by step.

Another example is cutting too much inventory too soon. Here again, the thought is that cutting inventory is good because less inventory is closer to the ideal state. However, too little too quickly and you generate chaos. The trick is understanding your processes, holding the right amount of inventory in a controlled fashion, and improving those processes step by step toward appropriate target conditions, so that, as an *outcome*, inventory can be reduced.

What Is the Time Horizon for a Target Condition?

One year. Some target conditions may reach a year into the future, which corresponds with the planning or policy deployment cycle in many companies. Or the target condition may be part of a long project. However, in my experience a one-year time frame is too long for a target condition to be effective, and such long-term target conditions should be supplemented with interim target conditions. You do not have to go too far at once, and it can be faster overall and more effective to take small steps rapidly than to try to make big leaps.

Three-month maximum. I suggest that the maximum time horizon for a production-process target condition should be three months. If a target condition extends further than three months into the future, you should probably look at breaking it into more manageable increments.

One to four weeks. I have had good success guiding people to establishing target conditions that are no more than one to four weeks out, particularly when they're first learning the improvement kata. This way a person can get more practice with full cycles of the improvement kata.

The further into the future your target condition reaches, the more you will need to lay out a plan for how you intend to move from the current to the target condition. For a one-week target condition, you can get going without much of a how-to-get-there plan. For a target condition three months out, you will need a well-thought-out plan.

What Is the First Step?

As you define a target condition, it will not be clear how to achieve it, but the next step should be clear. This is like "priming the pump."

In this regard, a Toyota person once told me to always focus on the biggest problem. However, when I tried to do this, I noticed a negative effect: we got lost in hunting for and discussing what was the biggest problem. When we tried gathering data and making Pareto charts, it took a lot of time and the biggest problem category in the Pareto chart was usually "other," which put us back to debating opinions. By the time we decided what the biggest problem was, the situation at the process had changed. This effect is called *Pareto paralysis,* and I encourage you to avoid it. Pareto paralysis delays your progress as people try to determine the "right" first step to take.

Fortunately, such delay is easy to avoid, because it matters more that you take a step than what that first step is. Do not worry so much up front about finding the biggest obstacle before you begin. Take a step, and when you've done that, the learning process begins and you will see further. If you are moving ahead in fast cycles, I assure you that you will soon find the current biggest problem. It will be waiting for you.

A related point in many instances is that the next step may *not* involve a countermeasure, but rather, getting more information through observation, data, or experiment. As mentioned before, if you are unsure, then go and see; again and again if necessary. This has helped me hundreds of times. Most steps you take will not be countermeasures, but efforts to see deeper and get more facts and data.

In setting the next step, a tactic I use is to ask the same person who conducted the process analysis and established the target condition to also define the next step. This eliminates those "what is the first step" discussions. The idea is to get started and then see further (Figure 5-32).

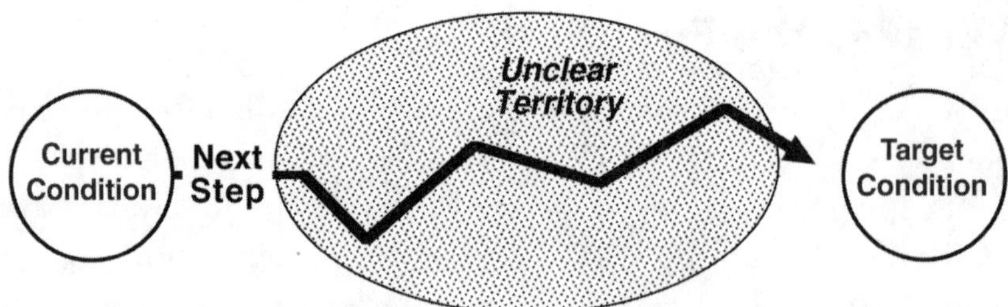

Figure 5-32. Once you take a step the learning process begins

Ready to Go

Once you have defined the target condition and the next step, you are ready to begin working toward the target condition. How Toyota does that is the other part of the improvement kata, and the subject of the next chapter.

Something you can do immediately is an analysis to assess the stability of a production process, which can be a good way to begin grasping the current condition. Do this at an assembly or "pacemaker" process if possible. (A definition of "pacemaker process" is in Appendix 1.) With a stopwatch, pencil and paper in hand, position yourself at the last workstation in the line, select a point, and time how often a part comes by that point. Do this for 20 to 40 successive cycles, recording the time for each cycle.

Then move upstream and time the cycle of each operator's work in a similar fashion. Select a single reference point in the operator's complete work cycle, which is where you will start and stop your stopwatch. Let the stopwatch run until the operator returns to that point in the cycle, regardless of how long it takes. Do this 20 to 40 times for each operator. Graph the findings for each position you timed as shown in the example in Figure 5-33. Do not calculate or use averages, which conceal process instability.

Now observe the process and ask yourself, "What is preventing the process and the operators from being able to work with a stable cycle?" Process stability alone is not a complete target condition, but making these observations can be a good start to understanding the current condition and developing a target condition.

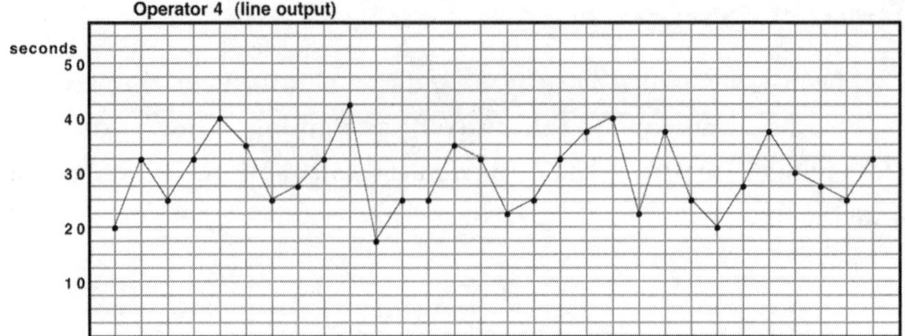

Figure 5-33. Checking process stability by timing successive cycles

Typical initial target conditions for manufacturing processes. Although there are many exceptions, the target conditions for a production process often initially progress through something like the following general categories. Within each of these categories there is typically a series of target conditions.

1. *Strive to develop a stable 1x1 flow to planned cycle time with the correct number of operators.* If the process is not stable or is unable to meet customer quality or quantity requirements, address this before trying to make other improvements. Until you are able to establish a stable process, do not worry too much about linking the process target condition to company targets.
2. *Strive for a level mix with small lot sizes.*
3. *Strive to connect the processes in the value stream to one another via kanban.*
4. *Further improvement.* This includes alignment with department targets, striving for a vision, reducing the gap between planned cycle time and takt time, moving the batch size closer to one piece, and so on.

Notes

1. Customer demand rates change over time, of course. Toyota recalculates takt time every 30 days, and reviews it every 10 days.
2. Assembly process diagrams from: Mike Rother and Rick Harris, *Creating Continuous Flow* (Cambridge, Massachusetts: Lean Enterprise Institute, 2001). Also at www.lean.org.
3. An item is produced only if a customer has ordered it. In practice this is either when an item has been pulled from finished goods inventory or, in the case of low-volume items, ordered. If a customer has not caused the card for a particular item to circulate and there are no "overflow" cards from earlier, then the assembly process would skip over that item's slot as it moves through the sequence.
4. To be able to assemble in a level fashion and still satisfy spikes in customer orders, there must be enough finished goods inventory to cover those spikes. In some cases customer spikes are so large that the required amount of finished-goods inventory would be unacceptably high. In this situation you can start pursuing the obstacle with the question, "Why does this customer's demand spike so much?"
5. In an emergency that threatens to affect an external customer, Toyota will temporarily run parts on a different machine than is specified, but not without initiating problem-solving activity that seeks to understand the problem.
6. H. Thomas Johnson makes this point when he refers to "managing by means," or MBM, a concept that he contrasts with "managing by results," or MBR. Western management thinkers tend to view the means as subordinate to results, whereas he argues for the view that the means, or process, is nothing less than results-in-the-making. See his *Profit Beyond Measure: Extraordinary Results through Attention to Work and People* (New York: The Free Press, 2000), especially chapter 2.

Chapter 6

Problem Solving and Adapting: Moving Toward a Target Condition

Setting a target condition is only one portion of the improvement kata. Working through obstacles that you then encounter as you try to move toward that target condition is the other, and where a lot of learning takes place (Figure 6-1). It is easier to set a target condition than it is to achieve it.

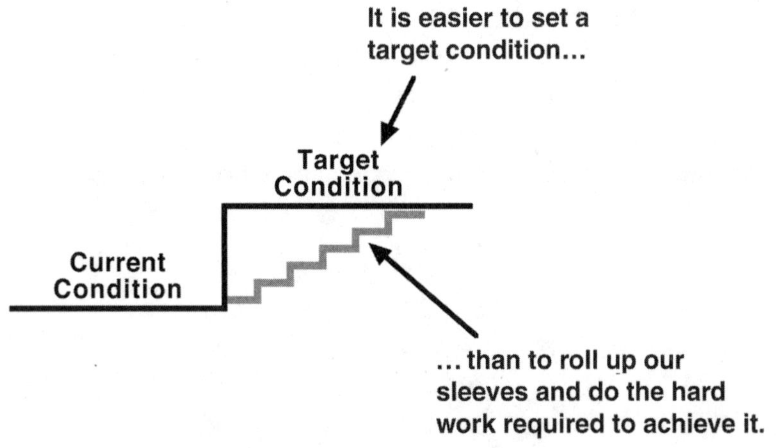

Figure 6-1. It takes work and learning to achieve a target condition

Number One: Assume the Path Is Unclear

To begin with we may need to calibrate our expectation of how the effort to achieve a target condition will proceed. We often make a plan and then intend to execute that plan, but reality is neither linear nor predictable enough for this to be an effective way to reach our target conditions. Consider, for example, landing an airplane:

Current condition:	Cruising at 30,000 feet altitude
Target condition:	Landed on the runway
Plan:	Intended flight path/trajectory down to the runway

How would you feel as a passenger if the pilot were to define the intended flight path for landing the aircraft, and after that allowed no further adjustments to it? On the way from 30,000 feet to the runway on the ground there are going to be many unpredictable wind gusts, and the aircraft will not actually reach the runway.

It is no different with target conditions—there too no one can aim so well up front as to always hit them. Regardless of how well you have planned, you will do well to assume that the way to the target condition is not completely clear; it is a gray zone (Figure 6-2).

Any step taken engenders reactions from the system, but because of interconnectedness, we do not know exactly what those reactions will be. What we are actually doing with a plan is making a prediction, and despite our best efforts, planning errors cannot be avoided. Unforeseen

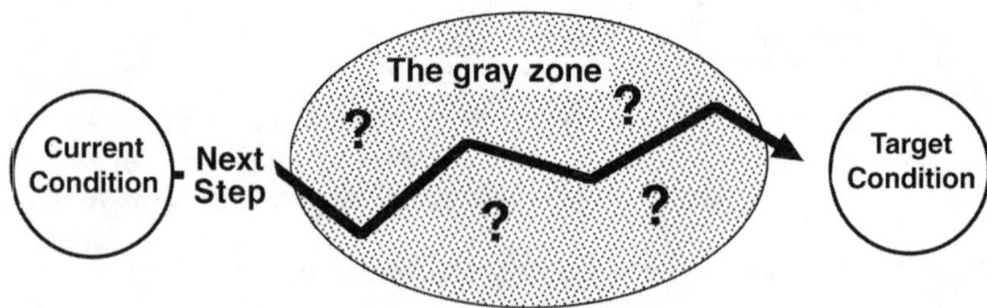

Figure 6-2. The way to a target condition is a gray zone

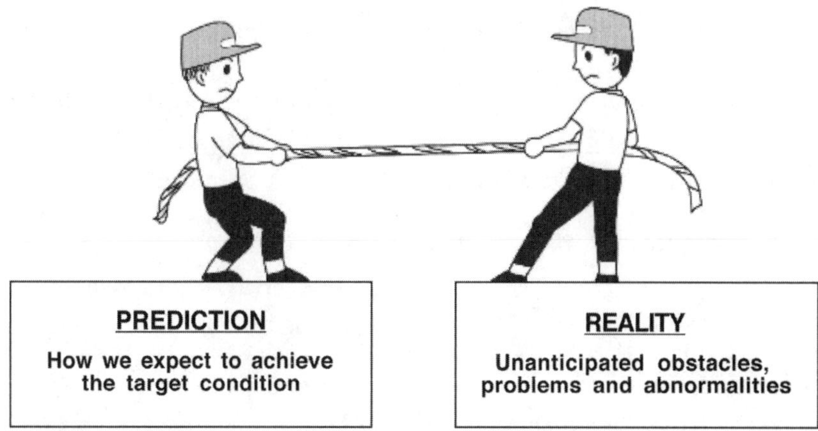

Figure 6-3. The tug-of-war between prediction and reality

problems, abnormalities, false assumptions, and obstacles will appear as we work to move forward (Figure 6-3). This is completely normal, and we should pay attention to them and make adjustments based on what we are learning along the way.

> *It is very difficult to make predictions, particularly about the future.*
>
> —Attributed to Niels Bohr

How Toyota Works Through the Gray Zone

Once a target condition has been established and a plan is made, Toyota then places considerable emphasis on the next step. There is no need for lengthy theoretical discussion or opinions about further activities or steps beyond that, because whenever one step is taken, the situation may be changed as a result.

What was learned in the last step may have an influence on the next step. For this reason, Toyota works toward a target condition in small, rapid steps, with learning and adjustments occurring along the way. This is the equivalent of placing one foot in front of the other, one step at a time, and always adjusting to the present situation as necessary, and is quite different than working through the predefined steps of a plan or action-item list.

By adjusting based on what is learned along the way, Toyota makes progress like a scientist. With each empirical insight, a scientist adjusts his or her course to take advantage of what has been learned.

> *I learn each day what I need to know to do tomorrow's work.*
>
> —Historian Arnold Toynbee explaining his high productivity

> *Nothing within a horizon can have a fixed definition. Every step taken alters the horizon, changes the field of vision, causing us to see what had been thus far circumscribed as something quite different.*
>
> —James P. Carse, Professor Emeritus, New York University

> *Plans are things that change.*
>
> —Fujio Cho, Chairman of Toyota Motor Corporation

Another way to visualize Toyota's way of working toward a target condition is the staircase diagram in Figure 6-4.

Here is a useful analogy: You have defined where you want to go (the target condition), but the way ahead between here and there is

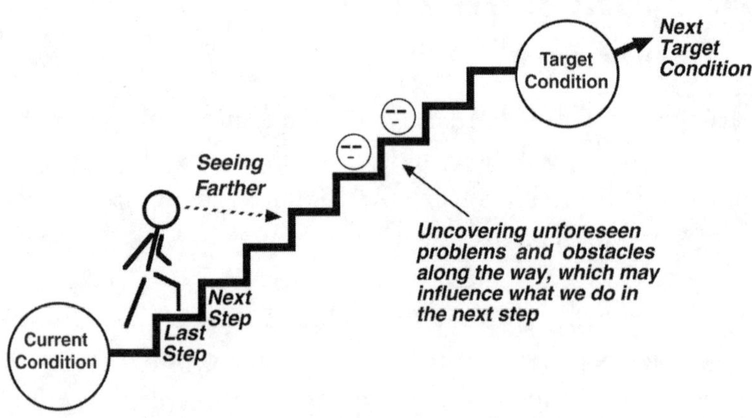

Figure 6-4. How Toyota works toward a target condition

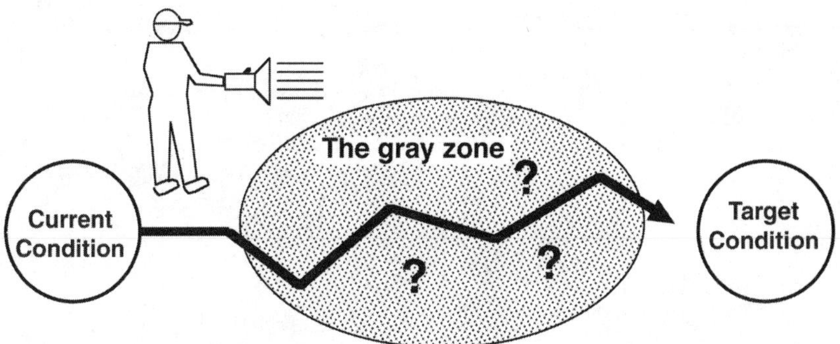

Figure 6-5. The flashlight analogy

dark. You are holding a flashlight, but it only shines so far into the darkness (Figure 6-5). To see further and spot obstacles hidden in the dark you have to take a step forward.

This Is PDCA (Plan-Do-Check-Act)

Because the target condition lies beyond the reach of our flashlight, the path to attaining it cannot be predicted with exactness. Thus, we have to find that path by experimenting. This is the scientific method, which consists of formulating hypotheses and then testing them with information obtained from direct observation.

The procedure or steps of experimentation are summarized by the well-known Plan-Do-Check-Act cycle (Figure 6-6):

1. *Plan*. Define what you expect to do and to happen. This is the hypothesis or prediction.
2. *Do* (or Try Out). Test the hypothesis, that is, try to run the process according to plan. This is often done on a small scale initially. Observe closely.
3. *Check* (or Study). Compare the actual outcome with the expected outcome.
4. *Act* (What's next?). Standardize and stabilize what works, or begin the PDCA cycle again.

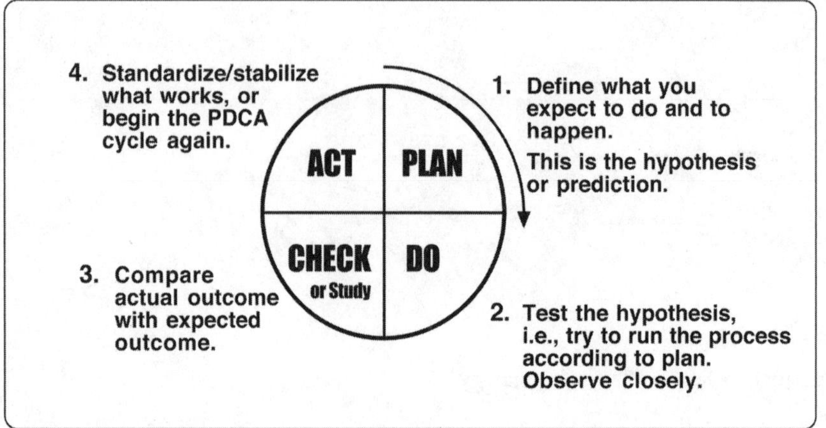

Figure 6-6. The PDCA cycle

The steps of PDCA constitute a scientific process of acquiring knowledge. PDCA provides us with a practical means of attaining a challenging target condition—it is the means for getting through the gray zone and characterizes a learning organization. But only if we use it the right way.

PDCA may have been introduced to the Japanese in the 1950s via lecture courses given in Japan by W. Edwards Deming, although at that time the terminology "PDCA" was probably not in use and Deming likely presented a version of the Shewhart cycle. This was Walter A. Shewhart's circular, or spiraling, depiction of "steps in a dynamic scientific process of acquiring knowledge," which appears in Shewhart's 1939 book *Statistical Method from the Viewpoint of Quality Control*. It is also certainly conceivable that persons in Japan already knew of Shewhart's writing and were familiar with the scientific method.

During his 1950–52 lecture activities in Japan, Deming provided training for engineers and statisticians, and gave lectures for top management. It is interesting to note that he presented the statistical techniques as *management* tools and emphasized overall managerial concepts like the Shewhart cycle. In other words, Deming's lectures

Figure 6-7. Toyota added Go and See to the center of the PDCA cycle

were delivered in the context of a way of thinking and managing, rather than simply as techniques. This is clearly also the fashion in which Toyota adopted PDCA, where it became a strategic approach and a basis for improvement and leadership at all levels.

Toyota later added the words "Go and See" to the middle of the PDCA wheel (Figure 6-7), because Toyota considers this to be important in all steps of PDCA. No matter how confident you are, you must always go and see the actual condition for yourself in order to understand it, because the situation is always changing as you move forward. If you were to only go and see one time, for example, you would become progressively more removed and distant from the real situation. The words spoken most often at Toyota may well be, "Show me."

I came across a good example of the necessity to go and see at an assembly process in Portugal. The engineers in the office said they knew from their calculation of machine capacities which workstation was the bottleneck in the assembly process. However, in the actual process on the shop floor, an entirely different workstation was the current bottleneck. The current real situation and problems in the process were not the same as those the engineers in the office were assuming based on their data. This is the reason that Toyota makes a distinction between facts and data, and prefers facts over data wherever possible.

Key Points About PDCA

We have known about PDCA for a long time, but we are not yet using it as does Toyota in its improvement kata. To start developing a deeper understanding, consider the following four points from the arena of scientific experimentation, discovery, and learning.

1. *Adaptive and evolutionary systems by their nature involve experimentation.* Since the way ahead is a gray zone, if we want progress, we must experiment. A target condition, for example, is only a setup for conducting experiments.

Hypotheses are nets: only he who casts will catch.

—Novalis (Friedrich Freiherr von Hardenberg) as quoted in *The Logic of Scientific Discovery,* by Karl Popper

2. *Hypotheses can only be tested by experiment, not by intellectual discussion, opinion, or human judgment.* This is what I call testing over talking. When you hear statements like, "I believe . . ." or "I think . . ." it is often better to stop talking and take a step; to test as quickly as possible, usually on a small scale first, so you can see further based on facts and data.

Neither the voice of authority, nor the weight of reason and argument are as significant as experiments for thence comes quiet to the mind.

—Roger Bacon

The moment of experience is the firmest reality.

—Composer Benjamin Boretz

3. *In order for an experiment to be scientific it must be possible that the hypothesis will be refuted.* This point is a little more difficult to understand, but it gets us closer to what Toyota is doing. The visiting executive who reviews an assembly process's heijunka leveling scheme and simply nods his approval, as mentioned in the last chapter, rather than asking, "What is currently preventing you from operating this way?" has not yet internalized this point. Neither has the plant manager who is planning to implement pull systems across his entire 6,000-person facility.

If we assume that at any time anything we have planned may not work as intended, that is, that it is always possible that the hypothesis will be false, then we keep our eyes and minds open to what we learn along the way. Conversely, if we think everything can work as planned, then we too easily turn a blind eye to reality—like the engineers at that factory in Portugal who thought they knew what the process bottleneck was—and tend to simply push for greater discipline in carrying out the plan. If we expect that everything can work as planned, then the effect is that we stop improving and adapting.

The game of science is, in principle, without end. He who decides one day that scientific statements do not call for any further test, and that they can be regarded as finally verified, retires from the game.

—Karl Popper

4. *When a hypothesis is refuted this is in particular when we can gain new insight and further develop our capability.* Envision a scientist in a laboratory wearing a white lab coat and heavy gloves, who is slowly pouring two beakers of clear liquid together under a fume hood. The scientist has predicted that combining these liquids will produce a blue liquid. If the resulting mixture does, in fact, turn blue, then the experiment was a confirmation of something the scientist already believed, and the scientist has not really learned anything new. If a hypothesis is not refuted, then the experiment was only a confirmation of already held ideas. Or, put in other terms, if there is no problem, there is not much improvement.

   On the other hand, if the mixture of the two liquids explodes and the scientist is covered in ash and holding two cracked beakers—an unexpected outcome—then he is about to learn something new.

Problems cannot be solved at the same level of awareness that created them.

—Attributed to Albert Einstein

> *There is no such thing as a failed experiment, only experiments with unexpected outcomes.*
>
> —R. Buckminster Fuller

We learn from failures because they reveal boundaries in our system's current capability and horizons in our minds. This is why Toyota states that "problems are jewels." They show us the way forward to a target condition. You need to miss the target periodically (again, preferably on a small scale that does not affect the customer) in order to see the appropriate next step. This is a fascinating point when you consider how much we as leaders, managers, and executives try to make it look like everything is going right and as planned. The main reason for conducting an experiment is not to test if something will work, but to learn what will *not* work as expected, and thus what we need to do to keep moving forward.

Learning to Ask a Different Question

As we take steps toward a target condition, one comment you sometimes hear is: "Let's see if this will work." This, erroneously, seems like a reasonable question since we are talking about experimenting. However, the question actually represents a circular argument, which is why it is utilized when people have a vested interest in preserving a status quo. Simply put, very few things work the first time, or even the second time.

I used to struggle with this question. We would go to the factory floor to try something and several people would fold their arms and say, "Well, let's see if this works." Of course within a short time the test failed. They were right, I was wrong, and the experiment would be over. At the first signs of problems, difficulties, or a failed step, it was announced that, "Well, that doesn't work," and often, "Let's go back to the way we did it before because we know that works."

Eventually it dawned on me how to deal with this question. Now, when arms fold up and people say, "Let's see if this will work," I say, "I can save you the time. We already know it probably won't work.

Despite our best efforts to plan this, we know that within a short time there will be 'charred and glowing pieces' lying around. We just don't know in advance when, where, or why it will fail."

At this point the arms usually start unfolding a bit, and I follow with, "What we should be asking ourselves is not will it work, but, let's see what we need to do to make this work." After calibrating a group's thinking in this way, I am always impressed with the smart ideas people from all levels come up with to get us closer to the target condition.

Toyota Is More Interested in What Does Not Go as Planned

The thinking reflected in Figure 6-8 is fundamental in Toyota's improvement kata.

Interpretation: if there is no problem, or it is made to seem that way, then our company would, in a sense, be standing still. Toyota's management wants the organization to see and utilize small problems in order to exploit the potential they reveal, and before they affect the external customer. If people are threatened by problems, then they will either hide them or conduct poor problem solving by quickly jumping to countermeasures without sufficiently analyzing and understanding the situation. The idea is to not stigmatize failures, but to learn from them.

To function in this way, the improvement kata should be depersonalized and have a positive, challenging, no-blame feeling. Toward that end, at Toyota an abnormality or problem is generally not thought of or judged good or bad, but as an occurrence that may teach us something about our work system. This can be somewhat difficult for westerners to understand: something can be a problem—a situation that we do not want—without it necessarily being considered good or bad. This is akin to the difference between "understanding" and "accepting." Trying to understand a situation and why it happens does

"NO PROBLEM" = A PROBLEM

Figure 6-8. A different way of thinking

not mean you have to accept it. Making this distinction will make you a better problem solver. Interestingly, if you look up *problem* in the dictionary, you won't find the negative connotation that we often assign to this word.

For example, at a Toyota assembly plant, I once was told that the normal number of andon pulls is typically around 1,000 per shift. Each pull is an operator calling for assistance from their team leader because the operator is experiencing a problem; a cross-threaded bolt here, a task that took a little too long there. Naturally, the number of andon pulls per shift varies, and I once heard of it dropping to only 700 pulls/shift. When I ask non-Toyota managers what they would do in this situation, I often get the answer, "We would celebrate the improvement."

According to my source, what actually happened when the number of andon pulls dropped from 1,000 to 700 per shift is that the Toyota plant's president called an all-employee meeting and said, "The drop in andon pulls can only mean two things. One is that we are having problems but you are not calling for help. I want to remind you of your responsibility to pull the andon cord for every problem. The other possibility is that we are actually experiencing fewer problems. But there is still waste in our system and we are staffed to handle 1,000 pulls per shift. So I am asking group leaders to monitor the situation and reduce inventory buffers where necessary so we can get back to 1,000 andon pulls per shift." This is quite a contrast to our current thinking.

Another example came while touring a U.S. vehicle assembly plant in Detroit with a group that included a former Toyota executive. At one point the plant manager remarked proudly, "Our vehicle assembly line runs three shifts and it never stops." To which the former Toyota executive responded with some irony, "Ah, they must all be perfect."

We hear about Toyota's successes, but not about its thousands of small failures that occur daily, which provide a basis for that success. Toyota makes hay of problems every day, where we tend to hide little problems until they grow into big and complex problems that are then difficult to dissect. Toyota has mastered the art of recognizing problems as they occur, analyzing their nature, and using what it learns to adapt and keep moving toward its target conditions.

Focusing On Process Instead of Blame

Toyota's approach of not stigmatizing failures, but instead utilizing them to learn and move forward, has an interesting effect: thinking that an abnormality or problem is neither positive nor negative shifts the focus from the individual to the process. We know that the vast majority of problems are caused by the system within which people work, rather then by the individuals themselves. Therefore, Toyota maintains a no-blame focus on the process, instead of on the people around the problem. The assumptions are:

- People are doing their best.
- A problem is a *system* problem, and if we were the other person, the same problem would still have occurred.
- There is a reason for everything, and we can work together to understand the reason for a problem.

An elegant question in this respect that I learned from Toyota is, "What is preventing the operators from working according to the standard?" I encourage you to utilize this question as you strive for a target condition, because it alters your thinking and changes where you look when a problem occurs.

Be hard on the process, but soft on the operators.

—Toyota

Note, however, that while an abnormality, problem, or unexpected result itself is not necessarily viewed as good or bad, and the system is considered the problem, Toyota does put intense and critical attention on both the problem and how people deal with it. Do we give it sufficient urgency and attention? Do we follow the improvement kata? We should not confuse Toyota's "no blame" culture with an easygoing "no worries" culture, as depicted in Figure 6-9.

Figure 6-9. Not stigmatizing failures does not mean "no worries"

How Toyota Utilizes PDCA

So what actually constitutes one PDCA cycle in real life? Consider the process of getting up and going to work, and a target condition of being in the car and ready to drive to work 60 minutes after waking up. Here is one possible PDCA cycle for that process:

Plan: Be in the car 60 minutes after waking up. (Target condition)
Do: Wake up and go through the morning routine, get into car.
Check: Once in the car check how long it took.
Act: (Next step to be determined)

As we sit in the car and check how long the morning routine took, we find that the total time was 64 minutes, or four minutes over the target condition. What have we learned about the process from this experiment? As depicted in Figure 6-10, not much! The total time taken was over 60 minutes (too long), but we cannot tell where in the morning routine the problem lies. Furthermore, it is too late to make an adjustment that would allow us to still achieve the target condition.

When I use this waking up and going to work example as a classroom exercise, participants invariably begin making improvement suggestions right away, such as setting the alarm clock four minutes

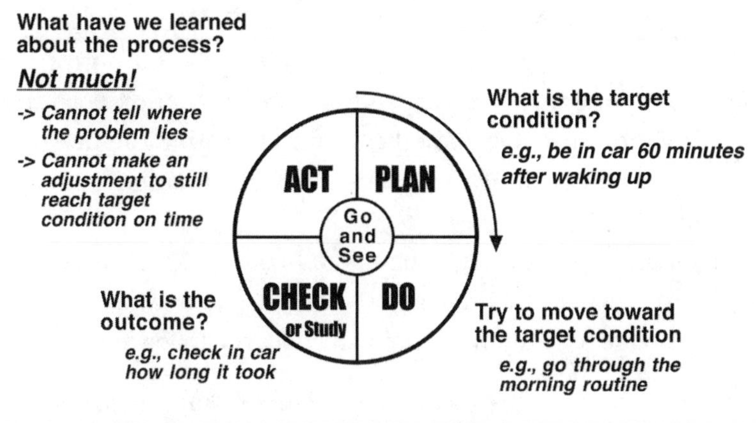

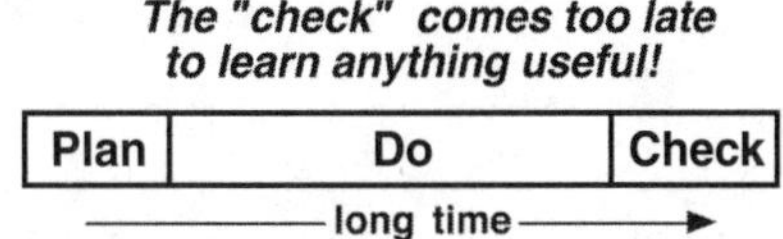

Figure 6-10. Only checking outcomes produces little learning

earlier or taking less time to shower, even though they have no further information about the problem. The urge to go directly to proposing and implementing countermeasures is surprisingly strong in us, and is fostered by our prevailing outcome- or results-based managerial system.

There are two things wrong with this PDCA experiment: (1) The "check" comes too late for us to learn anything useful about the process, or to make adjustments on the way. (2) The target condition specifies only an outcome, which means that it is not actually a target condition at all.

History shows that many seemingly large and sudden changes developed slowly. The problem is that we either fail to notice the little shifts taking place along the way or we do not take them seriously. In contrast, Toyota states clearly that no problem is too small for a response. For an organization to be consciously adaptive, it would ideally recognize abnormalities and changes as they arise and are still small and easy to grasp.

Consider, for example, the dieting quote, "I got fat slowly, then suddenly." If you are gaining unwanted weight and notice it when you're one pound overweight, you can see the causes, correct easily, and hit your target. On the other hand, if you only notice the gain, or take it seriously, after 15 pounds, then the situation is much more difficult.

Turning back to the getting-up-and-going-to-work process: to be able to experiment in shorter cycles, we need a more detailed target condition. A target condition generally includes the following information:

- The steps of the process, their sequence and their times
- Process characteristics
- Process metrics
- Outcome metrics

Ensuring that there are both process metrics and outcome metrics allows Toyota to have shorter and finer PDCA cycles (Figure 6-11). There is a longer overall cycle that checks the outcome, and, more important, many short PDCA cycles that check process metrics along the way. If that sounds too complicated, it simply means this: every step on the staircase toward a target condition is a PDCA cycle (Figure 6-12). Each step is a hypothesis, and what we learn from testing that hypothesis may influence the next step.

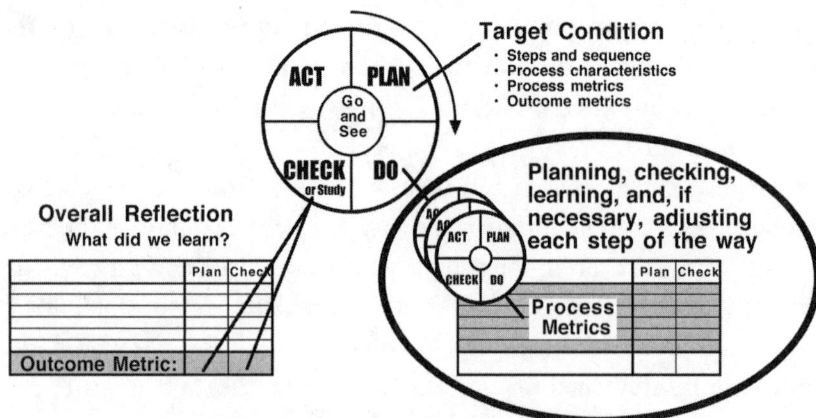

Figure 6-11. Outcome metrics and process metrics

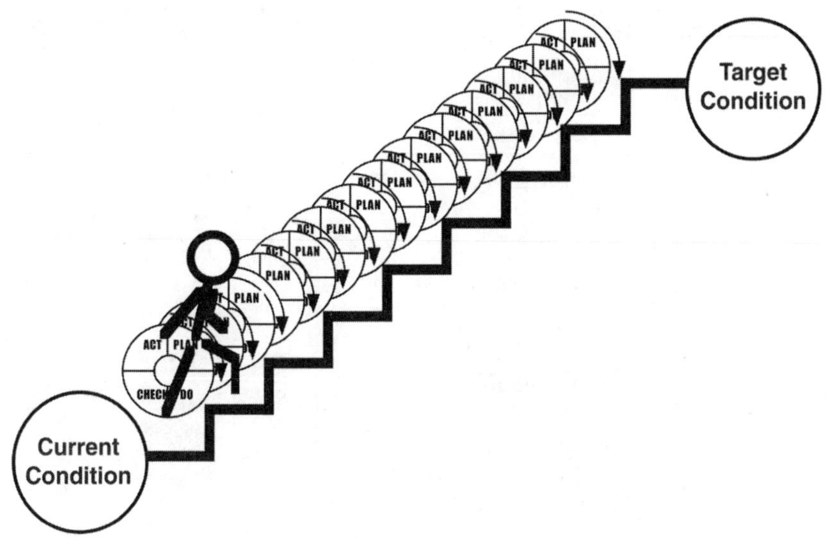

Figure 6-12. Every step = a PDCA cycle

With the shorter PDCA cycles that check process metrics, we have now reached the level in an organization—the fractal—at which continuous improvement, problem solving, and adaptation can be done effectively. For example, natural selection may favor one family of birds over another, but this is played out at the detail level, such as the length of their beaks or other attributes. We can have a vision of ending hunger, but achieving that will involve details like trucks having gasoline, roads being passable, and so on. We may want to develop and offer an electric automobile, but it is at the detail level that this desired condition will or won't be achieved.

Interestingly, the detail level is something that many popular management concepts—such as management by objectives as we practice it, employee motivation schemes, and so on—do not reach. This may explain some of the difference in the improvement and adaptiveness performance of Toyota versus its competitors.

Of course, to work this way you will have to define in advance the expected result of any step. This then puts you in a position to recognize abnormalities early and make the necessary adaptations and improvements on the way to a desired condition.

Steps, sequence, times		Plan minutes	Actual minutes
	Alarm rings / Snooze-button cycles	5	
	Start coffeemaker	3	
	Bathroom routine	15	
	Get dressed	10	
	Make breakfast	7	
	Eat breakfast and read newspaper	10	
	Clean up breakfast	5	
	Check calendar and briefcase contents	3	
	Leave house and get into car	2	
	Outcome metric:	60	

Figure 6-13. Experiment setup for the getting-up-and-going-to-work process, including steps, sequence, process metrics (step times), and an outcome metric

Let us put together a more effective experiment for the process of getting up and going to work, beginning with a better target condition that looks like the chart in Figure 6-13.

Now we have set ourselves up to make checks and learn and adapt along the way. As you can see in Figure 6-14, the step "Make breakfast" has taken four minutes longer than the planned time. Now we not only know where the problem is, but we can also make adjustments to the remaining steps to allow us to still achieve the 60-minute outcome.

Compare this approach to the first experiment, which only checked the outcome. Adding process metrics and short PDCA cycles is like putting on a pair of glasses and seeing clearly for the first time. It is no wonder that process operators sometimes get annoyed when managers visit a process for a short time, create performance incentives, drop some random suggestions for eliminating waste, and then head back to their offices.

Steps, sequence, times		Plan minutes	Actual minutes
	Alarm rings / Snooze-button cycles	5	5
	Start coffeemaker	3	3
	Bathroom routine	15	15
	Get dressed	10	10
	Make breakfast	7	11
	Eat breakfast and read newspaper	10	
	Clean up breakfast	5	
	Check calendar and briefcase contents	3	
	Leave house and get into car	2	
	Outcome metric:	60	

Figure 6-14. A clearer view of what is happening

In the getting-up-and-going-to-work example, we are still not yet ready to introduce a countermeasure, because we do not yet know what it is about making breakfast that caused the problem. The next step would be to pay close attention to the current breakfast-making routine and ask, "What is preventing us from making breakfast in seven minutes?"

Consider a manufacturing example. Say a process target condition includes producing 32 boxes of product over two shifts. If we check the outcome at the end of each shift and find a shortfall, we will have difficulty tracing and understanding the cause. A variety of small problems will have occurred during the shift (think of those 1,000 andon pulls per shift at a Toyota assembly plant), and the context that caused those problems is gone. We are not adaptive and also have few options now to make up for the shortfall in time for delivery to the customer.

On the other hand, each box or associated kanban card represents 30 minutes of production time and can be used as a process metric—an

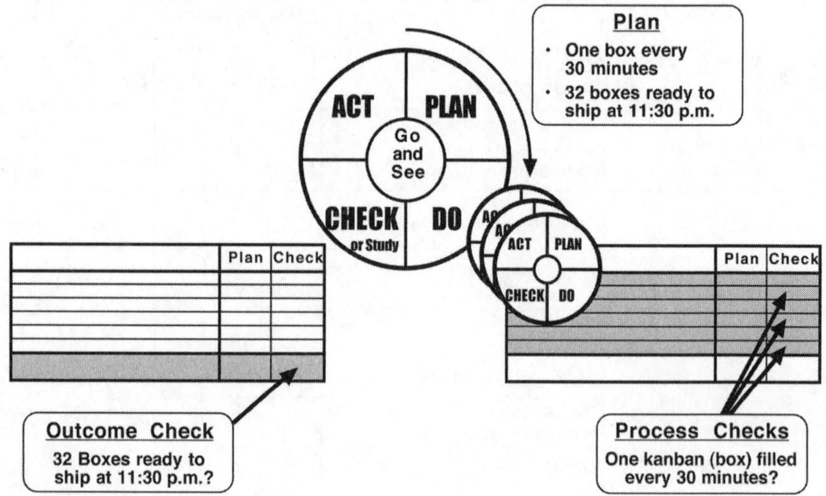

Figure 6-15. Kanban cards can be process metrics

early warning indicator (Figure 6-15). We can check every 30 minutes, and if there is a shortfall on one of those checks, the root cause trail is still hot and we can still make up for the shortfall.

This is an interesting contrast to how we work in our factories. In many cases we instruct the operators to call for a logistics pickup when a pallet of boxes is finished. Not only is this too infrequent for effective PDCA, but the logistics person comes by when the boxes are actually ready rather than when they are *supposed* to be ready. In this setup there is no experiment whatsoever. Why do we work this way? What are our assumptions? How do these assumptions differ from Toyota's assumptions?

If we want to check in short increments and utilize the information, then support personnel must be able to respond appropriately. For example, many of our factories have whiteboards for checking hourly production at their processes, which look exactly the same as such boards in a Toyota factory. But in many of our factories the comments written on these boards are used more to justify why a target production quantity was not reached, rather than to trigger quick response during the shift. A good example of copying a technique rather than the thinking behind it.

The right heart. Frequent process checking is sometimes interpreted as a means for policing people to keep them working hard (Figure 6-16). Ironically, this would create an artificial situation that obscures the true condition and inhibits our ability to improve. For example, if people tighten up and alter their behavior when the leader approaches, then the leader loses sight of the true condition. To improve in the Toyota style we will need to adopt the right heart: we are checking for problems because we *want* to find the problems.

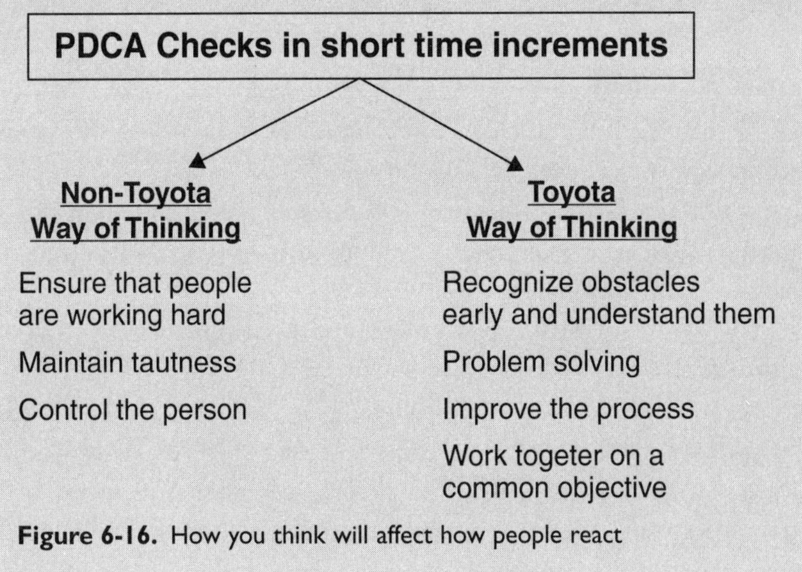

Figure 6-16. How you think will affect how people react

Rapid Cycles

Since it is the refuted hypotheses—the problems, abnormalities, and unexpected results—that show us the way forward, Toyota is highly interested in seeing the next problem or obstacle as soon as possible. Since we can only see the next obstacle when we take a step (one PDCA cycle), we should take that step as soon as possible.

As mentioned in Chapter 2, at Toyota you are generally taught to strive for single-factor experiments, that is, to address one problem at

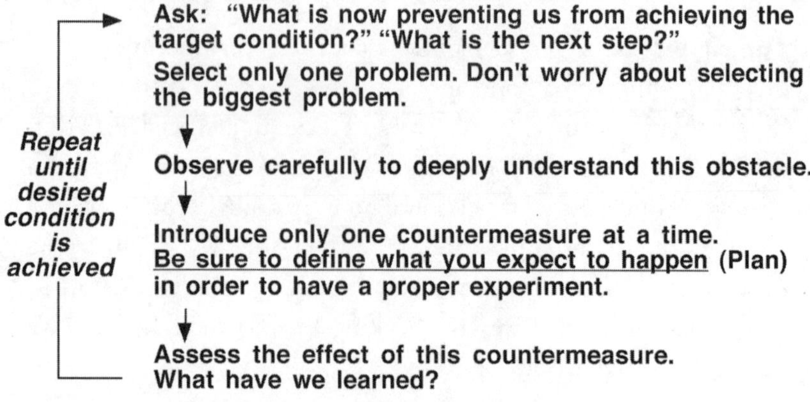

Figure 6-17. Experimenting in rapid cycles

a time and only change one thing at a time at a process. This helps us see cause and effect and better understand the process. But this would be too slow if each cycle takes a long time.

For these reasons, individual PDCA cycles are turned as quickly as possible, sometimes even taking only minutes for one cycle, along the lines articulated in Figure 6-17.

The desire to turn rapid PDCA cycles has an influence on the nature of the steps that we take toward a target condition. The idea is to not wait until you have a perfect solution, but to take the step now, with whatever you have, so we can see further (Figure 6-18). A provisional step now is preferable to a perfect step later, and investing in prototypes and experiments up front, which may seem like extra expense, often reduces overall cost in the long run.

One example is from the factory in Germany, mentioned in Chapter 5, where part of the target condition for the assembly process was a planned cycle time of 16 seconds. The pair of observers timed 20 successive cycles asked themselves, "What is preventing us from having a part come by this point every 16 seconds?" They noticed that the operator had to periodically walk away from the line to get trays of parts, which caused instability in the line cycle time.

The next step proposed by the two observers was to develop a better logistics concept, whereby the parts would be brought to the operator. But how long will it take before this can be done? If we wait

Figure 6-18. Do it now, with whatever you have on hand

until the material handling department develops cyclical material routes with point-of-use delivery, that will take weeks, at least, during which time we would not eliminate this variable (Figure 6-19). Make a logistics concept and plan, okay, but don't wait for that to be completed. If possible, make the change right now in a temporary fashion, so you can then see the next problem and keep moving forward.

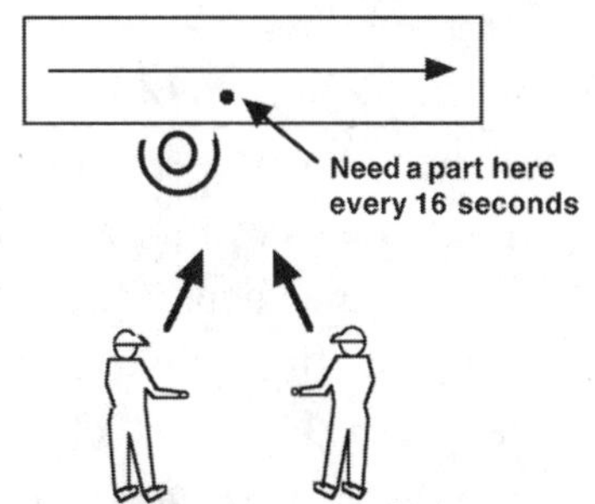

Figure 6-19. Don't wait to take a step

Another example comes from a factory that makes hydraulic cylinders for a nearby customer factory that assembles earth-moving equipment. Finished hydraulic cylinders come in a variety of sizes and are packed on pallets by size, one size per pallet. Each pallet has a special fixture to securely hold several cylinders, but only of one size. Therefore, the minimum shipping quantity for each cylinder size is a one pallet quantity. The customer, however, only requires two cylinders of any size at a time, and thus has an aging inventory of several opened pallets of cylinders in its receiving area.

A proposal for the next target condition closer to a 1x1 flow between the two factories was to ship only pairs of cylinders the customer actually needed. This would require a different fixture, so that several pairs of different size cylinders could be packed on one pallet. However, such a fixture would have to be designed and built, which would take several weeks.

In the Toyota way of thinking, this delay is not acceptable, and a provisional fixture solution—even if it temporarily adds some waste—would be introduced as quickly as possible. Not only can Toyota then see the next obstacles to achieving a 1x1 flow between the factories, but the fixture idea can be fine-tuned before expensive fixtures are fabricated. Perhaps even smarter solutions will be developed and fancy fixtures will not be needed after all.

Many years ago I learned the hard way the benefits of fine-tuning a provisional step rather than going right into full implementation. At a large automobile supplier factory, we had designed a new assembly process and needed some flow racks for parts presentation at the line. When I showed the maintenance department—which fabricates such things in this plant—our sketches of the racks, I was told building them would take three weeks. However, since our project had some priority, the maintenance department agreed to fabricate the racks over the weekend as a favor.

Monday morning our racks were there exactly as we had specified them. They were made out of angle iron, with some of the finest welds I have seen, and nicely painted the same blue color as other equipment in the plant. Once we had the racks at the line, we started our production trials. Of course, the trials led to many little adjustments in the line, which included shifting some work elements from one operator to another. This meant that the associated parts would now have to be moved to a different flow rack. We also found the need for adjustments to the flow racks as we moved things around, changed reach heights, and so on.

Imagine the good cheer with which I was greeted at the maintenance department when I now brought back the beautiful, weekend-made flow racks for some changes. This time it did take three weeks. Clearly, we should have started with some provisional racks, even though up front that seemed like extra time and expense, and worked up to something more fancy if necessary when the situation stabilized.

Again, we often leap ahead with too much faith in our planning, and thereby fail to leave room for learning and adaptiveness.

Keeping an Open Mind

The next step may not be what you expect, so you need to be as open-minded and scientific as possible as you go through PDCA cycles. It is difficult to not be biased in looking at a situation, and it is probably a lifetime's effort to teach oneself to view occurrences without preconceived notions about those occurrences.

The Results

We have misunderstood why Toyota is more successful than other organizations in achieving the challenges (target conditions) it sets for itself. It is not primarily because Toyota people have greater discipline to stick with a plan or experience fewer problems, as is often thought. Rather, they spot problems at the process level much earlier, when the problems are still small and you can understand them and do something about them (see Figure 6-20). Toyota's success is not due to sudden innovation or having airtight plans, but about the ability to execute more effectively in the face of unforeseeable obstacles and difficulties.

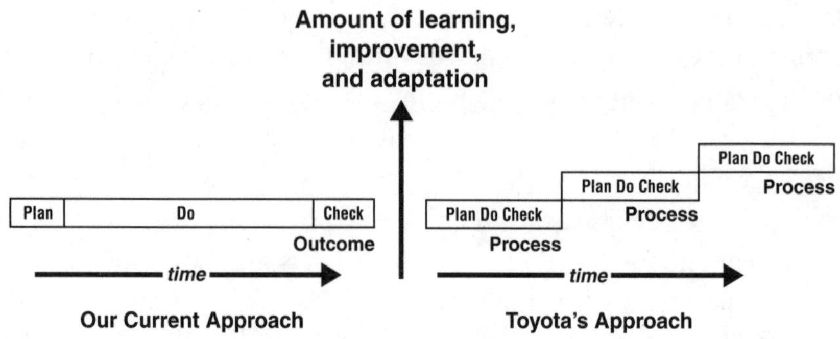

Figure 6-20. Short PDCA cycles = more learning

In contrast, we find out late that a plan has failed (although frequently this is not even admitted). Information about the little problems along the way was never picked up and acted upon. What do we then assume is the cause of the plan failing? Poor planning, poor discipline in execution, and human error.

What do we think is the solution? Make a new plan. Plan better. More discipline in implementation. More countermeasures. Motivate people to be more careful or work harder. We may apportion blame, to increase pressure on people to be more careful, or even replace people. Unfortunately, none of this addresses the actual causes of the plan failing. I once heard a colleague summarize our approach as: "It's always 'no problem' until the end, and then we have a big problem."

While taking problems at face value is a basis for Toyota-style continuous improvement and adaptation, inside many other companies I find way too much of either sweeping little problems under the rug or placing blame, both of which inhibit the ability to see reality and adapt to actual conditions. When you combine hiding problems with the popular idea of trying to manage from afar via targets and managerial accounting metrics, it means that even less accurate information gets through to managers, who thereby either fail to lead in the making of appropriate adjustments—small course corrections—or try to do it too late.

A lot has been said and written about learning organizations. With the way it applies PDCA, Toyota has developed a learning organization in a pragmatic way.

1. **What is the target condition? *(The challenge)***
2. **What is the actual condition now?**
3. **What obstacles are now preventing you from reaching the target condition?**
   Which one are you addressing now?
4. **What is your next step? *(Start of next PDCA cycle)***
5. **When can we go and see what we have learned from taking that step?**

Figure 6-21. The five questions

The Five Questions

The five questions in Figure 6-21 are a summary of Toyota's approach for moving toward a target condition, and are perhaps the most useful information in this book, now that you know what they mean. They are highly effective in practice.

The five questions come into play once you are "on the staircase," that is, in the PDCA phase of the improvement kata, after a target condition has been established. The questions build upon one another. The better you've defined the target condition, the better you'll be able to assess the current condition. The better you assess the current condition, the better you can recognize obstacles. The better you recognize obstacles, the better you can define your next step. Note that *before* a target condition has been established, the order of questions 1 and 2 is reversed from what is shown here.

This sequence of five questions is a device to give you a routine and mental pattern for approaching any process or situation, and to help you learn the improvement kata. The questions distill part of the improvement kata down to a point where it becomes accessible and usable by anyone. They are a "minikata," if you will, perfect for practicing. I keep the five questions in mind any time I visit a process, and apply them to many other activities as well. I highly recommend that you use and internalize them.

What Toyota Emphasizes in Problem Solving

Despite what the words "problem solving" might lead us to think, the primary focus in problem solving at Toyota is not solutions, but understanding the current situation in a work system so deeply, firsthand, that the right solution (called a countermeasure) becomes obvious and practically falls in your lap. Most of the effort of problem solving at Toyota is placed in grasping the situation—deeply understanding the conditions that led to the problem—as opposed to hunting for solutions.

We often mistakenly think that good problem solving means *solving the problem*, that is, applying countermeasures, and we may even propose and apply several countermeasures in the hope that one of them will stop the problem. In contrast, in Toyota's way of thinking if the solution to a problem is not yet obvious, it means we have not yet understood the situation sufficiently. Time to go and see again (Figure 6-22).

An example: A factory that makes precision-cast turbine blades for aircraft engines was experiencing a quality problem. One of the last processes in the turbine-blade value stream is a spray-coating line, much like a paint line, and some blades were coming out of the coating process with dents from banging against one another. Due to the damage, these expensive parts would have to be scrapped. Engineers quickly put forth a number of potential countermeasures, such as

	Toyota	Us
Focus	Learn about the work system. Understand the situation.	Stop the problem!
Typical Behavior	Observe and study the situation. Apply only one countermeasure at a time in order to see cause and effect.	Hide the problem. Quickly move into countermeasures. Apply several countermeasures at once.

Figure 6-22. What does "problem solving" mean?

hanging the blades farther apart on the coating line chain conveyor, putting a protective shield between each blade, and so on.

One engineer took a different approach and simply observed the coating process in action. After about three hours of watching he noticed something at a point in the process where the chain conveyor makes a 90-degree turn. As the turbine blades went around this corner, some of them would rotate counterclockwise a little and slightly unscrew the hook upon which they were hanging. When the hook became unscrewed far enough, it allowed the blade to swing and on occasion contact the neighboring blade. Once the engineer understood the problem, then the right countermeasure became obvious: prevent the hooks from unscrewing.

Few of us actually take the time to keep observing a process until the cause of a problem becomes clear. We tend instead to reward firefighters and expediters who temporarily fix a problem. We will explore Toyota's thinking about problem solving in more detail in a case example in Chapter 8.

It Keeps Going

Once you begin working with the improvement kata at a process, there is no end (Figure 6-23). If the target condition is achieved with some consistency day in and day out, it may be time to develop the

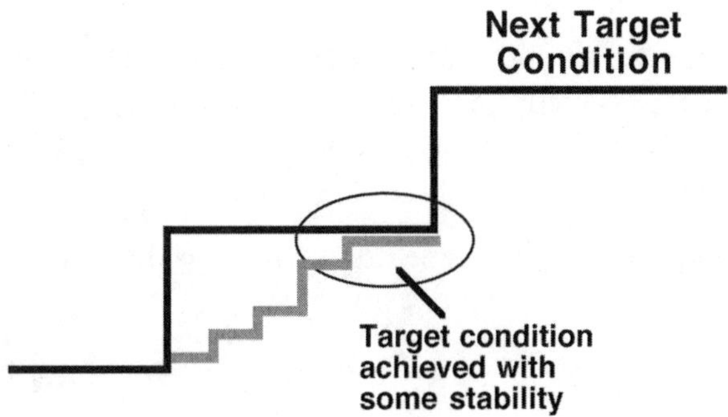

Figure 6-23. Reaching one target condition sets the stage for the next target condition

next target condition for this process. Without a target condition (challenge) to strive for, a process will tend to slip back.

This is the time to make an overall reflection, to summarize what was learned in this complete improvement kata cycle in preparation for the next. While you are working to achieve the current target condition, you will usually begin to see elements of what should be the next target condition. If not, then you're probably not struggling enough with process details.

You may not arrive at a target condition 100 percent. For example, it is unlikely that a production process can ever be 100 percent stable. At production processes you may reach a state where you are just reacting to deviations and abnormalities, rather than still striving to reach a challenging target condition. A question I sometimes ask myself is: "Are we still working under a challenge here?" If not, then it may be time to define the next target condition.

Occasionally you will not achieve a target condition on time, but this is sometimes acceptable. Why? Because we learn the most from failures.

For a few years I chaired a manufacturing conference in Munich, and one year several speakers, in presenting improvements they had made, ended their presentations with a photograph of the award—a trophy or plaque—they had won. After this happened a few times in a row, I felt compelled to point out that sure, Toyota too would show its awards, but this would not be the last slide in its presentation. Toyota's last slide would describe the next challenge. It is okay to celebrate successes, but we should always be looking ahead and focusing on a target condition and the next step. If we decide to use awards, then they should not be seen as an end, but rather as a beginning, a doorway to more learning.

The benchmark to beat is yourself and your current condition.

Summary of Part III

Part III explains Toyota's improvement kata, the fundamental approach for continuously improving and evolving throughout the organization. The improvement kata cannot be described in a few sentences, but now that it has been explained in Part III, it can be summarized with the simple diagram in Figure P3-3.

The improvement kata operates within an overall sense of long-term direction, which may represent an ideal state that might not ultimately be achievable. It is a direction giver. From day to day, however, the improvement kata often operates within the scope of a nearer and more specific target or need.

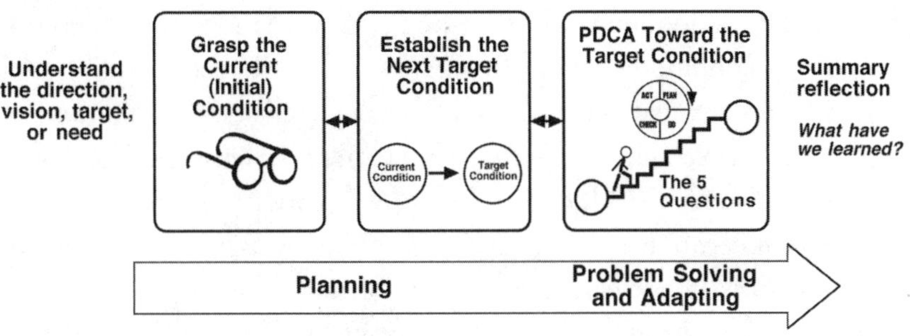

Figure P3-3. The improvement kata

With the direction in mind, the improvement kata itself is then often applied at the process level. It begins with developing an understanding of the current condition at the process, which typically requires firsthand observation and analysis of the situation.

With a good grasp of the current condition established, and the overall direction or target in mind, the next target condition for the process is described. In other words: "How do we want this process to be operating?"

Once the target condition is defined, a series of PDCA cycles toward that condition begins. These cycles uncover unforeseen obstacles, which are what need to be worked on in order to achieve the target condition. It is in particular here that learning and adaptation take place, based on feedback from the PDCA cycles.

These three stages of the improvement kata build upon one another. The better your analysis of the current situation, the more precise your definition of the target condition will be. The more precisely you define the target condition, the better and more quickly you can recognize obstacles to it.

Once the target condition is achieved, these stages of the improvement kata are repeated, of course, since the long-term vision has not yet been reached. Before that is done, however, an overall summary reflection on what has been learned in the last pass through the improvement kata takes place.

Note that the horizontal axis in the diagram is not to scale. Adequately grasping the current condition, for example, may take a long time. In reality the stages of the improvement kata also overlap. As you try to establish the target condition, you will often find you need more information on the current condition. As you PDCA toward the target condition, you may gain insights that allow you to add detail to the target condition.

The improvement kata is presented here via examples primarily from manufacturing, which is where the research took place, but the same routine can find application in many situations. By learning about Toyota's improvement kata, we are no longer copying Toyota's solutions. Now we are learning the procedure, repeatedly applied, by which Toyota develops its solutions, and how those impressive Toyota statistics mentioned at the start of Chapter 1 are achieved.

Adaptive Persistence

By embedding the improvement kata into daily work, Toyota has done something elegant: it has developed a practical and universal method for evolving along unforeseeable routes toward only generally defined long-term visions. This could be called "Adaptive Persistence," a fitting phrase coined by Richard T. Pascale in his famous 1984 *California Management Review* article.

To paraphrase Mr. Pascale, Toyota's continued success is not due to perfect up front decisions and plans (that is, perfect aim). Many priorities become clear only as you strive to move toward something, rather than through advance planning. Thousands of PDCA cycles toward target conditions contribute incrementally and cumulatively to Toyota's cost, quality, and market position. Toyota finds the path along the way based on what is being learned along the way. In hindsight, then, what seems to be strategy emerges.

Toyota does not really have any solutions to offer us, but rather a means for us to sense situations and develop appropriate, smart responses. Toyota's executives, managers, and leaders are operating on the basis that organization survival arises from adaptation to unfolding events, on the way to a desired condition. They do not think of good versus bad situations, but of problems as something to be expected and as opportunities to more deeply understand and further develop our work processes. Toyota's strategy for moving toward a vision is target conditions + PDCA; which is to say, the improvement kata. Furthermore, Toyota's executives, managers, and leaders see as perhaps their main task teaching people the improvement kata in a learn-by-doing mode, which will be the subject of Part IV.

A Way of Thinking and Acting

It is important to realize that the improvement kata is about behavior routines (Figure P3-4). It is a routine of thinking and acting that harnesses our human capability to improve and to solve problems. When we view and interpret what Toyota is doing in this light, it becomes easier to grasp, and we can go further in our own efforts to compete on a similar basis.

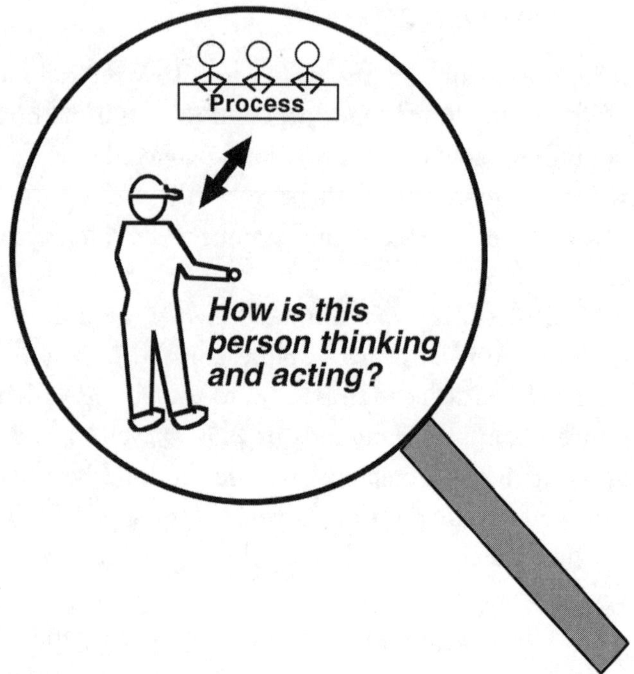

Figure P3-4. The improvement kata is about behavior routines

I did not know these things in my early days of trying to benchmark Toyota, and in hindsight it showed in my efforts to communicate with Toyota people. For example, in the early 1990s, I was involved in a lot of setup-time reduction projects at stamping processes in Detroit. During a trip I made to Japan at that time Toyota people would ask me, "How are those setup-time improvement projects going?" I would of course proceed to tell them about the most successful projects, where teams were able to reduce setup time by 70 percent or more. Yet our Toyota hosts never seemed impressed with what I was saying. They would sort of shrug and soon change the subject. I assumed I was not improving enough for their standards and that I needed to generate even greater setup time reductions.

Today I can understand better what was happening in those conversations: that we were operating with two different mental models. I was not presenting my setup-time improvement efforts in a format

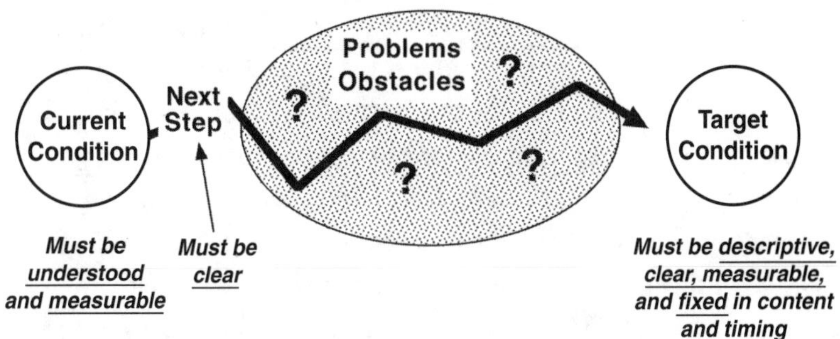

Figure P3-5. The improvement kata is a mental model

that the Toyota people could relate to or understand (as depicted in Figure P3-5). While I was explaining outcomes—how much improvement we had achieved—what they wanted to hear was something like, "The original condition was *x*. We set a target condition of *y*. We achieved *z*, and learned the following in the process." The degree of improvement was actually not that important to them. What they were interested in was what we were striving to achieve, why, how we were approaching it, what we were learning, and how we were teaching people.

Sometimes I wish I could go back and redo some of the conversations that I had on those Japan trips. But then maybe they served their purpose, since we learn from problems.

What Kind of Discipline Is Needed?

Sometimes managers and senior leaders remark that "we just need more discipline." The thinking seems to be that if people in the organization would adhere more closely to their work standards and do what they were supposed to do, there would be fewer problems.

Unfortunately it does not work this way. Keep in mind the second law of thermodynamics, or entropy, which states that even if we follow the work standard, a work process will tend to slip toward chaos if we leave it alone. No matter what, there will be problems that the operators, if left alone, will have to work around. The process will decay.

Discipline is needed, certainly, but not in the way we have perhaps been thinking. The kind of regimen we need is for everyone—and especially executives, managers, and leaders—to follow and stick to an improvement kata; to a thinking and behavior routine for how we go about improving and adapting. At this point it should become clear to you that (1) Toyota's success is about behavior routines; (2) if you want to emulate Toyota, then changing people's behavior patterns is the task; and (3) this is a different undertaking than trying to implement tools, techniques, or introduce a series of principles.

For many of us, the improvement kata is different than our current way of thinking, and it takes practice to change that way of thinking. But once you do get it, the improvement kata in itself is not that complicated. This makes sense too. Since Toyota wants to have everyone in the organization involved in continuous improvement and adaptation, they would not utilize a method that is only accessible to specialists.

The pattern of the improvement kata also simplifies a manager's or leader's job. Once leaders have learned the behavior pattern, they can be clear about what they need to do in any situation—how to proceed—to manage people. A leader using the improvement kata also does not need to know the solution to a problem, and in fact it is detrimental for the development of people in the organization to be given solutions by their leaders. What the leader needs to know is *how people should go about understanding a situation and developing solutions.* The leader should have firsthand experience with the improvement kata pattern, and know how to guide people through it so they learn it.

Learning about the improvement kata has given me a more effective way of engaging and leading groups of people, and I am more relaxed in the face of uncertainty because I know how to proceed. Take the case of the stereo speaker factory mentioned in Chapter 5, where getting the time it takes to hammer in brass inserts to be the same, whether there are eight or as many as 18 inserts, was part of the target condition. An initial response and push-back you may often get in response to a challenge like this is a somewhat provocative, "Well, please tell us how you think that is supposed to be possible!"

In the past I would try to answer that question by describing possible solutions. Not only would I fail at that, I would also be failing to tap and develop the capability of others. Today I answer such questions easily by saying: "I don't know, and that is how it is supposed to be. If we already knew the answer, it would just be an implementation question, and anyone—including any of our competitors—could do that. I don't know the solution to the problem, but I know how we can go about developing a solution."

> *I was gratified to be able to answer promptly and I did. I said I didn't know.*
>
> —Mark Twain, *Life on the Mississippi*

Toyota's improvement kata involves teaching people a standardized, conscious "means" for sensing the gist of situations and responding scientifically. This is a different way for humans to have a sense of security, comfort, and confidence. Instead of obtaining that from an unrealistic sense of certainty about conditions, they get it from the means by which they deal with uncertainty. This channels and taps our capabilities as humans much better than our current management approach, explains a good deal of Toyota's success, and gives us a model for managing almost any human enterprise.

> *... it is my impression that, after many contacts with Toyota employees, they view new situations in daily life—whether new problems, solutions elsewhere, partial solutions to the present problems, or chance events—as potential opportunities to improve competitiveness more often than those in other firms.*
>
> —Takahiro Fujimoto[1]

Comparison with Our Current Management Approach

If the process level is the fractal at which continuous improvement and adaptation can occur most effectively, then organizations that are able to improve constantly and systematically at this level should, in crowded market situations, realize a competitive advantage. If so, then this has implications for both management and management education.

Many companies experience a subtle disadvantage when it comes to continuous, incremental improvement and adaptation, because they rely heavily on managing by setting outcome targets, reporting of metrics, incentive schemes, and ROI-formula-based decision making. The evidence is mounting that, by themselves, management by objectives—at least as we currently practice it—and formulaic decision making do not make an organization sufficiently adaptive and continuously improving for long-term survival in highly competitive markets.

One problem is that reported numbers arrive after the fact, are manipulated to look better than they are (because of incentives), and, as Professor H. Thomas Johnson points out, are only abstractions of reality. Metrics are abstractions made by man, while reality is made by nature. Only process details are real and allow you to grasp the true situation.

Many executives and managers—reinforced by their MBA education—put their faith in those quantitative abstractions, pursue financial outcome targets, and in many instances have lost connection with the reality from which those abstractions emerge. Decision makers are poorly informed about the actual situation, and as a result they make incorrect assumptions, set inappropriate targets, and do not see problems until they have grown large and complex.

Managing from a distance through reported metrics leads to overlooking or obscuring small problems, but it is precisely those small problems that show us the way forward. Overlooking or obscuring small problems inhibits our ability to learn from them while they are still understandable, and to make timely adaptations in small steps. Over time this can adversely affect the company's competitive position.

I meet many managers, executives, and academics who continually hunt for the right mix of performance metrics that will stimulate Toyota-style continuous process improvement. This may seem logical from the perspective of the current management paradigm, but those metrics simply do not exist. There is no combination of outcome metrics and incentive systems that by themselves will generate continuous improvement and adaptation.

Setting targets and performance metrics alone usually does not generate the desired behavior or result in real improvement of work process. And how could it? The people trying to achieve the quantitative targets are not taught or guided by any sort of improvement kata. My colleague Robert Austin has studied this phenomenon and makes it nice and clear with the following comments:

> *The manager relies on signals that he or she assumes are good results measures. In fact, the employee knows ways to make signals look good that the manager hasn't thought of and that have nothing to do with results.*
>
> *Another lousy feature of such systems is that they punish workers who have too much integrity to game the measures.*[2]

If we want our organization to be adaptive and continuously improving, we should develop ways of maintaining more focus on the details of the real situation in real time. Toyota's improvement kata does this well. It provides a means for people to work empirically and creatively toward objectives that may not be easily or readily achievable, and that would often not initially pass one of our formulaic ROI decision-making calculations.

Toyota's shop floors are not connected to the IT system. Managerial accounting control systems can exacerbate the negative effects of managing from a distance via metrics, since reported data arrives late and leaders interact even less with the reality of the situation. This is why accounting control systems have little or no place on factory floors at Toyota. Factory leaders at Toyota do not refer to accounting reports to get an understanding of a situation. They are taught to go and observe the situation firsthand. In order to develop and guide good improvement practice, Toyota leaders interact with the unfolding situation at the process level, by following the improvement kata.

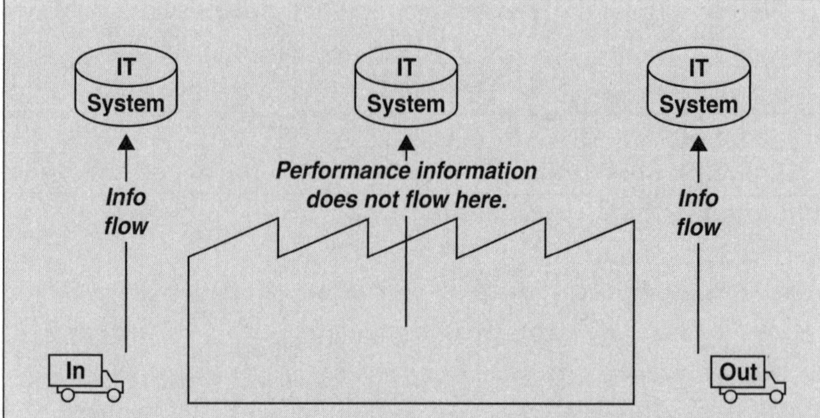

Figure P3-6. IT systems have little place on the factory floor

The factory in Figure P3-6 is treated like a "black box," but of course a large amount of process performance data is utilized in Toyota plants; on thousands of charts, boards, documents, alarms, etc. However, this data is maintained near the place of occurrence, and leaders have to go to the process to get the information they need and understand the situation there. To manage an organization with the improvement kata, many leaders may have to organize their workdays differently. There is an organizational impact.

In summation, the improvement kata gives people a means for working together. Consider, for example, some managerial concepts of the late twentieth century proposing that managers and leaders should seek out and respect the ideas of their subordinates. I have witnessed dozens of organizations that sincerely tried to employ this logical but vague advice and got nowhere with it, or worse. In an unmanaged—or "self-directed"—environment, the scope of ideas about what to do is often so wide-ranging and even conflicting that it frustrates progress. In contrast, when groups of people strive for a target condition—not just an outcome metric—and also have a common routine for working to achieve it, then they are brought into a channel that focuses their thinking and taps their capability. Not only does this make it more practical to seek out and respect other people's ideas, it makes it natural to do so.

Here is an interesting observation to consider. At Toyota, how to act in going through the improvement process is defined by the improvement kata, whereas the subject matter is open and varies depending on what one is working on. To a degree this is the opposite of how we so far have been trying to emulate Toyota: we defined the subject matter, the production techniques like kanban or heijunka that were to be implemented, but left "how to act" up to everyone to decide for themselves.

How does Toyota ensure that everyone in the organization learns and follows the improvement kata? That is the subject of Part IV.

Notes

1. Takahiro Fujimoto, *The Evolution of a Manufacturing System at Toyota* (New York: Oxford University Press, 1999).
2. Jim Austin, "Robert Austin: An Interview," *Science Career Magazine* (April 26, 2002).

Part IV

The Coaching Kata: How Toyota Teaches the Improvement Kata

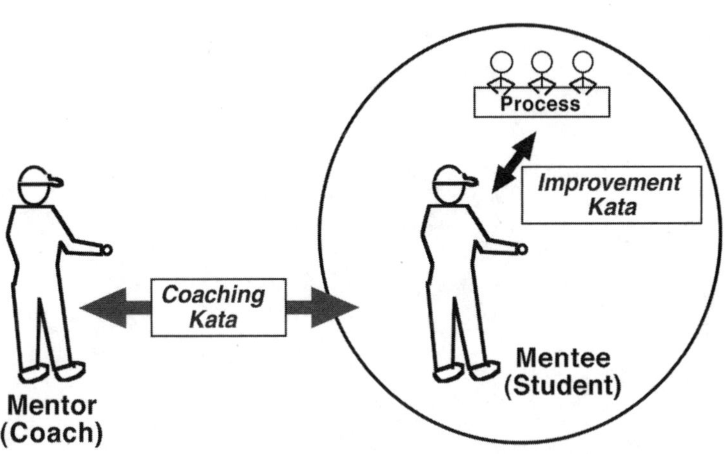

Introduction to Part IV

Once we become aware of Toyota's improvement kata, described in Part III, it gives rise to several new questions, such as:

How do we teach everyone in the organization the improvement kata?

How do we ensure people are engaged in the improvement process and utilize the improvement kata correctly in their daily work?

How will we know what skills individuals need to work on?

How do we ensure that appropriate challenges/target conditions are developed?

How do we ensure that the PDCA cycle is carried out correctly and effectively?

How will we ensure that leaders have a grasp of the true situation at the process level in the organization?

How will we pass on the improvement kata from generation to generation?

Toyota's answer to these questions is its coaching kata, which is the subject of Part IV. The purpose of the coaching kata is to teach the improvement kata and bring it into the organization. We will look into the role of managers and leaders at Toyota in teaching the improvement kata to everyone in the organization and making that kata work as effectively as possible every day. Part IV is not about how Toyota trains production workers in their jobs. It is about how Toyota works to develop and maintain improvement kata behavior across the organization.

In Chapter 7 we will first take a brief look at *who* is actually applying the improvement kata to production processes in Toyota factories. There have been a lot of misconceptions about this. Then, in Chapter 8, we will look at *how* application of the improvement kata is taught and managed at Toyota.

Chapter 7

Who Carries Out Process Improvement at Toyota?

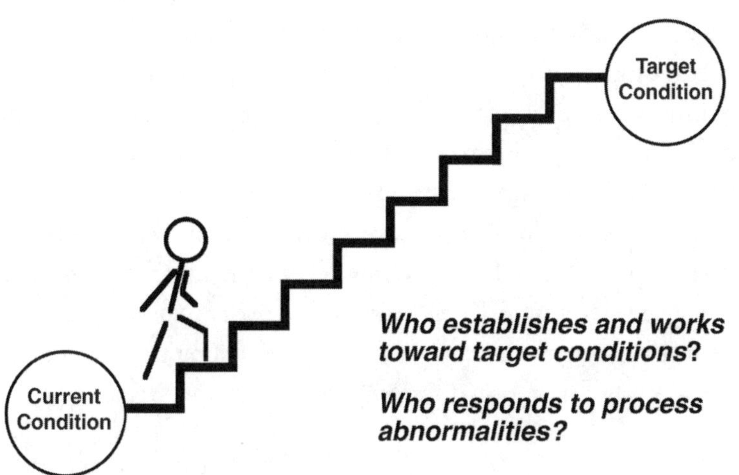

Figure 7-1. Working toward a target condition

A question that has been debated for many years is: "Who should carry out process improvements?" (Figure 7-1). Here are three common but problematic answers to that question.

1. *The process operators?* One of the widely held opinions about continuous improvement at Toyota is that it is primarily self-directed, with teams of production operators autonomously

making improvements in their own processes. Some typical comments along these lines are:

"The operators are closest to the process and are empowered."
"How can we get our line operators to solve problems?"
"How can we make continuous improvement run by itself?"

Operator autonomy is a commonly held and unfortunate misconception about Toyota's approach. It is not at all how operators and improvement are handled at Toyota. For one, it is unfair and ineffective to ask operators on their own to simultaneously make parts, struggle with problems, and improve the process, which is why Toyota calls autonomous operator-team concepts, "Disrespectful of people." It is physically impossible for production operators to work fully loaded to the planned cycle time in a 1x1 production flow and simultaneously make process improvements. Furthermore, many operators are just beginning to develop their understanding of the improvement kata and their problem-solving skills. There are currently no autonomous, self-directed teams at Toyota.

This does not mean that we should not empower or engage process operators. In fact, teaching people the improvement kata by engaging them in it is critical to Toyota's success. It only means that concepts like self-directed work teams are not such an effective way for an organization to empower and engage people.

2. *Leave it to chance?* I have not heard anyone actually give this answer, but in many cases our comments and actions—comments like these—indicate this is exactly what is happening:

"Andon gives everyone in the plant information."
"This alerts everyone that there is a problem."
"Any person walking through the area can see ..."

The number of andon-style warning-lamp systems that have been installed in our factories in the last 20 years, for example, is astonishing. Yet in many factories the red lamps are lighting up and no one is responding. The basic point here is that if we assume anyone (or everyone) is responsible, then no one is responsible.

3. *A special team?* As we have already discussed, this will not work if we want improvement to occur at every process every day. At Toyota, factory staff includes no specific continuous improvement agents. The improvement kata is embedded into every work process, and everyone is taught to work along the lines of the improvement kata.

Who Does It?

In schematic form, a typical Toyota factory's line functions are organized as shown in Figure 7-2. There are, of course, additional support

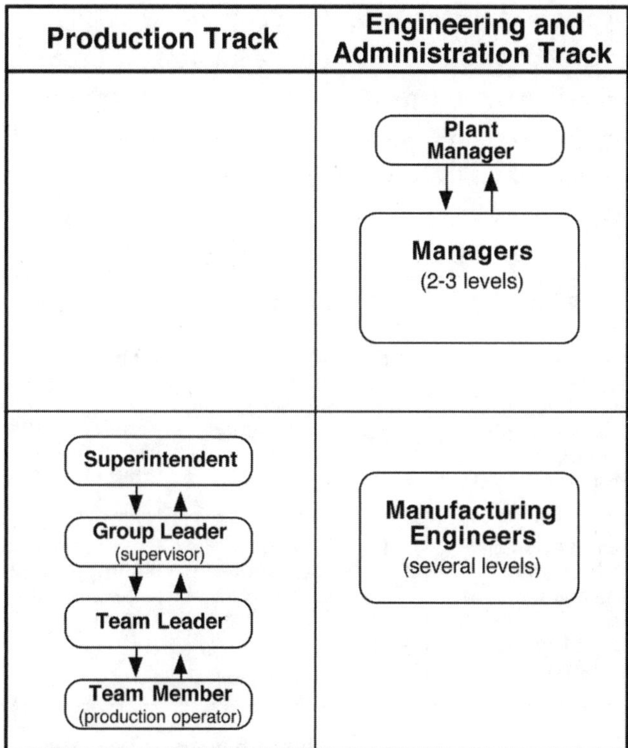

Figure 7-2. Schematic of Toyota factory line organization

functions such as maintenance and production engineering that are not shown, but this diagram is detailed enough for our purposes.[1]

In 2004, Professor Koichi Shimizu of Okayama University published a paper about continuous improvement of production processes in Toyota factories. In his paper, Shimizu classifies process improvement activity at Toyota in two categories:

- Improvement carried out by production operators themselves through quality circles, the suggestion system, and similar initiatives. Shimizu calls this "voluntary improvement activity."
- Improvement carried out by team leaders, production supervisory staff, and engineers as part of their job function.

There are some surprises in Shimizu's paper (Figure 7-3). Specifically, his research suggests that only about 10 percent of realized improvement in productivity and cost at Toyota comes from the first category, whereas about 90 percent comes from the second. In addition, the main purpose of the first category—improvements carried out by production operators themselves—is not so much the improvement itself, but rather to train production operators in kaizen mind and ability, and to identify workers who are candidates for promotion to team

Who	Impact	Purpose
Production operators themselves through quality circles and suggestion system	Only 10% of realized improvement comes from this	Training of kaizen mind and ability Identify workers to promote to team leader
Team leaders, production supervisory staff, and engineers as part of their job function	90% of realized improvement comes from this	Cost reduction via improvement in productivity and quality

Figure 7-3. Who carries out process improvements at Toyota?

Source: Koichi Shimzu, "Reorienting Kaizen Activities at Toyota: Kaizen, Production Efficiency, and Humanization of Work," *Okayama Economic Review,* vol. 36, no. 3, Dec. 2004, pp. 1-25.

leader. The purpose of the second category of improvement, on the other hand, is clearly cost reduction via diligent and constant improvement of productivity and quality.

What I have been able to learn so far about who makes process improvements on Toyota shop floors fits with Shimizu's findings. The great majority of shop floor improvement in a Toyota factory is generated by the functions circled in Figure 7-4. These team leaders, group leaders, superintendents, and various levels of manufacturing engineers are the primary people who apply, and coach application of, the improvement kata to production processes. This process improvement activity represents well over 50 percent of their work time, which is not surprising since at Toyota the improvement kata is actually a way of managing.[2]

Toyota production operators, called "team members," are of course also regularly involved in making process improvements, but these are usually improvements in the operators' immediate work envelope, which are carried out in collaboration with, and under the guidance of, the team leader. It's the responsibility of team leaders to encourage and get improvement suggestions from their team members, and, conversely, operator promotion to team leader is determined in part on

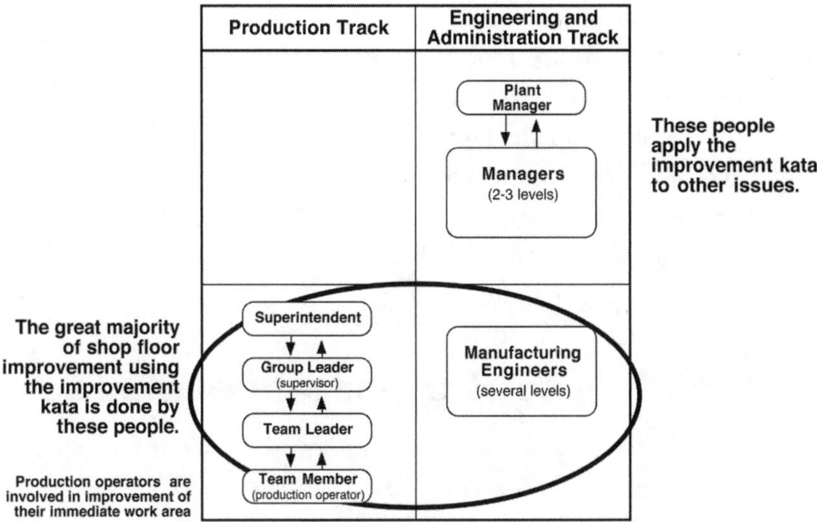

Figure 7-4. In the factory organization, process improvement activity is mostly here

how much improvement initiative and skill an operator demonstrates. Both operator and team leader, in other words, have incentive to work together on process improvement.

Working with Target Conditions

In the case of a new process or product, management sets a target cost and a target date for production. The first process target condition (that is, work standard) is typically established by the process's group leader and a production engineer. This is then given to the production team (the team leader and team members).

As the production stage begins, the production team and their group leader work to achieve that target condition, which can take several weeks. Once regular production stabilizes, then further target conditions, called "standards" or "targets," are developed:

- Group leaders, team leaders, and team members focus on target conditions in their process, and on understanding and resolving daily production problems.
- Themes, targets, plans, and initiatives are announced by senior management. These are worked down into the organization via mentor/mentee dialogues (more on this in the next chapter), and are converted into process target conditions. The conversion of outcome targets into process target conditions generally begins at the "superintendent" level. Managers at this level ensure that target conditions, improvement efforts, and projects at individual processes follow improvement-kata thinking, fit together for a flowing value stream, match with the organization's targets, and serve customer requirements.

Responding to Process Abnormalities

A common way of reacting to process abnormalities in our factories is to have production operators record them, so they can be compiled into summaries and Pareto charts. Sounds like a good idea, but it is not effective for improvement. I once listened to a plant manager proudly explaining a Pareto chart of problems and how the top problem was being worked on. One of my colleagues said in response, "Oh, and the rest of those problems you are shipping to the customer?" which I thought was a pretty good insight.

The information provided by Pareto charts usually comes too late to be useful for process improvement efforts. By the time a problem has risen to the top of a Pareto chart, it has already caused a lot of damage and grown complicated, the root-cause trail is cold, and we become involved in analyzing postmortem data instead of understanding what is actually happening on the shop floor now. It is interesting to note how often the largest category in a Pareto chart is "other," that is, an accumulation of smaller problems.

This does not mean that Pareto charts should be abolished, but that they should not be thought of as our first choice for becoming aware of and dealing with process problems.

Here are two aspects of how Toyota thinks about dealing with process problems:

1. *The response to process abnormalities should be immediate. Why?*

   - If we wait to go after the causes of a problem, the trail becomes cold and problem solving becomes more difficult. We lose the opportunity to learn.
   - If left alone, small problems accumulate and grow into large and complicated problems.
   - Responding right away means we may still be able to adjust and achieve the day's target.
   - Telling people that quality is important but not responding to problems is saying one thing but doing another.
   - Lean value streams are closely coupled, and a problem in one area can quickly lead to problems elsewhere.

2. *The response to process abnormalities should come from someone other than the production operators. Why?*

   An example helps here. Imagine a 1x1 flow assembly cell in one of our factories with an "autonomous" team of operators. In the cell, there is a status counter that displays two numbers. One number is the actual quantity produced, which increases each time a finished item is scanned. The second number is the target quantity, which increases automatically as each takt time interval passes.

What happens in this process when one operator experiences a problem? The cell stops. What do the operators do? They try to fix the problem so they can resume production. Say it takes a few minutes to do that, during which time the target-quantity counter continues to advance. Now the problem is fixed and the cell is able to run again. What do the operators do? Naturally they resume production, probably as quickly as possible since the line is now a little behind according to the status counter. Yet the moment the problem occurred, while the trail is hot, is the best time to learn why it happened. Looking into it later will be fruitless.

Can you see the conflict in our thinking? Do we want the operators to make parts, or do we want them to go into problem investigation? They cannot do both simultaneously. Problems are normal, and if we set up autonomous processes, there is no way the operators can be successful. These kinds of autonomous production processes seem to reflect a flawed assumption that if everyone did what they were supposed to do, there would be no problems.

In order to be able to respond to process problems as they occur, production processes at Toyota-group companies are supported and monitored by a team leader. This team leader is the designated person to respond first and immediately to any process problem. Although team leaders respond to every abnormality, each response does not trigger problem-solving activity, which is usually initiated in response to repeating problems. The process's work standard—the target condition—is owned by the team leader, who uses it to help spot abnormalities in the process. The team leader is not monitoring the process to police its failings, but to be acquainted with how it is working.

With team leaders at its processes, Toyota has—in comparison to many other factories—one official extra level of indirect staffing. This does not sound "lean," but it is an enabler for process improvement because there is someone to respond as problems occur, and the root cause trail is still hot. As mentioned earlier, you can expose problems only to the degree that you can handle them. With its team leader approach, Toyota can handle more problems and can thus learn and improve more.

Having a fast-response system in place then gives Toyota the ability to staff its production processes with no more than the correct number of operators, which in turn quickly reveals problems. This combination represents an improving system. Conversely, manufacturers with autonomous teams of operators generally need to have extra operators in their processes, which, as already mentioned, causes work-arounds, obscures problems, and leads to a static system.

Interestingly, at Toyota, having this improvement and response system—team leaders—does not equal having more people in total compared to other companies. On the contrary. There are two reasons for this:

- Because of the team leader's presence, the process can be staffed with only the correct number of operators; no extra.
- Because there is an improvement and response system in place, beginning with the team leader, over time productivity is improved and even fewer operators are needed.

We should be careful with overly simple, quick-benefit statements such as "cut indirect labor" or "flatten the organization chart," because they can lead to suboptimization and a dangerously static system.

Notes

1. The information under this heading comes from observations and interviews at Toyota facilities, and discussions with several former TMEMNA employees.
2. Manufacturing engineers at Toyota are responsible for improvement in shop floor operations. This is different from what the words "manufacturing engineer" mean to us. Toyota also has what it calls "production engineers," who, like manufacturing engineers in our factories, are responsible for developing tools, processes, machines, and equipment.

Chapter 8

The Coaching Kata: Leaders as Teachers

Coaching Is Required

Suppose we would like to teach a team of athletes some new skills and have them do well in competition. In this case, we would certainly not expect that simply explaining a different way of doing something, no matter how well that explaining is done, will be sufficient for altering their behavior. It is not possible to objectively assess one's own performance and see what skills you need to work on. This is because we tend not to perceive our own habits and do not know what we do not know. In the case of athletes, we naturally expect them to practice under the observation and guidance of an experienced coach, and that the necessity of having a coach will not go away. If no one observes them and provides feedback, they can end up internalizing the wrong routines.

It is the same at Toyota, where the improvement kata does not happen automatically or autonomously. Toyota's managers and leaders work hard every day to both teach it and to keep improvement going in an effective manner. Since improvement and adaptation are central to Toyota's business philosophy (normal daily management = process improvement), it is not surprising that managers and leaders there work to ensure that improvement happens. What is surprising, however, is how they go about it.

The Role of Leaders at Toyota

The primary task of Toyota's managers and leaders does not revolve around improvement per se, but around increasing the improvement capability of people. That capability is what, in Toyota's view, strengthens the company. Toyota's managers and leaders develop people who in turn improve processes through the improvement kata.

> *We now accept the fact that learning is a lifelong process of keeping abreast of change. And the most pressing task is to teach people how to learn.*
>
> —Peter Drucker

Developing the improvement capability of people at Toyota is not relegated to the human resources or the training and development departments. It is part of every day's work in every area, and it is managers and supervisors who are expected to teach their people the improvement kata. The improvement kata is part of how people are managed day to day. This means, of course, that the managers and leaders must themselves be experienced in using the improvement kata.

Because the improvement kata is a set of behavioral guidelines, it is something that we learn through repeated practice. It takes conditioning to make behavioral routines become second nature, and consequently a lot of Toyota's managerial activities involve having people practice the improvement kata with their guidance. For team leaders and group leaders, this teaching occupies more than 50 percent of their time, and for higher-level managers it can also occupy up to 50 percent. Developing people in this manner is part of a manager's or supervisor's evaluation, bonus, promotion, and salary.

Training While Working On the Real Thing

We may think of taking classes and seminars to learn, but Toyota thinks of working through actual improvement challenges as how one learns. There are some classroom training courses at Toyota, but to ensure that improvement happens and that people internalize the improvement kata the primary emphasis is on doing: managers and

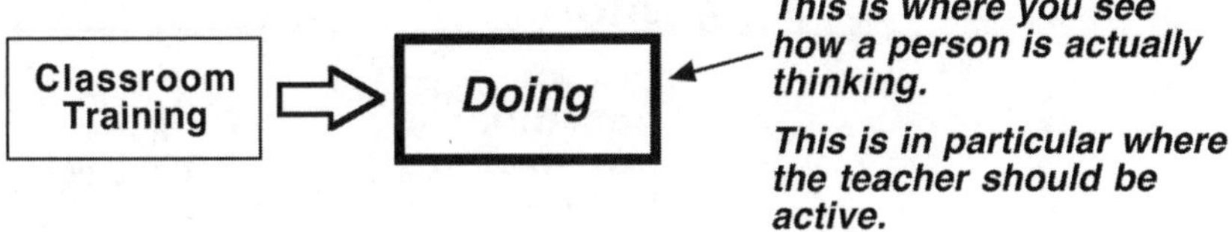

Figure 8-1. At Toyota, training and doing are not separated

leaders at Toyota teach people the improvement kata by guiding them in making real improvements in real processes. This approach is not unlike skills training in sports, where "training" means athletes performing an actual activity over and over under the observation and guidance of an experienced coach.

By comparison, in many of our companies the concept of training seems to have devolved to classroom teaching and simulation exercises. Unfortunately, classroom training and simulations cannot ensure change, mastery, and consistency. Classroom training alone, even if it includes simulations, at best only achieves awareness. We can only discern what people are actually learning and how they are thinking—and hence what they need to learn and practice next—as they try to apply in real life what they are being taught (Figure 8-1).

Toyota does not make a distinction between learning the improvement kata and improving processes. Toyota's teachers—that is, managers and leaders—observe and work with their students as those students are doing the actual activity day to day. Of course, as you might expect, at Toyota there is a kata for how managers and leaders do this.

The Coaching Kata

Toyota's kata for teaching the improvement kata is a mentor/mentee dialogue (Figure 8-2), which probably has its roots in the Buddhist master/apprentice teaching method. Like the improvement kata, the coaching kata is often not directly visible to visitors and benchmarkers. Yet the development of continuous improvement and adaptation at Toyota, through application of the improvement kata, has depended to considerable degree on such coaching.

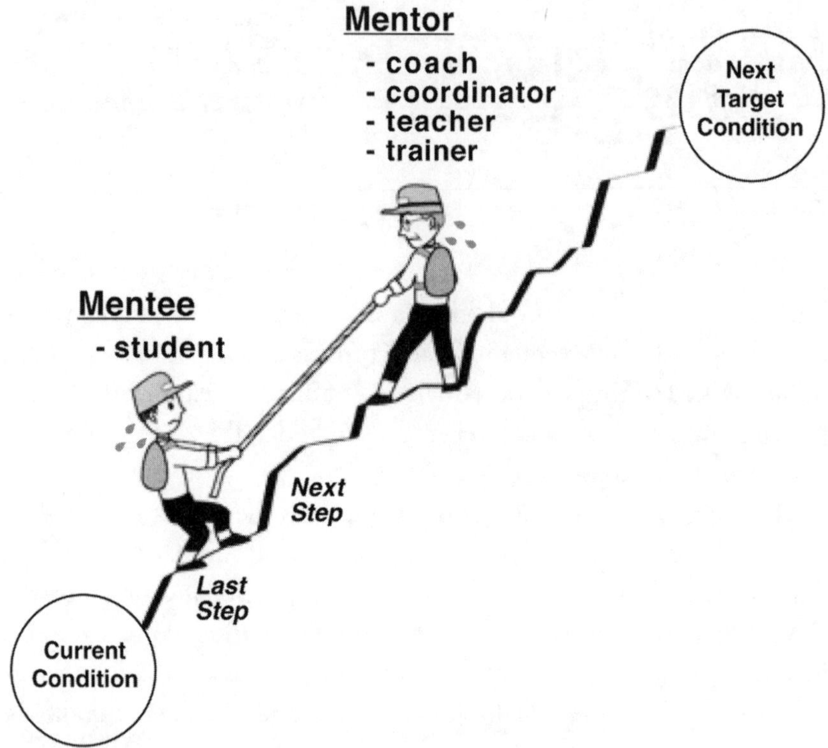

Figure 8-2. Toyota's classic depiction of its mentor/mentee approach
Note: Labels and current- and target-condition circles were added by the author.

Everyone at Toyota Has a Mentor

Mastery is the objective of any kata, and even people at higher levels in Toyota are honing their skills and working toward that goal. Like the improvement kata, the pattern of the coaching kata is also practiced at all levels throughout Toyota. Each employee is assigned a more experienced employee—a mentor—who provides active guidance through the process of making actual improvements or dealing with work-related situations. That mentor, in turn, has his or her own mentor who is doing the same. It is the buddy system, or two-man rule, with one buddy being the mentor.

These mentor/mentee relationships are not necessarily linked to the organizational hierarchy. For shop-floor operators, their mentor is their team leader, who is in turn supported by the group leader. However, above these levels in the organization you may get mentored not only by your immediate superior,[1] but also by someone else, who may be assigned to you based on your current activities and development needs. Over the years, you will have different mentors.

It easily takes 10 years of practicing the improvement kata and the coaching kata before both become so ingrained that one can be a good mentor. This is one reason why Toyota has in the past avoided bringing managers in from outside the company, and instead preferred to develop them from within. One of Toyota's key challenges while growing rapidly is to have enough mentors.

A person's need for coaching never goes away. Regardless of how much experience one has gained, it is unlikely that anyone can become so good at discerning the reality of a situation and applying the improvement kata that coaching will no longer be necessary. The intention is that both the improvement kata and the coaching kata increasingly become second nature (automatic and reflexive) as a person rises in the organization.

The Mentor/Mentee Dialogue

The mentor (coach) guides the mentee in applying the improvement kata through a back-and-forth dialogue over a period of time, which has sometimes been compared to a game of catch:

Mentor→Mentee→Mentor→Mentee ...

The mentor/mentee dialogue is utilized, for example, when a current situation is being assessed, when a target condition is being developed, and then when the routine of the five questions comes into play.

One key element in Toyota's mentor/mentee dialogue is that the intention is for the mentee to figure things out for him- or herself under guidance, which is a well-known teaching method. The dialogue often begins with the mentor giving the mentee a purposely vague assignment, need, or challenge. For example, the mentor may ask the mentee to have a look at a problem or situation, or suggest something like, "We should wash parts within the one-by-one assembly flow at this process, rather than in batches." The mentor then asks what the mentee proposes. The mentee's answer helps the mentor discern how the mentee is thinking and what input the mentor should give next. That is why the mentor's assignment or challenge is often vague at the start—so he can see how the mentee is approaching the situation.

The mentee gives her observations or proposal, sometimes in bullet form in a single-page document (more on this later). After this is presented to the mentor, it is often pushed back to the mentee in the first cycle, with a suggestion such as, "Please think about this some more," or simply, "Why?" This is only the first of several catch cycles, through which the mentee's analysis and proposal become progressively more developed and detailed. Once the current situation has been analyzed and the target condition defined and detailed to the mentor's satisfaction, then the mentee's role becomes planning and carrying out PDCA cycles, also with the oversight of the mentor. In doing this, the mentee often has to justify actions to her mentor, and to define in advance the expected result of an action.

The point to remember here is that the mentor is asking questions of the mentee not to direct the mentee to a particular solution—although it may appear that way—but rather to learn what and how the mentee is thinking and how the mentee is approaching the situation. The mentor works to teach the mentee the routine of the improvement kata by providing step-by-step guidance, based on the mentee's reactions and responses along the way. The mentor guides the mentee through the improvement kata, but in a manner that has the mentee learn for him- or herself the routine and thinking inherent in that kata. The mentee is learning by personally gaining insight. The highest, though somewhat bittersweet, praise for a mentor is if the mentee feels he or she learned and achieved the target condition independently. As an aside, from my observations I can say that the mentor's job is as difficult as the mentee's.

A second, and clever, element of mentor/mentee dialogues at Toyota is that while the mentee is responsible for the doing, the mentor bears considerable responsibility for the results but should not give solutions to the mentee. This overlap of responsibility creates a bond between mentor and mentee, because if a mentee fails, then it is the mentor who will get the scrutiny.

If the learner hasn't learned, the teacher hasn't taught.

—Common expression, which is frequently used at Toyota

The mentee is the person who works on the problem, whereas the mentor's task is to keep the mentee "in the corridor" of the improvement kata routine. This is what is illustrated in the Toyota picture of the two mountain climbers shown earlier in Figure 8-2. Of course, to be able to guide the mentee in this way, the mentor must also be looking at the situation and often thinking one step ahead of the mentee; but no more than a step ahead. The mentor works to bring the mentee into the behavior corridor prescribed by the improvement kata, but ultimately the mentor must accept the solution that the mentee develops. Leading the mentee to a solution would block the development of the mentee's capability, that is, the purpose of the mentor/mentee dialogue approach.

Although Toyota mentors are usually not directive about solutions, they can, however, be directive about how to go about understanding a situation and developing solutions. For example, once he has heard from the mentee in one cycle, the mentor may, at times, be directive about the next step.

A third element of the mentor/mentee dialogue is that it is not just learning by doing, but that people learn when they make discoveries through small errors (see Chapter 6). The mentor expects the mentee to make small mistakes in applying the improvement kata, and it is especially at these points that the mentee will learn, and that the mentor can see what coaching input is required. In other words, the mentor lets the mentee make small missteps—as long as they do not affect the customer—rather than giving the mentee answers up front.

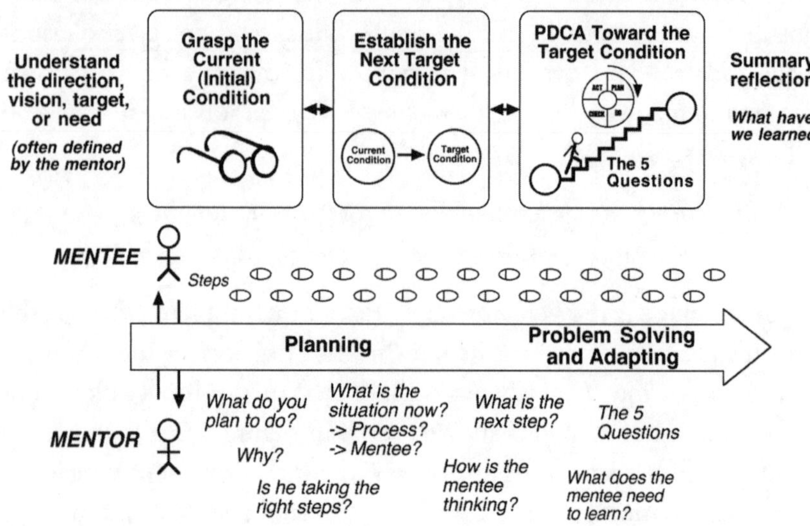

Figure 8-3. Mentor/mentee dialogue (the coaching kata) to teach the improvement kata

With the mentor/mentee teaching approach, as depicted in Figure 8-3, Toyota has developed a smart answer to the question of how an organization can teach its members the improvement kata and keep improvement going. The mentor/mentee approach has several benefits:

- Leaders can discern how a mentee is thinking and thereby determine the appropriate next step and what skills the mentee needs to practice to become a better problem solver. We do not recognize people's current skill-development needs when we tell them what to do.
- This approach—learning by doing with trial and error, under guidance—is more effective than relying on written documentation, classroom training, or telling someone what to do for passing on organizational culture—that is, developing specific behavior patterns.
- This approach develops alignment between company goals and workplace behaviors. It provides focus, direction, and control,

but with a considerable amount of leeway that helps people develop their own capability. It is not top-down or bottom-up; it is both, simultaneously. The mentor/mentee approach develops individual responsibility and initiative while also providing common direction and approach. This is what I mean when I refer to "operating in the desired corridor."

- The needs of the mentee and the situation determine the next mentoring and training that the mentor provides. This means that information is flowing both down and up in the organization. As a result, strategic decisions can be more in sync with the actual situation at the process level.

Mentor/Mentee Case Example

The best way to explain Toyota's mentor/mentee teaching approach is to show it in action. The following case example provides a close look at a Toyota-style mentor/mentee dialogue. Simultaneously, it also does a good job of demonstrating how Toyota thinks about problem solving, which is important for deepening our understanding of the improvement kata. The case example is similar to one that was used to help teach problem solving at Toyota's Georgetown, Kentucky, factory, although this one is greatly expanded.

Keep in mind that this case is just one example of a Toyota mentor/mentee dialogue. Although these dialogues typically mirror the pattern of the improvement kata in some way, they can take on a variety of forms depending on the situation. The objective here is not to give you a mechanical script for a Toyota mentor/mentee dialogue, but to give you some a sense for the pattern, or routine, and thinking inherent in the coaching kata.

Setup

Start by taking a look at the five-step problem-solving approach in Figure 8-4, called "Practical Problem Solving," which is commonly used at Toyota. This is problem solving as applied in everyday operations. I will refer to these problem-solving steps as we go through the case example.

Steps of Toyota's Practical Problem Solving

1. Pick Up the Problem: Problem Consciousness

- Identify the problem that is the priority.

2. Grasp the Situation (Go and See)

- Clarify the problem.
  - What should be happening?
  - What is actually happening?
  - Break the problem into individual problems if necessary.
- If necessary use temporary measures to contain the abnormal occurrence until the root cause can be addressed.
- Locate the **point of cause** of the problem. Do not to go into cause investigation until you find the point of cause.
- Grasp the tendency of the abnormal occurrence at the point of cause.

3. Investigate Causes

- Identify and confirm the direct cause of the abnormal occurrence.
- Conduct a 5-Why investigation to build a chain of cause/effect relationships to root cause.
- Stop at the cause that must be addressed to prevent recurrence.

4. Develop and Test Countermeasure

- Take one specific action to address the root cause.
- Try to change only one factor at a time, so you can see correlation.

5. Follow Up

- Monitor and confirm results.
- Standardize successful countermeasure.
- Reflect. What did we learn during this problem-solving process?

Figure 8-4. The problem-solving approach used in the case example

As you can see from the five steps, there is no magic in this problem-solving approach. The basic steps are well known and similar to what is described in many problem-solving books and training courses. Most managers and engineers I meet have already had some kind of problem-solving training and even still have the course documentation on their office bookshelf. Yet I find almost no one following the problem-solving approach properly. This is a good example of how ineffective classroom training alone is for changing our behavior.

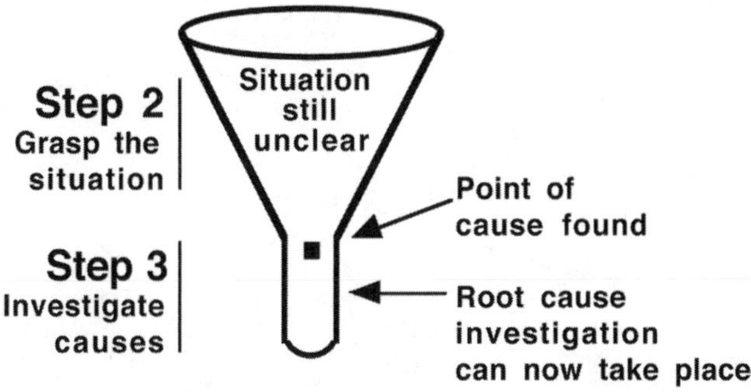

Figure 8-5. A funnel to illustrate the "point of cause" concept

Within the Practical Problem-Solving approach, Toyota often uses a funnel to illustrate the "point of cause" concept, which is mentioned under Step 2, Grasp the Situation (Figure 8-5). This concept may have arisen because Toyota vehicle assembly factories have long assembly lines. The idea is that when you become aware of a problem, you then need to trace it back up the line or value stream until you find the point where the cause may lie. Try not to go into cause investigation until you think you have found this point.

Cast of Characters

The mentor/mentee case example takes place in a section of the final vehicle assembly line, called the "trim line," at a Toyota assembly plant. The people noted in the Cast of Characters in Figure 8-6 are involved.

Cast of Characters		
Paul	Trim Shop Assistant Manager	*Your mentor*
Tina	Trim Section B Group Leader	*You*
Dan Bob Judy Mary Jeff	Trim Section B Team Leaders	*Your mentees*

Figure 8-6. Persons involved in the case example

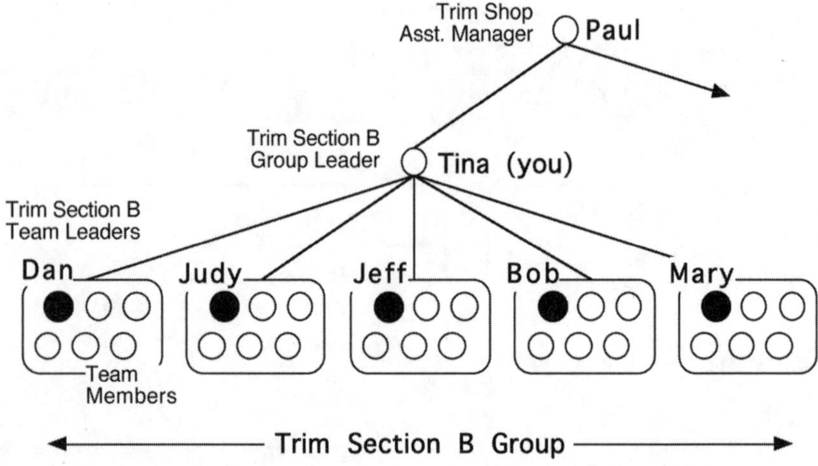

Figure 8-7. Case example organization structure

The organization looks as diagrammed in Figure 8-7, which is a typical organization structure at a Toyota assembly plant production line. This is the same Toyota line-organization structure that is mentioned in Chapter 7.

How to Read the Case

In this case you take on the role of the mentor—the Coach—whose task it is to teach the improvement kata. Your character is Tina, the group leader, and your mentees are the five team leaders: Dan, Judy, Jeff, Bob, and Mary.

The case has 11 chapters. After Chapter 1, each chapter is presented as a unit consisting of a situation (in a box) and a corresponding analysis of Tina's mentoring behaviors. Proceed through the case as follows:

1. Read the situation in the box.
2. Then read the analysis of Tina's mentoring behavior for that chapter, where I will point out several aspects of the coaching kata.
3. Wherever you are asked the question *If you were Tina what would you do next?,* write your response to this question on a piece of paper before moving on.

Summary Discussion

At the end of the case there is a summary discussion of key points on the subject of mentor/mentee dialogue and Toyota-style problem solving.

BEGIN HERE

Chapter 1

Paul, the trim shop assistant manager, met with all the trim-line group leaders (one of whom is you) to discuss a troubling trend in trim-line scrap. Scrap costs had increased 8 percent over the last two months. Paul requested that each group leader initiate problem solving in their groups to reduce scrap cost generated from their processes. He set the target of returning each group's scrap cost to its earlier level within 30 days.

If you were Tina what would you do next?

Chapter 2

After the meeting with Paul, Tina, the trim section B group leader (you), decided to analyze her scrap costs to identify where increases in her group had occurred. Tina reviewed her scrap reports from the previous four weeks to determine what part her group was scrapping most often and which of the parts being scrapped created the highest cost. She also asked each of her five team leaders to sort through the scrap records they had written in the current week to determine the same information.

The analysis showed that a side panel interior trim piece in Dan's team was the part that Tina's group had scrapped the most. Due to the quantity of the part scrapped, it was also the highest scrap expense to the group. Tina decided to target her initial activity at scrap reduction on this trim piece.

In what step of Practical Problem Solving is Tina?

Analysis

What mentoring/coaching behaviors is Tina using?

- Show me.
  Mentors prefer facts and data over opinion.
- The mentor must see deeply him/herself.
  If Tina tells her team leaders to observe their processes and then report back to her, she will not be in a position to evaluate their comments. More on this in a moment.
- Single-factor experiments.
  Tina prefers serial rather than parallel countermeasures. The goal is to learn about the work system, not just shut off the problem via a shotgun blast of countermeasures. Within one contiguous flowing production process, like Tina's group along the assembly line, mentors encourage mentees to only change one thing at a time and check the results. Changing more than one thing simultaneously increases the number of variables and makes cause and effect harder to see, which makes problem solving difficult. If you try to reduce scrap everywhere in the group, you lose sight of cause and effect and don't develop an understanding of the system.

  Tina has decided to identify and focus on the biggest problem and not unleash chaos in her group by creating multiple variables.

Inappropriate actions by the mentor in this cycle would have been:

- Simply ask the five team leaders what they think is the problem.
- Tell the team leaders that we must reduce scrap.
- Tell the team leaders to observe their processes, to go and see.

In what step of Practical Problem Solving is Tina?

- Tina is trying to identify the priority problem. She is in Step 1: Pick up the problem.

If you were Tina what would you do next?

Chapter 3

Tina decided to talk with Dan, the team leader of the team that installs the trim, to get a sense of his grasp of the situation.

Dan told Tina that he wasn't sure what was going on with the side panel trim piece. He noticed that the team had been scrapping more of the parts lately. He also knew that one of the team members on the process had complained that the parts seemed harder to install. He also felt that he had been answering more andon-cord pulls (calls for assistance) at that process lately and that they were usually related to the side panel trim.

In what step of Practical Problem Solving are Tina and Dan?

Analysis

What mentoring/coaching behaviors is Tina using?

- Leading with questions.
  Tina's task as a manager and mentor is not to solve the problem, but to develop her mentees' improvement capabilities through practice. Tina would garner no praise or credit from her superiors if she were to solve the scrap problem herself, because by doing that she would have wasted an opportunity to further develop the capability of the organization. Tina's job is to develop Dan as a problem solver.

  Since a mentor's job is to develop the mentee, they tend not to quickly tell the mentee what to do. Although mentors are experienced in problem solving, they do not point out solutions or give detailed instructions.

  The mentee is given a challenge, a problem, and is expected to make mistakes along the way, on a small scale. Those very mistakes show the mentor what behaviors the mentee needs to practice and what inputs the mentor should give. By asking questions and observing how the mentee responds, the mentor learns what the mentee is thinking. The mentor then provides guidance to move the mentee into the corridor of thinking and acting prescribed by the improvement kata.

For these reasons, in this cycle Tina will not tell Dan to go and observe the process. She will ask Dan what next step he proposes and observe how he answers. Dan is thinking about the problem, but Tina is thinking about how Dan is approaching the problem.

The power of teaching by asking questions goes back to Socrates, but it is a difficult skill to learn. The method fails if it is used by someone in authority who is simply trying to convince others of a particular solution or answer. People can detect the difference between authentic, neutral inquiry versus an effort to persuade them. There is a big difference between using questions to get a person to come to your preconceived solution versus using questions to discern how a person is thinking and what they need to learn.

Inappropriate actions by the mentor in this cycle would have been:

- Tell Dan to go and observe his process.
- Tell Dan how to proceed.

In what step of Practical Problem Solving are Tina and Dan?

- They are about to get into Step 2: Grasp the situation.

If you were Tina what would you do next?

Chapter 4

In talking to Dan, Tina realized that he had not picked up the problem with the side panel trim even though there were indications that a problem existed. Tina realized that she needed to work with Dan to further develop his problem-solving skills.

Tina and Dan went to the scrap area to look at the most recent side panel trim pieces to be scrapped. She asked him to look at all the scrap trim pieces and tell her what he observed. The first thing Dan noticed was that a nylon clip was broken on most of the parts. He showed the clip to Tina and proposed that they call Incoming Inspection to check if the parts were being delivered from the supplier with cracks in the nylon clip.

Analysis

What mentoring/coaching behaviors is Tina using?

- Sometimes the mentor is directive about the next step.
  After hearing Dan's response, Tina proposed they go look at the scrapped pieces, rather than waiting for Dan to suggest this step. Toyota's mentoring approach is not done exclusively through questions. It is not supposed to be a guessing game for the mentee. The mentor is asking questions in order to see what the mentee is thinking. Once that has occurred, the mentor may make a directive statement regarding the next step (but not about solutions).
- Go and see. Tina went with Dan to see the situation.
  Had Dan in the past proven himself to be a highly experienced problem solver, it is possible that Tina may have let him go alone and then report back to her. But she knew from his response that he was a beginner in problem solving and needed more of her coaching help.

If Tina had sent Dan to the production process and scrap area and asked him to report back his findings without going and looking for herself, she would have effectively nullified her ability to manage further. If a mentor does not have firsthand understanding of the situation, then they cannot lead. This is an important point. Tina would have no way to evaluate whether what Dan was saying and proposing was on the right track or not. She would essentially be out of the picture and could only nod and say, "Okay, let's do that." (This points out an Achilles' heel in management by objectives as we have been practicing it.) Although Tina's job is to develop the improvement capability of her mentees, she must understand the real situation deeply enough to evaluate what her mentee is telling her, in order to see what the mentee needs to learn and what the mentee's next step is. So mentors are generally paying attention to two things: the situation under scrutiny, and how the mentee is approaching the situation.

- Observe, don't interview.
  Many of us would interview the operators in the process, to see what they think might be the problem. As we have already discussed, this only gives you people's opinions, not facts and data. Mentors and mentees must learn to see deeply for themselves and understand what is happening.

Inappropriate actions by the mentor in this cycle would have been:

- Have Dan go observe the process and report back to Tina.
- Ask or interview the workers in the process.

If you were Tina what would you do next?

(Dan has made a proposal, to which you must respond.)

Chapter 5

Tina responded that when they had finished their investigation and established that in fact it was a parts-quality problem, they would call Incoming Inspection. In the meantime she asked Dan not to jump to conclusions too soon and to look at the parts again.

When Dan looked at the scrapped parts again, he noticed that one of the three mounting studs on every part had damaged threads on its end.

In what step of Practical Problem Solving are Tina and Dan?

Analysis

What mentoring/coaching behaviors is Tina using?

- Guide the mentee to "work it back" to the point of cause.
  If Dan were to contact the parts-receiving department at this early point, it would initiate a lot of activity, but the situation is not yet understood. Imagine how much waste would result if people from many different areas were contacting Incoming Inspection so early in their problem solving. Engaging the parts-receiving department in this way is, incidentally, not uncommon.
  Mentors will guide their mentees to first grasp the condition where the problem was discovered, and then work it back from there if the evidence suggests doing that.

In what step of Practical Problem Solving are Tina and Dan?

- Tina and Dan are still trying to clarify what is happening. They have not yet found the point of cause and are still in Step 2: Grasp the situation.

Chapter 6

Tina suggested to Dan that they go and observe the side panel trim installation process. They checked the line-side parts for the damaged stud threads, and did not find any, before watching the operator perform the process.

Then Tina and Dan went to look at the work standard for the side panel trim process. The standard required that the team member pick up the part and the nut driver at the parts rack before moving to the vehicle to install the part. The driver is placed on the vehicle floor, and the part is then positioned so the nylon clips line up with holes in the body panel. The team member then knocks the clips into the panel with his hand. Next, the team member picks up the driver and loads its socket with a nut. He then installs a nut onto each of the three studs.

After watching the team member install several parts, Tina asked Dan if he noticed anything that could be a potential problem with the installation. Dan said that everything looked normal to him. He could see no deviation from the work standard.

Tina asked him to look again but this time to focus on what specific actions the team member takes to install the nuts to the studs.

In what step of Practical Problem Solving are Tina and Dan?

Analysis

What mentoring/coaching behaviors is Tina using?

- Refer to the work standard or target condition before observing a process.
  Tina and Dan checked the work standard before observing the process. Be sure to understand the way the process should be operating, so you have a point of comparison. This is why the first of the five questions is, "What is the target condition / standard at this process?"

- When the mentee makes a proposal or statement, the mentor should respond quickly.
  When I first received this advice from a Toyota person, I mistakenly thought it meant that the mentor must fully understand the situation and know the solution. Try as I might, that was something I could almost never achieve.
  Tina has asked Dan to look again at the process and focus specifically on what the team member does to install the nuts to the studs. It seems like Tina knows the solution, doesn't it? A young American working at Toyota in Japan once told me how it initially drove him crazy that his Japanese mentors would ask him questions and seemed to already have a solution in mind. "If you know what you want me to do then just tell me!" he wanted to say.
  After some time the American learned that the mentor does not, and should not, have a preconceived solution in mind. The mentor must answer quickly, but he only has to see *what the next step is*. The mentor cannot fully know the way ahead, but he must grasp the situation deeply enough to know what the next step is so he can lead his mentee to and through it. And if the next step is unclear, then the answer is almost always, "Let's go and see." In most cases the next step is in fact to get more specific facts or data. Once I learned this, my own efforts to experiment with mentoring became considerably more effective.
  Tina does not have in mind a solution to the problem. It is Dan's responsibility to solve the problem and her responsibility to develop Dan's capability to do that. But she does know that the damage to the threads on the studs is likely to be occurring when the nut is driven onto the stud. She has an inkling about the point of cause, and is guiding Dan in that direction.
- Go and see.
  Imagine in what direction this effort might be going if Tina had stayed in her office and Dan was reporting his impressions to her there. Tina could not do this mentoring if she was not at the process with Dan understanding the current situation firsthand.

- Overlap of responsibility.
  Although Dan is responsible for the doing and Tina cannot just tell him what to do, since her job is to teach Dan, she knows that she in turn bears a lot of the responsibility for the results.

In what step of Practical Problem Solving are Tina and Dan?

- Tina has recognized that the point of cause is probably where the nut is driven onto the stud, but Dan has not. Tina would be ready to enter Step 3 (Investigate causes), but since Dan is the one who has to solve the problem, they are still in Step 2 (Grasp the situation). Tina is guiding Dan to the next step in a way that allows him to learn the lesson for himself.

Chapter 7

Then Dan noticed that the team member had to install the nut through a hole in the side panel, and that the team member could not see the end of the stud to assure that the nut was correctly located. The team member had to rely on feel to determine if the nut was aligned. Dan told Tina that now he knew what the problem was. The side panel trim installation had two new team members working on it in the past month. The new team members just didn't have the feel for the nut alignment yet, and that was why the threads were getting damaged and the parts were being scrapped.

Dan suggested that they would need to do a better job of training new team members so they wouldn't strip the threads on the studs.

Analysis

No mentoring activity by Tina in Chapter 7

If you were Tina what would you do next?
(Dan has made a proposal, to which you must respond.)

Chapter 8

Tina suggested that first they should confirm the relationship between the number of scrap parts and new team members on the process. She and Dan reviewed the scrap records for the group and compared any increase in the amount of scrapped side panel trim pieces to the dates that new team members were on the process. They found a direct relationship. Each time there was a new team member, there was a significant increase in the number of trim pieces that were scrapped.

Dan told Tina that he would have a meeting with all the team members who worked on that process immediately and tell them they needed to be more careful. He also said he would retrain all of them on installing the nut.

In what step of Practical Problem Solving are Tina and Dan?

Analysis

What mentoring/coaching behaviors is Tina using?

- Show me.
  Mentors prefer facts and data over opinion.

In what step of Practical Problem Solving are Tina and Dan?

- Tina and Dan have reached Step 3: Investigate causes.

If you were Tina what would you do next?
(Dan has made a proposal, to which you must respond.)

Chapter 9

Tina asked Dan if he knew what the team members were doing when the threads stripped. Dan replied that he didn't know what they were doing but he knew they weren't doing it correctly. Tina suggested they revisit the process and take a closer look at what the operators were actually doing and what the circumstances were when the threads stripped out.

When they observed the process again, they saw the team member on the process load the nut into the driver socket. Next, the team member started the driver to spin the socket and improve the setting of the nut in the socket. The trigger is then released to locate the nut on the stud. Then the driver trigger is depressed again to install the nut on the stud. Tina and Dan didn't see anything abnormal about the way the team member they were observing did the process. This team member didn't create any stripped threads while he was on the process that shift.

Tina suggested to Dan that they observe one of the new team members on this process. Then they saw a different technique being used. This team member kept the trigger of the driver depressed while he was locating the nut on the stud.

Tina suggested that she and Dan conduct an experiment to confirm that what they had seen could create stripped threads.

In what step of Practical Problem Solving are Tina and Dan?

Analysis

What mentoring/coaching behaviors is Tina using?

- Focus on understanding the process, not on implementing countermeasures.
  Tina and Dan are at Step 3 (Investigate causes), but with his proposals, Dan is skipping over this and going right into Step 4 (Develop and test countermeasure). This is not unusual.

We often think that good problem solving means applying countermeasures. In contrast, the focus in problem solving at Toyota is on understanding the current situation so deeply that the countermeasure becomes obvious. Mentees are prevented from introducing countermeasures before they sufficiently grasp the situation.

If we introduce countermeasures before understanding the situation, we create more variables, which interferes with identifying root causes. In the worst case, the wrong countermeasure might temporarily reduce occurrence of the problem, making us believe our effort was a success.

- Focus on the process, not the people.
  Mentors know that the vast majority of problems are caused by the system within which people work, not by the individuals themselves. They assume that the operators are doing their best, that if they were in the operators' shoes, the same thing would still have happened, and that training alone does not improve a process.

  An important point to realize here is that if we did carry out Dan's suggestion of retraining the new operators, then the scrap rate is likely to decrease. However, this would not be because the root cause had been identified and eliminated, but because extra managerial attention had been paid to the process. The same problem would return again later, because the process itself has not actually been improved in any way.

  To instill this thinking in their mentees, mentors will ask questions such as, "What is preventing the operator from working to standard?" or, "Do you know what the person was doing when the problem occurred?"

  Dan is proposing training, but training in what? How does the process, the standard, need to be changed so the process is actually improved? He has not yet answered this question.
- Testing over talking.
  Conduct small-scale tests before implementing something on a broad scale. As always, seek facts and data.

In what step of Practical Problem Solving are Tina and Dan?

- Tina and Dan are in Step 3: Investigate causes.

Chapter 10

Tina and Dan took some scrap trim pieces and a driver over to a vehicle and tried installing the trim using the method they had seen at their process. They noticed a feeling in the driver when the nut was properly located. This was an important point, because the positioning of the nut to the stud is a blind operation in the installation of the side panel trim. Next they tried installing the nut using the method they had seen at the other process.

During the second trial, they kept the driver running while trying to align the nut and stud. Of the 10 tries, four resulted in stripped threads. Tina and Dan now knew that the only way to be sure the nut and stud are properly aligned is to perform the positioning with the driver in the off position.

Next, Tina and Dan went to look at the work standard for the side panel trim process again. There was no information that instructed the team member to make the positioning of the nut and stud before triggering the driver. Dan told Tina that now he could hold a meeting with the team members to discuss the results of their investigation and instruct each of them on the correct procedure for installing the nuts.

Tina directed Dan to also correct the work standard based on their findings. In addition, she asked him to report their findings the next morning at the team leader meeting and to work with the other team leaders to identity other processes in the group with the potential for having the same problem.

In what step of Practical Problem Solving are Tina and Dan?

Analysis

What mentoring/coaching behaviors is Tina using?

- Conduct small-scale tests before implementing.
- Refer to the work standard or target condition.

In what step of Practical Problem Solving are Tina and Dan?

- Tina and Dan are now in Step 4: Develop and test countermeasure.

If you were Tina what would you do next?

Chapter 11

Tina and Dan tracked the Section B scrap for the next three months and had no further occurrences of assembly-damaged side panel trim pieces.

Dan confirmed the adoption of the new standard by observing the operators and the process. The team leader on the second shift was instructed to do the same.

Tina reported her experiences in the problem solving to Paul, the trim shop assistant manager.

Why did Tina insist on three months of follow-up tracking on the trim scrap?

- To confirm that the root cause was found and eliminated.

Summary Discussion of the Mentor/Mentee Case

Now that you have gone through the case example, we can get into a somewhat deeper discussion about the mentor/mentee dialogue and problem solving at Toyota.

1. How Did You Feel as You Read Through the Case?

I have taken a few hundred people through this case example in a classroom setting, and a common feeling among many participants was some exasperation that Tina and Dan's effort to solve the problem seemed to proceed slowly. As Tina sends Dan back to look at the situation again and again, some participants start visibly shifting around in their seats. "When are they going to implement something?"

It is important to see that at Toyota the emphasis in problem solving is on Step 2 (Grasp the situation) and Step 3 (Investigate causes). If these steps are done thoroughly, then the countermeasure (Step 4) often comes quickly and almost by itself. Conversely, if the countermeasure is not yet obvious, then it usually means that more study of the situation is necessary, rather than more thinking about countermeasures. It is a classic case of greater diligence up front being more effective and, overall, quicker. To really solve a problem, you have to understand why it is happening.

Supposedly, Albert Einstein was once asked, "You have one hour to solve a problem, how do you proceed?" According to the story, his answer was something like, "I would analyze the problem for 55 minutes and in the last five minutes I would introduce my countermeasure." The funny thing is that in our companies, we proceed in exactly the opposite manner. Within a very short time after recognizing a problem, we are proposing a variety of countermeasures in the hope that one of them will stop the problem. This is a very different approach from Toyota's, where the goal is not to implement countermeasures but to better understand the work system so we can improve it based on what we are learning about its processes.

If we throw countermeasures at a problem or have a list of countermeasures, then what that really means is we do not know enough about the situation causing the problem. Instead of causing more chaos and complicating our analysis by introducing several countermeasures, we would be better off more carefully observing the situation before deciding and acting. We have taught our managers to think about *what* will solve the problem, whereas Toyota managers like Tina are thinking about *how* their mentees should be approaching the problem.

2. How Long Do You Think the Story in the Case Took?

I do not have information about the actual elapsed time that Tina and Dan took, but most of the story is likely to have occurred, from beginning to end, within only one shift. This is a critical point, and one that has implications for how our managers and leaders organize their work days.

If mentors want their mentees to grasp the situation thoroughly, proceed step by step, and change only one thing at a time, then the cycles from step to step should be short and follow without delay. If our managers and leaders try to fit this mentoring into their existing schedules—for example, waiting for a prescheduled weekly review to come around—it will be far too slow and mechanical. Two things will happen:

- The situation in and around the process is likely to change.
- Because it takes so long to move forward, the pressure to solve the problem increases, which causes us to skip steps and jump to countermeasures.

For effective PDCA, the mentor's review of the last step should occur as soon as possible, so you can adapt based on what you find. As described in Chapter 6, progress is by rapid small steps, always adjusting to the present situation. Toyota mentors tend to insist on a short deadline for taking the next step, and to review the result of that step immediately through short, often stand-up, meetings at the process. Turnaround time is minutes or hours, with the mentor placing particular emphasis on the next step. There is no need for lengthy discussions about activities or steps beyond that, because whenever one step is taken, the situation may be new anyway.

I have observed a Toyota mentor asking the fifth question, "When can we go and see what we have learned from taking that step?" and when the mentee responded with, "In two days" the mentor simply repeated his question until the mentee finally said, "How about this afternoon?" To that, the mentor said, "Okay, good.

3. What Would Have Happened If Tina Had Stayed in Her Office Instead of Going to Observe the Process Herself?

Tina would very quickly have not been able to give good advice to Dan if she had relied on his reports alone, rather than going to see for herself. Going and seeing keeps the mentor closer to the real condition at the process—not so the mentor can develop a solution, which is the mentee's responsibility, but so the mentor can use the details of that condition to appropriately guide the mentee into improvement-kata thinking and acting.

4. How Was Tina Teaching Dan?

Tina was teaching Dan by making an actual improvement in an actual process, rather than in a classroom. This kind of teaching occurs one-on-one on the shop floor, in contrast to periodic project reviews conducted in an office.

5. What Do You Think of the Countermeasure Dan Developed?

The countermeasure was: "Hold a meeting with the team members to instruct each of them on the correct procedure for installing the nuts, update the job instruction sheet to indicate positioning of the nut with the gun in the off position, and report the findings at the team leader meeting."

Many people who have gone through this case example wanted a more fail-safe countermeasure, such as a device that would prevent the gun from spinning while the operator is locating the nut on the stud. Yet the countermeasure in the case example is acceptable at Toyota. Why? Keep in mind that Toyota's production processes are closely managed by team leaders, who observe the process every shift and compare its operation to the work standard. If our production processes are largely unmanaged—and many of ours are—then of course we will tend to prefer fail-safe mechanisms, or "poka yoke," as they are often called. Interestingly, Toyota does not like to add too many poka yoke devices to its processes because they increase maintenance requirements, and because Toyota wants its operators to have to think as they do their jobs.

There is also another more subtle but important point here. Sometimes in our experiments with Toyota's mentoring routines the mentor would see an even better or more elegant solution than the mentee had developed. The mentor would then be inclined to propose his solution over what the mentee had developed.

At Toyota the goal is not necessarily to develop the very best solution today, but to develop the capability of the people in the organization to solve problems. The mentor gets no extra points for having a better idea than the mentee. Of course the solution must be good enough to serve the customer, but beyond that, having the most perfect solution now is not what Toyota is thinking about. Toyota is thinking about developing the capability of its people.

Although the mentor is often a tough customer who leads the mentee through the problem solving via questioning—like Tina in the case example—ultimately the mentee is the person who must analyze the problem and develop the countermeasure. It may be tempting, especially for inexperienced mentors, to try to lead the mentee to a different solution that the mentor has in mind. But this is not Toyota-style mentoring. If the mentee sufficiently solves the problem in a way that meets the target condition, then the mentor must accept this.

Here is the point: How well the mentee does reflects the current capability of the organization, and if possible this should not be obscured, because we always want to understand the true current situation as clearly as possible. The solutions the mentees develop reflect the current level of capability in the organization, and that can be an important input for mentors. It may tell them what skill sets they need to work on next with their mentees. Artificially creating perfect solutions would disguise the true state of affairs and make it more difficult to understand what we need to do next to move our organization forward.

I hope you are having as much of an ah-ha moment right now as I did when this penny dropped for me.

Management does not need to bring solutions to problems. What management should bring into the organization is a kata for how people should act when faced with a situation. If the ability to apply the kata is developed in the organization correctly, then management will not need to worry about the outcomes. Conversely, if the results are not satisfactory, then it is the kata that is not being applied correctly.

6. Imagine This Approach Happening at Every Process in an Organization for Decades

In the case example, we are looking at an occasional stripped thread on one component of a product (an automobile) that has thousands of components, inside a huge company that makes many different products. In that light the effort that Tina and Dan went through could seem disproportionate, like too much effort. Yet imagine small effective steps of continuous improvement happening at every process every day for 50 years, and you begin to get a sense of how Toyota has achieved the position it holds today.

7. Caution! Good Coaching Skills Take Practice to Develop

Toyota's mentoring is a unique coaching and teaching approach, and it takes practice (under the guidance of an experienced mentor) to develop such mentoring skills. I have seen a few pitfalls in experiments with developing mentors, including:

- You have to be a mentee before you can mentor. In order to accompany and guide others through the improvement kata, the mentor must have sufficient experience in carrying out the improvement kata him- or herself.
- It is difficult for new mentors to adopt the right mind-set. When you go and see, your mind should be open, without preconceived notions about what could be the situation and what might be solutions. The mentor should know very well how the improvement kata proceeds (the how), but should have an open mind in regard to the content of the particular improvement effort (the what).

  For example, inexperienced mentors often ask questions designed to get the mentee to adopt the mentor's preconceived solution. This is sort of like the guessing game: "I'm thinking of a number between 1 and 10." Unfortunately, this does not develop the mentee's capability. Remember, the mentor is asking *what* the mentee is thinking in order to discern *how* the mentee is thinking.
- Mentees often feel pressure to give an answer, even if they don't know the answer. The mentor should get himself and the mentee to the point where "I don't know" is an acceptable and valid answer. And when "I don't know" is the answer, then go and see!

A Written Document to Support Mentor/Mentee Dialogue

Cycles of coaching should ideally be frequent, short, and conducted face-to-face. In the case example, Tina and Dan's communication was all verbal. However, it is often advisable to use a simple, one-page written document in support of mentor/mentee coaching. Verbal communication alone can rely too little on data, and during verbal communication a mentee may naturally, and unconsciously, adapt what he is saying to what he thinks the mentor wants to hear.

By asking the mentee to summarize information in writing on one page *in advance of coaching,* the mentor can more clearly see how the mentee is approaching an issue and how she is thinking. This in turn helps the mentor see the next step and what coaching is required at this time. Limiting the document to one page compels the mentee to be clear in describing her analysis and proposal.

Typical items in mentor/mentee dialogue that make it onto a written document include:

- Summary of observations or current condition
- Target condition
- Proposals
- Plans
- Key points from reflections

At Toyota such one-page documents are called A3s because they are often made on a sheet of ledger-sized paper, referred to as A3-size in many countries.

The format of an A3 generally mirrors the steps of the improvement kata. They are written in a succinct, bulleted, and visual style that tells a story with data. Although the A3 is typically on one page, there can be additional pages of backup documentation. It is the "story" itself that is built up and presented on the single page.

The format of an A3 varies depending on the purpose and theme. Figure 8-8 presents the typical sections of an A3.

You may notice that in this example A3, "Current Condition" comes before the "Target Condition," which is a reversal of their order in the

The A3 preparer needs a mentor to work with in developing the story.

Theme and Business Case

What is this A3 about?

Why are we doing it?

Current (Initial) Condition

Describe based on analysis conducted at the site. Go and See.

Bullets are sufficient.

Must be measurable in some aspect(s).

Target Condition

Describes a condition at a point in time in the future

Must be clearly and specifically defined.

Must be measurable in some aspect(s), so we can know if we are there or not.

Moving from Current to Target Condition

Describes planned activities.

A plan is a prediction, so PDCA along the way will be important.

Metrics

Signatures *Ceremonial sign off gives OK to proceed with this plan.*

Figure 8-8. Example of the A3 format

five questions at the end of Chapter 6. The reason for this is that the five questions come into play *after* a target condition has already been defined, whereas an A3 is from the beginning, where understanding the current condition precedes defining the target condition. Each section of the A3 builds upon the previous one. The better you define the theme, the better you can assess the current condition. The better you assess the current condition, the better you can develop an appropriate target condition. And so on. As the mentee develops the A3, the mentor typically has the mentee focus on one section of the A3 at a time, and that section may be rewritten several times. That section is then the foundation for the next section.

Purpose of an A3

The purpose of A3 documents is to support the mentor/mentee dialogue. This is done by:

- Having the mentee carefully think through something.
  It is surprisingly difficult to distill our understanding about something down to one sheet of paper. Preparing a succinct and

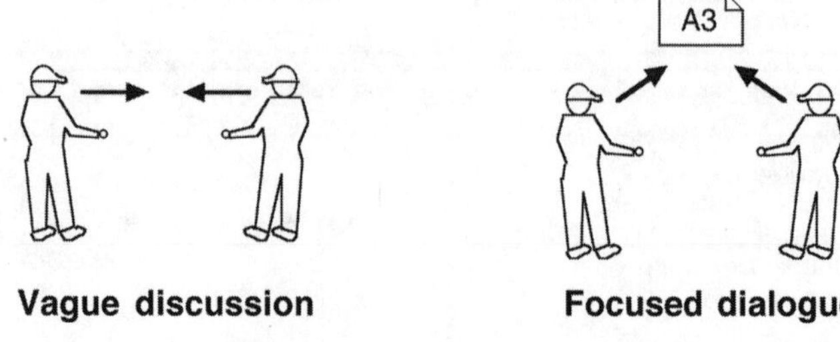

Figure 8-9. An A3 can help mentor/mentee interaction stay focused

precise A3 forces you to develop a deep and clear understanding of a situation.

I would have written a shorter letter, but I did not have the time.

—Attributed to Blaise Pascal, Johann Wolfgang von Goethe, and others

- Showing the mentor how the mentee is thinking, so the mentor can see what the next step is for the mentee, and what skills the mentee needs to develop.
- Keeping coaching focused and efficient (Figure 8-9). An A3 helps create a neutral, no-blame situation by giving both mentor and mentee a focal point. If there is an important issue, question, or lesson learned, then it should be noted in the A3.
- Achieving consensus and clear action
- Providing milestones for process checks

Lessons Learned About A3s

This is another one of those instances where we can easily miss the point while trying to copy a Toyota practice. We tend to focus on the tool—the format of *completed* A3s that we see at Toyota—rather than on the less visible *how and why* an A3 is developed and used. Upon learning that Toyota utilizes A3s, some managers and consultants have singled them out as a lean tool and suggested that people use them. The result in many cases has been a lot of paper generation and not much more than that.

There is no magic in the A3 documents themselves. The trick is in how they are used, and here are some key points in that regard from our experimentation:

- An A3 is a tool that is used within and in support of the mentor/mentee dialogue, that is, the coaching kata, which in turn is being done to teach and drive application of the improvement kata. The improvement kata in turn is applied in pursuit of a long-term direction or vision, which exists because of an organization philosophy of improvement and adaptation. An A3 by itself may not be so effective.
- An A3 is put together through a highly iterative, back-and-forth process between mentor and mentee. It is not just filled in at once and signed, because then it would just be a meaningless formality. Imagine the document being slid back and forth between mentor and mentee several times as they develop a progressively better understanding of the current and target conditions, and step-by-step build up the sections of the A3. If there are not several push-backs, then the A3 document is not being used correctly.

  Much of the benefit of an A3 lies in this process of creating it, because it forces you to work with facts and data and think through what you are doing. The objective and benefit is not so much to have a completed A3, but to go through the iterative, step-by-step process of developing it.
- It takes more time to develop a good A3 than you may think; sometimes weeks or even months.
- As already mentioned, in developing the A3, the mentor typically has the mentee focus on one section at a time, because each section of the A3 sets the framework for the next. You will probably go back and make adjustments often. Keep your eraser handy.
- Once the A3 is completed and signed it becomes a tool for making process checks as the mentee works toward the target condition. The A3 then becomes a tool to help mentor and mentee better identify problems along the way.

- A good way to start is to simply ask the mentee for a proposal on one blank sheet of paper, rather than predefining the A3 format. Wait and see what the mentee produces. Then you can discern how the mentee is thinking and guide him accordingly from there. This is like in the case example, when Tina started by giving Dan a vague assignment. She then waited for his response in order to see how he was thinking, before guiding him into the next step.
- Caution: a written document can encourage e-mail communication over face-to-face communication, or be used as a substitute for Go and See. Communication should remain face-to-face, and you should seek facts over data at the process.
- Talk less and communicate more, by staying focused on what is written in the A3. Avoid ad-lib discussion, which is typically not based on facts and data, is quickly forgotten, and therefore wastes time. If there is no data, there is no basis for discussion. Have the mentee summarize the necessary points and data *before* coaching in order to help prevent this effect.

For more on the A3 process within mentor/mentee dialogues, see the book *Managing to Learn*, by John Shook.[2]

Notes

1. I use the word *superior* here, but as we will see, in many ways it is the mentor who is supporting the mentee.
2. John Shook, *Managing to Learn* (Cambridge, Massachusetts: Lean Enterprise Institute, 2008), and www.lean.org.

Summary of Part IV

There is a significant difference between the approach and activities of managers at Toyota versus managers in our organizations. Both work with goals, targets, and outcome metrics, of course, but that is only a start for the Toyota manager/mentor, because she or he is charged with teaching. As the diagram in Figure P4-1 illustrates, the difference lies at the interface, the interaction, between manager and subordinate.

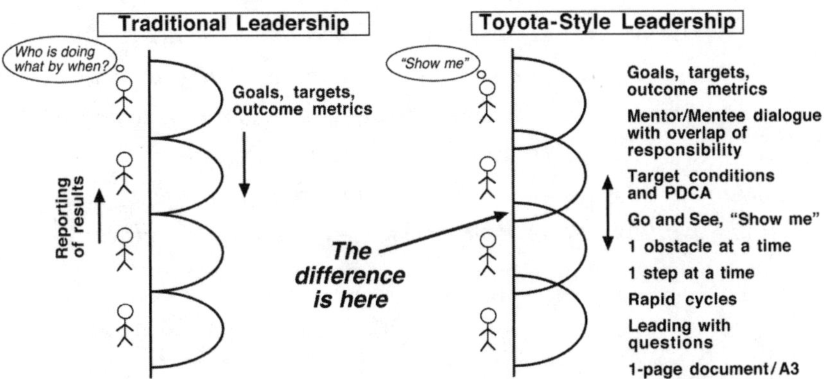

Figure P4-1. A difference, at the point where managers and the people they manage interact

The teaching requirement and the overlap of responsibility—mentee responsible for doing and mentor responsible for results—binds leader and subordinate together like the pairs of runners in a three-legged race, where the right leg of one runner is strapped to the left leg of the other. It is a game of interdependency, learning, and coordination between teammates. And lest you think this is just an exercise for some people in the organization, keep in mind that everyone at Toyota has a mentor.

In some respects what Toyota has done with its improvement kata and coaching kata is to grow management by objectives into its full potential, while in the same period of time we sometimes seem to have sought to reduce it to "manage by the numbers" or "manage by results."

In Toyota's Own Words

Toyota has a unique corporate culture that places emphasis on problem solving and preventative measures, such as making decisions based on the actual situation on the ground and highlighting problems by immediately flagging and sharing them. Toyota's management team and employees conduct operations and make decisions founded on that common system of checks and balances and on high ethical standards.

A distinctive feature of Toyota's system is that senior managing directors do not focus exclusively on management. As the highest authorities in their areas of supervision, they also act as links between management and on-site operations. Retaining an emphasis on developments on the ground—one of Toyota's perennial strengths—helps closely coordinate decision making with actual operations. Management decisions can be swiftly reflected in operations, while overall management strategy is able to readily incorporate feedback from frontline operations.

—Toyota 2004 Annual Report, page 16

With regard to Toyota's improvement kata as described in Part III, it is a scientific approach, and thus universal in nature and applicable in many organizations and to many different situations. I have utilized it successfully many times. It works, and I have no hesitation in recommending it to you as described in this book.

With regard to Toyota's coaching kata, on the other hand, we do not yet have enough experience with it to know if that approach is always necessary for developing improvement kata behavior. Some kind of coaching is undoubtedly required in order to teach people the improvement kata, but more research—experimentation—on teaching methods is probably necessary. Perhaps Toyota's coaching kata is not the only way to do it.

The distinction between the improvement kata and the coaching kata is important, since the main objective is not "management by questions," per se, but to have members of the organization think and act along the lines of the improvement kata. Making the distinction between the two kata allows a mentor to clearly ask him- or herself:

(a) How is this person doing with the improvement kata?
And then:
(b) What coaching do I need to do now?

Is the Coaching Kata in Flux at Toyota?

The mentor/mentee approach has traditionally been Toyota's method for passing its improvement kata on to all organization members. Toyota utilized this approach when it opened its first manufacturing facility in North America, the NUMMI plant in Freemont, California—a 50-50 joint venture with General Motors that commenced production in 1984. Approximately 400 "coordinators" were sent from Japan to the California site. These were mentors who essentially took Toyota's new American hires by the hand and taught them Toyota's improvement kata through the mentor/mentee learn-by-doing approach presented in this chapter. A similar number of coordinators were later sent to Kentucky, when Toyota established its second North American production site there.

In more recent years, however, Toyota has been growing so rapidly around the world (factories in 28 countries at last count) that it is faced with a need to bring many more new employees into its way of thinking and acting. Toyota's coaching kata—the mentor/mentee approach—has not always been able to keep up, because it requires experienced mentors, a limited resource, and it takes time.

> *. . . a vital aspect of our reinvention is changing how we choose and develop our leaders. Obviously, using only Japanese advisors cannot be done anymore. We are stretched thin here and elsewhere around the world.*
>
> —Toyota President, Fujio Cho, in a speech given in Traverse City, Michigan, August 3, 2004

Since Toyota utilizes problems as opportunities to evolve and improve, we can assume that it is in the process of adapting its way of teaching the improvement kata. On the other hand, an organization's intentionally cultivated behavior patterns are a fragile thing, and Toyota is no exception. Adapting in this area will probably work for Toyota as long as there are still enough key people in the organization who understand and have mastered the adaptive behavior pattern—the improvement kata.

What Is the Next Step for Us?

The evidence from experimentation suggests that some kind of coaching will be necessary in order for groups of people to learn to use the improvement kata, as well as to keep it operating every day at every process. If you want to integrate an improvement kata into an organization's way of doing things, then you will have to develop some kind of coaching approach. We will tackle this subject in the next, and final, chapter.

Part V

Replication: What About Other Companies?

Chapter 9

Developing Improvement Kata Behavior in Your Organization

The second overarching question mentioned in the introduction to *Toyota Kata* is: How can other companies develop similar routines and thinking in their organizations? At this point we have a basic awareness of what Toyota is doing to achieve continuous improvement and adaptiveness, as described in Parts III and IV. There is, of course, more to learn there, but we would perhaps do well to shift some of our attention away from the question of what Toyota is doing and more onto that second question. While it is interesting to study and discuss Toyota, even more important may be the experimentation, learning, and development we do for ourselves in our own situations.

Be Clear About What You Are Undertaking

Some other ways to phrase the second overarching question might be:

> How do we get everyone in the organization to think and act along the lines of the improvement kata described in Chapters 5 and 6?
>
> How do we get this behavior routine into an organization?

A Different Challenge

Not to implement or add on some new techniques, practices, or even principles

→ To develop consistent behavior patterns across the organization

Figure 9-1. The task

How do we spread improvement kata behavior across the company so it is used by everyone, at every process, every day?

How do we learn a new way of thinking and acting?

Which is to say that before we go any further, we should be clear about the challenge. Knowing about the improvement kata that lies behind Toyota's success, and that it is about behavior patterns and developing such behavior patterns, ask yourself: *Is this what you intend to do?*

Developing new behavior patterns across an organization involves a more significant effort and further-reaching change—particularly in leader behavior—than what you may have assumed that "lean manufacturing" is about. It should be clear to you at this point that bringing continuous improvement into an organization—"lean" or the "Toyota Production System"—involves a different kind of challenge than we originally thought. Toyota's embedding of the improvement kata and the coaching kata into daily work represents more than just adding something on top of our existing way of managing. It means changing how we manage (Figure 9-1).

Organization Culture

Trying to get each person in an organization to think and act in certain ways means you are working on organization culture. Most organizations that are interested in Toyota's approach probably do not need to completely change their existing culture, but rather, to make an adjustment, like maneuvering a curve in the road, as shown in Figure 9-2. So how does one make such a change in organization culture?

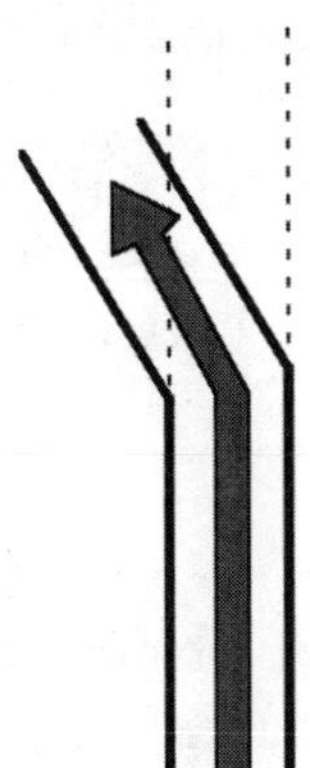

Figure 9-2. Making a shift in organizational culture

What Do We Know So Far About This Challenge?

Since the late 1980s, Toyota has successfully—though not without difficulty—been spreading its approach to local citizens at new Toyota Group sites around the world; that is, *inside* Toyota. This includes North America and Europe, and it suggests that Toyota's improvement kata should be practicable for organizations and people outside of Toyota. However, in Chapter 1, I stated the following:

> *To date, it appears that no company outside of the Toyota group of companies has been able to keep improving its quality and cost competitiveness as systematically, as effectively, and as continuously as Toyota.*

Astute readers may have already been wondering as they started this chapter: "If no company outside Toyota has succeeded in bringing such systematic continuous improvement into all processes every day across the organization, then how can anyone answer the question being raised at the beginning of this chapter and tell us how to do it?"

The fact is we simply do not yet have authoritative answers to the second overarching question, and that includes Toyota itself too. For example, Toyota's efforts to spread its approach to its *outside* suppliers have achieved many point successes in a wide variety of processes and value streams, but even those efforts to integrate the improvement kata into everyday operation across the organization at these other companies have so far not met expectations.

What I can do in this chapter is share with you what we have learned with regard to the second overarching question—which in fact is quite a lot—and how we are working on issues raised by that question.

You Need to Become an Experimenter

The goal of this chapter—and this book overall—is to set you up to experiment and thereby develop your management system in accordance with the needs of your situation. If you want to change behavior patterns and organizational culture, then it is quite likely there is no other way:

- There is probably no approach that fits all organizations. Each company should work out the details by developing its management system to suit its particular situation.
- There is great value in striving to understand the reality of your own situation and experimenting, because it is where you learn. No one can provide you with a solution, because the way to answering the second overarching question—as with any challenging target condition—is and should be a gray zone.

But we do know how to work though that gray zone. The improvement kata, the means by which processes are improved, is a way of experimenting, and we can apply it to almost any sort of process. So when I say you need to become an experimenter, it does not mean that you have to start a separate activity. We can continuously improve and adapt, train people, and develop our organization culture simultaneously, with the same activity. In fact, this describes quite well how Toyota goes about it.

There is now a growing community of organizations that are working on this, whose senior leaders recognize that Toyota's approach is more about working to change people's behavior patterns than about implementing techniques, practices, or principles. In fact, as you strive to develop improvement kata behavior and thinking in your organization, that step-by-step effort will have an effect on your techniques, practices, and principles. That is a good way to look at it.

What Will Not Work

Some of the early lessons from our experimentation were about approaches that do not work for changing people's behavior. Let us get those out of the way from the start. If you wish to spread an improvement kata (a new behavior pattern) across your organization, then the following tactics will not be effective:

- *Classroom training.* Even if it incorporates exercises and simulations, classroom training will not change people's behavior. It seems for several years now we have assumed that simply comprehending Toyota's system would automatically lead to its adoption—*because it makes sense!* This approach has been decidedly ineffective. Intellectual knowledge alone generally does not lead to change in behavior, habits, or culture. Ask any smoker.

  As mentioned in Chapter 8, the concept of training in sports is quite different from what "training" has come to mean in our companies. In sport it means repeatedly practicing an actual activity under the guidance of a coach. That kind of training, if applied as part of an overall strategy to develop new behavior patterns, *is* effective for changing behavior.

  Classroom training has a role, but the best that we can probably achieve with it is awareness. And even that tends to fade quickly if it is not soon followed by repeated, structured practicing. Classroom training should probably be kept short and provided mostly for information purposes and to participants who are about to go into hands-on practicing with a coach.

- *Workshops.* These are designed to make point improvements, not to develop new behaviors. Furthermore, as discussed in Chapter 2, results naturally tend to slip back after a workshop ends.
- *Having consultants do it for you.* Developing internal routines and capability for daily continuous improvement and adaptation at all processes involving all people—culture—is by definition something that an organization must do for itself. An experienced external consultant can provide coaching inputs, especially at the beginning, and even experiment together with you. But to develop your own capability, the effort will have to be internally led, from the top. If the top does not change behavior and lead, then the organization will not change either. More on that later in this chapter.
- *Looking to metrics, incentives, and motivators to bring the desired change.* As we have discussed, there is no combination of metrics and incentive systems that by themselves will generate improvement kata behavior and change your culture to one like Toyota's.
- *Reorganizing.* Many companies have tried unsuccessfully to reorganize in the hope of finding organizational structures that will stimulate continuous improvement and adaptiveness; for example by bringing departmental functions into value-stream-oriented organizational structures.

  As tempting as it sometimes seems, you cannot reorganize your way to continuous improvement and adaptiveness. What is decisive is not the form of the organization, but how people act and react. The roots of Toyota's success lie not in its organizational structures, but in developing capability and habits in its people. It surprises many people, in fact, to find that Toyota is largely organized in a traditional, functional-department style.

  Anything unique about Toyota's organizational structures, such as their team leader approach, evolved out of Toyota striving for specific behavior patterns, not the other way around. First figure out how you want people to act—for example, along the lines of the improvement kata—and strive to develop those behavior routines. If, then, along the way, making organizational adjustments is a necessary or useful countermeasure, that's okay. But these should be seen for what they are: countermeasures, not target conditions. Keep your attention on the target condition of developing improvement kata behavior, and let the needs of your efforts there drive the evolution of your structures.

All these tactics have their place, but they will not generate improvement kata behavior, nor the cost, quality, and adaptiveness benefits that accrue from daily application of that kata. Culture change is not achieved through books, intellect, classroom training, discussions, or anything similar.

How Do We Change?

The field of psychology is clear on this: we learn habits, automatic reactions, by repeatedly practicing behaviors. In order to build new mental circuits, we must practice a desired behavior pattern and periodically derive a sense of achievement from that behavior. The canon that we *learn by doing*, by experiencing, has given rise to the well-known and widely accepted change model depicted in Figure 9-3.

Much of what we do is routinized and habitual. Repeated practice—conditioning—creates neural pathways and, over time, an organization's culture. This change model is particularly important with regard to the improvement kata because several aspects of that kata are

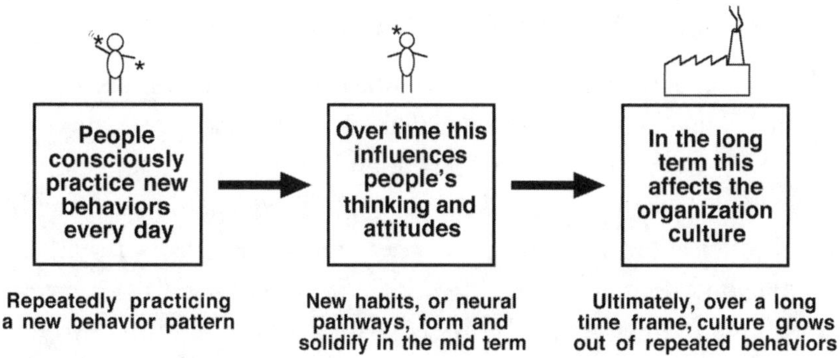

Figure 9-3. A model for changing organization culture

so different, and even counterintuitive, from the perspective of our current management approach. The only way to truly understand its underlying meaning and learn to apply it in different situations is by personally and repeatedly practicing it in actual application.

Ideally, following the improvement kata pattern would become automatic and reflexive, and our mindfulness thereby freed to be applied to the details of the situation at hand. This is the ideal that Toyota's coaching kata, described in Chapter 8, strives to achieve, and a reason why Toyota people have had difficulty explaining to us the underlying pattern of what they do.

> *We are what we repeatedly do. Excellence, then, is not an act, but a habit.*
>
> —Aristotle

> *To know and not to do is not yet to know.*
>
> —Zen saying

Fortunately, kata are designed specifically for passing on. In martial arts, kata were apparently created so the masters could pass on their most effective fighting techniques to further generations. In other words, kata are a way of doing exactly what we are discussing here: practicing behaviors and learning new habitual routines.

How to Experiment

Use Actual Work Processes

This is something we adopted one-to-one from Toyota's approach: training and doing are not separated (Figure 9-4). To practice the improvement and coaching katas, students apply them in actual situations at actual work processes. In this manner your experimentation will be real, not theoretical. You can perceive where the student truly is with his thinking and skills, and take appropriate next steps. And the degree or lack of improvement in the processes serves as a metric for the effectiveness of your effort to coach and develop the desired behavior routines.

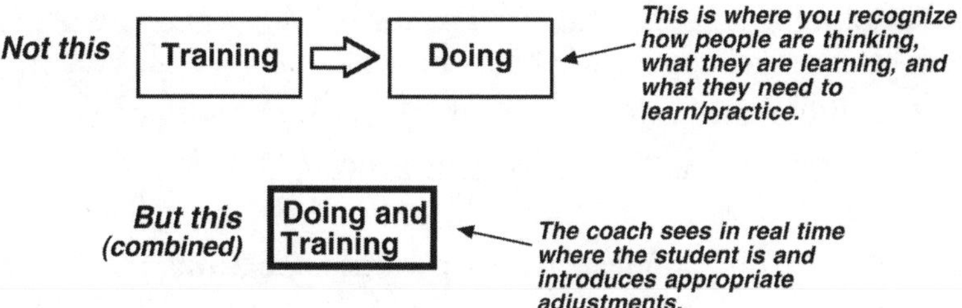

Figure 9-4. Experimenting with real processes

Focus On Three Main Factors

If we want to get people, including ourselves, to think and proceed along the lines of the improvement kata, I propose three main factors that we can influence in order to achieve this (Figure 9-5).[1]

Focusing on any one of these three areas alone is not effective for changing to a desired organization culture, and conversely, if any one of them is left out, the effort is also not effective. For instance, just

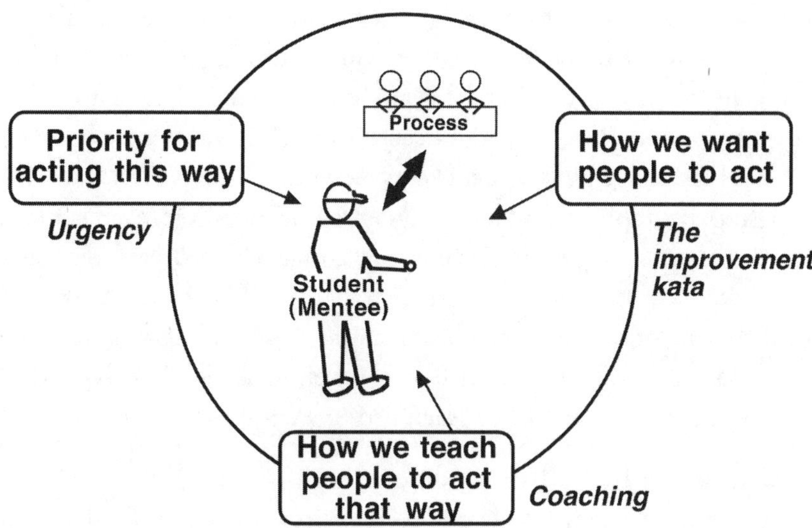

Figure 9-5. Three factors that we can influence

establishing urgency for change typically generates a wide range of behavior reactions. The result is often no real change at all or something quite different from the improvement kata. We should not expect that simply pushing people will generate improvement-kata behavior.

Likewise, coaching alone achieves very little. Coaching in what?

Finally, just defining and explaining the improvement kata, even if we were to combine that with a sense of urgency, will also not change people's behavior. It would be like saying to an athletic team, "You should play this way in order to win," and then leaving the team alone.

Use the Improvement Kata to Develop Improvement Kata Behavior

This is the most important advice in this chapter: to develop improvement kata behavior in your organization, you should utilize and follow the improvement kata *in this development process itself.* Simply put, the improvement kata is your means for experimenting.

This is not about "implementing" a new management system and culture. The way to any target condition, including culture change, is unclear, and practicing good PDCA will be a key factor in successfully achieving that condition. In other words, while working toward a target condition that includes a changed culture, it is just as important to frequently check the current condition and adjust accordingly. Developing new behavior patterns is a change process that occurs over time via PDCA.

Using the improvement kata in order to introduce improvement kata behavior is an example of applying it at a higher fractal level than at a production process. The improvement kata can be used at all levels, and anyone in the organization can be asked the five questions (Figure 9-6).

Let us take a closer look at how this can be done. As described in Part III, the improvement kata is applied to a *work process* by:

- Grasping the current condition
- Defining a measurable target condition

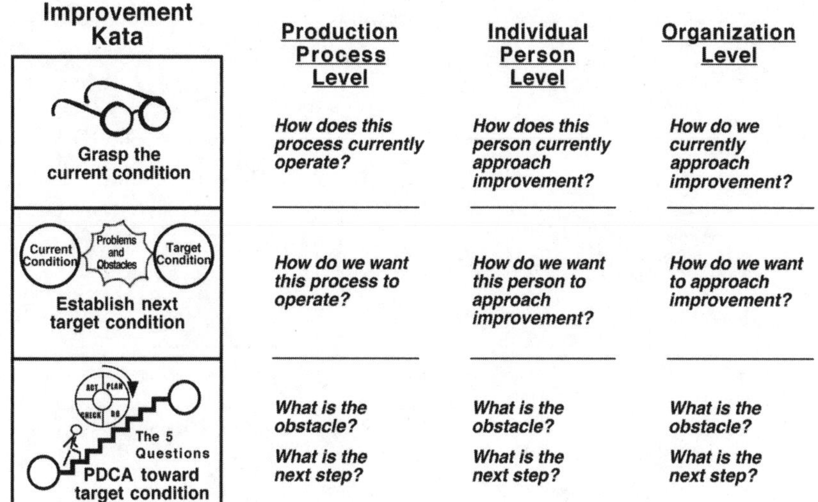

Figure 9-6. The improvement kata finds application at all levels

- Utilizing short PDCA cycles to move toward that target condition

The point to realize is that precisely the same kata can be applied to a *coaching process*. A target condition can be established for coaching, and you can PDCA toward that target condition.

A baseline assumption we should make here is that the improvement kata works. In other words, our experimenting is not done in order to test if the improvement kata is effective, but to learn what we need to do in order to develop effective improvement kata behavior. Ergo, if the improvement kata is not yet operating as desired, then it is the teaching/coaching of it that needs to be adjusted via PDCA. As shown in Figure 9-7, our coaching approach is perhaps the main knob we can adjust in order to develop desired behavior patterns. If you do not like the results at the work process, then scrutinize the coaching. In this regard, I encourage you to keep in mind: "If the learner hasn't learned, the teacher hasn't taught."

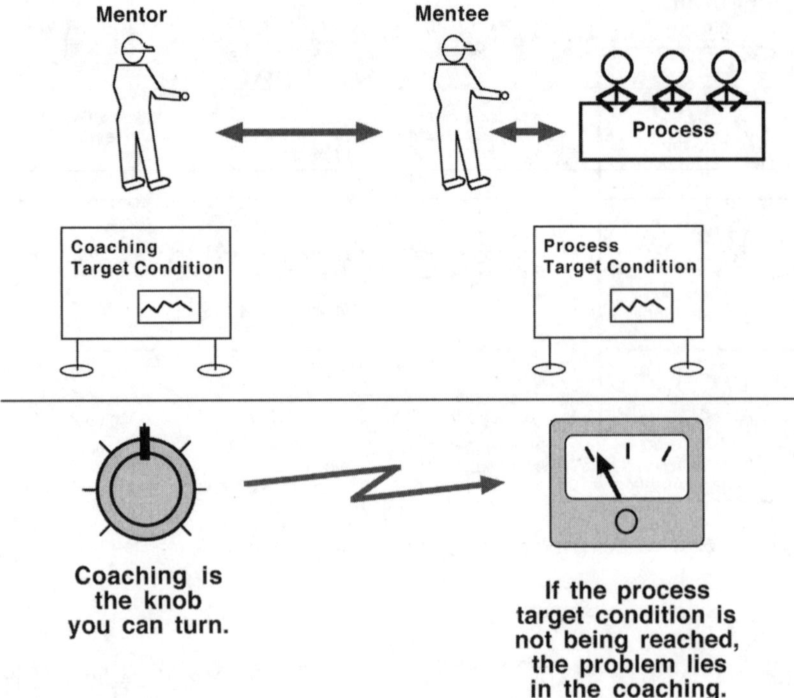

Figure 9-7. If the improvement kata is not working properly, the coaching needs adjusting

Tactics

The remainder of this chapter describes specific tactics I have been using, which may be generic enough to be applicable at other organizations. Since a discussion of tactics is essentially a discussion of solutions (countermeasures), I urge you to view them as thought starters, ideas and inputs to your own efforts to develop improvement kata behavior in your organization. It would not be appropriate or effective for me to propose countermeasures without understanding your specific current and target conditions, nor for you to jump directly into applying someone else's countermeasures. Again, the best advice here is to utilize and follow the improvement kata routine as you try to develop the improvement kata routine in your organization. Then you can adapt to what you are learning in your situation and find your own appropriate path to the desired condition.

Learning to Do Before Learning to Coach

Coaches should be in a position to evaluate what their students are doing and give good advice; to bring their students into the corridor of thinking and acting prescribed by the improvement kata. In other words, coaches should be experienced. It is only after they have practiced improvement kata themselves that coaches will be able to see deeply enough to provide that useful advice.

If a coach or leader does not know from personal experience how to grasp the current condition at a production process, establish an appropriately challenging target condition, and then work step by step toward that target condition, then she is simply not in a position to lead and teach others. All she will be able to say in response to a student's proposal is, "Okay" or "Good job!" which is not coaching or teaching.

The catch-22 is that at the outset there are not enough people in the organization who have enough experience with the improvement kata to function as coaches. This is not unlike Toyota's problem as it grows rapidly. It will be imperative to develop at least a few coaches as early as possible. (See "Establishing an Advance Group" later in the chapter.)

Who Practices First?

At Toyota, the improvement kata is for everyone in the organization and everyone practices it. No one group is singled out. However, Toyota is not trying to change its kata; it is continuing with the same basic approach it has been following since the 1950s.

On the other hand, if an organization wishes to effect a change in culture rather than continuing on the same path, it requires leadership from one group in particular: the senior level. In such a change situation, the senior managers should practice the improvement kata ahead of others in the organization.

Managers and leaders at the middle and lower levels of the organization are the people who will ultimately coach the change to the improvement kata, yet they will generally and understandably not set out in such a new direction on their own. They will wait to see, based on the actions (not the words) of senior management, what truly is the priority and what really is going to happen.

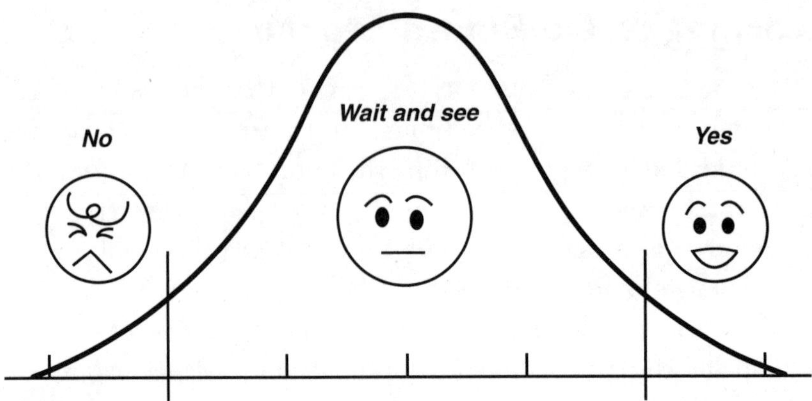

Figure 9-8. Distribution of reaction to change

George Koenigsaecker, an early lean thinker in the United States, has depicted this effect using the normal distribution curve in Figure 9-8.

What Mr. Koenigsaecker's diagram suggests is that only a small percentage of people in the organization (the right tail of the curve) will welcome a change effort and actively participate. Another small group (the left tail) will fight it actively. And the great majority—although they may nod and indicate their support—will be on the fence and waiting to see what is going to happen. Although many have criticized mid-level management for avoiding change, if you think about it, the wait-and-see attitude is an understandable reaction to uncertainty by managers who are on a career ladder in an organization. Also, do you want your managers to easily jump from one way of managing to another?

The point is:

(a) The way the majority of managers and leaders behave—the people in the middle of the normal curve—will determine how people in the organization act, and thus determine the organization's culture.

(b) If the senior managers do not go first in personally practicing and learning the improvement kata, then it is unlikely that they will be able to effectively enlist, mobilize, and guide those managers and leaders toward the desired behavior pattern. The kind of cultural shift we are talking about cannot be delegated by the senior leaders.

Establishing an Advance Group

Before starting to teach senior managers the improvement kata, we have tended to first establish a small advance group. The initial purpose if this group is to develop familiarity with the subject and how it works. It is this advance group that actually goes first with practicing the improvement kata.

I include a senior executive—*the* senior executive in the case of small and mid-sized companies—as a member of this group. The advance group is not a staff group or lean manufacturing department that will be responsible for all mentoring and training, or for making improvement happen at the process level. That will be the responsibility of the local managers and leaders at each level and in each area in the organization. Do not create a lean department or group and relegate the responsibility for developing improvement-kata behavior to it. Such a parallel staff group will be powerless to effect change, and this approach has been proven ineffective in abundance. Use of this tactic often indicates delegation of responsibility and lack of commitment at the senior level.

The advance group is responsible for monitoring, fine-tuning, and further developing (via PDCA) the organization's teaching approach. The advance group is the organization's "keepers of the kata," so to speak. However, this group will to some degree also assist with coaching at all levels of the organization so that it can maintain a grasp of the true current situation in the organization.

To be a workable size, the initial advance group should consist of no more than about five people. This group needs a mentor—for example, an external consultant. If you utilize an outside coach, it is important that you hire this coach specifically to help you get started and develop your internal coaching capability. Do not hire an external person to do the coaching work for you, because then you will not build this important capability in your organization. An external coach's job is to accelerate and help guide the development of your capability.

A good first step for the advance group is to simply try applying the improvement kata to a few assembly processes, all the while reflecting: "What are we learning about the improvement kata, our processes, our people, and our organization?" This allows the group to develop a better understanding of what the improvement kata entails and to simultaneously gain a firsthand grasp of the current condition at the process level in the organization. A good place to begin practicing the improvement kata is at a "pacemaker process." Appendices 1 and 2 explain what that is and provide detail for assessing the current condition of a production process, which is the beginning of the improvement kata and prerequisite for establishing a target condition.

Something this group can do immediately, for instance, is to assess the stability of a production process, as described in Chapter 5. This involves timing and graphing 20 to 40 successive cycles at several points in the process and then asking, "What is preventing this process and the operators from being able to work with a stable cycle?"

These initial efforts to try out the improvement kata can easily occupy the advance group for two to six months. That may sound like a long time, but consider that we are talking about how we want the organization to operate; its culture. The advance group should not go into this task with only a shallow understanding of what is involved and where the organization is.

These initial shop-floor activities of the advance group are also a good opportunity to get started in training your first few internal coaches. We have tended to attach two or three potential coaches to the advance group, in addition to the four to five advance group members. These coaches in training do not participate in all advance group activities, such as planning activities. They participate in the shop-floor efforts to apply and learn about the improvement kata.

Training Through Frequent Coaching Cycles and the Five Questions

To develop new habits, the field of psychology tells us it is preferable to practice behaviors for a short time frequently—such as every day—rather than in longer sessions but less frequently. Ideally, of course, every encounter and interaction in the organization would radiate the kata, as in the mentor/mentee case example in Chapter 8.

To get people to frequently practice and think about the routine of the improvement kata, I currently use a concept I call a "coaching cycle." These cycles come into play after a process target condition has been established, and utilize the five questions. The five questions are a regimen to train improvement-kata behavior. They simplify a part of the improvement-kata routine and thus make it easier to apply, understand, and transfer. One coaching cycle essentially entails the mentor going through the five questions once while standing at the process with the mentee (Figure 9-9). In most cases, we have been striving to

The Five Questions Make Up One Coaching Cycle

1. **What is the target condition? *(The challenge)***
   - What do we expect to be happening?
2. **What is the actual condition now?**
   - Is the description of the current condition measurable?
   - What did we learn from the last step?
   - Go and see for yourself. Do not rely on reports.
3. **What problems or obstacles are now preventing you from reaching the target condition? Which one are you addressing now?**
   - Observe the process or situation carefully.
   - Focus on one problem or obstacle at a time.
   - Avoid Pareto paralysis: Do not worry too much about finding the biggest problem right away. If you are moving ahead in fast cycles, you will find it soon.
4. **What is your next step? *(Start of next PDCA cycle)***
   - Take only one step at a time, but do so in rapid cycles.
   - The next step does not have to be the most beneficial, biggest, or most important. Most important is that you take a step.
   - Many next steps are further analysis, not countermeasures.
   - If next step is more analysis, what do we expect to learn?
   - If next step is a countermeasure, what do we expect to happen?
5. **When can we go and see what we have learned from taking that step?**
   - As soon as possible. Today is not too soon. How about we go and take that step now? (Strive for rapid cycles!)

Figure 9-9. Contents of a coaching cycle

do this at each focus process at least once per shift. The purpose of a coaching cycle is:

- To allow the coach to quickly grasp the current condition in both the process being improved and the mentee so that the coach can judge what is an appropriate next step
- To provide a routine for conditioning training
- To recognize the mentee's efforts

With practice and experience, one coaching cycle should not take very long. Novice coaches sometimes mistakenly let the cycle get into lengthy discussions that cover many different factors and can run into hours. I have been shooting for 15 minutes per coaching cycle in many cases. As soon as a *single* next step—not a list of steps—is clear to both mentor and mentee, then the coaching cycle is over. As in the mentor/mentee case example, the next step can and often should be very small. That is perfectly acceptable, as long as the cycles are rapid.

A coaching cycle is not all there is to coaching, of course. Get through the five questions one time relatively quickly and take stock: "What is the situation now? Where are we in the improvement kata, in the process being improved, and in the development of this person's capabilities? What is needed next?" After a coaching cycle, the mentor can then, for example, decide whether he should stay on with the mentee during the next step—to observe and provide guidance as Tina did in the mentor/mentee case example in Chapter 8—or return later for a check by means of another coaching cycle. The next coaching cycle should follow as soon as possible, often within hours or even minutes on the same day. If the next step can be taken right away, then by all means do that.

A few lessons learned about coaching cycles:

- It is a good idea to limit a student's first few target conditions to a time horizon of only one week. This way, the student can get more experience with the entire improvement kata, experience some success, and begin to develop a rhythm. After some practice you can begin to lengthen the target condition horizon a bit to, say, one to four weeks out.

- Do not wait until the end of a shift to conduct coaching cycles. Think of a check as a beginning, not an end, and do it early in the workday if possible. You can specify the time of day as part of a coaching target condition. If we're always putting off coaching cycles until the end of the workday, it suggests the lack of a specific coaching target condition and a low level of priority.
- Whenever you approach any process, go through the five questions. In this manner you will not only be teaching others the way of thinking, but you'll be teaching yourself as well.
- The fifth question—"When can we go and see what we have learned from taking that step?"—has been a sticking point. New coaches often ask this question thinking that the next step must be a countermeasure or solution. Likewise, the mentee often thinks this is what the coach wants. In many (or even most) cases, however, the next step is just to get a deeper grasp of the situation, as was illustrated in the case example in Chapter 8.
- Another lesson is to coach only one target condition at a time, which generally means one mentee at a time. If you try to coach several mentees at once, the dialogue tends to become too general and mentees may become less open about discussing problems. Every mentee is potentially in a unique situation and usually has unique development needs.

Sense of Achievement

Developing a new mindset also involves periodically deriving a feeling of success from practicing the behavior patterns. While we may think that success only comes at the end of something, there are important opportunities for positive reinforcement at all stages of the improvement kata, as shown in Figure 9-10. These opportunities should be utilized, since the objective is not just solutions, but building the capability to follow the improvement kata routine, to understand situations and develop appropriate solutions.

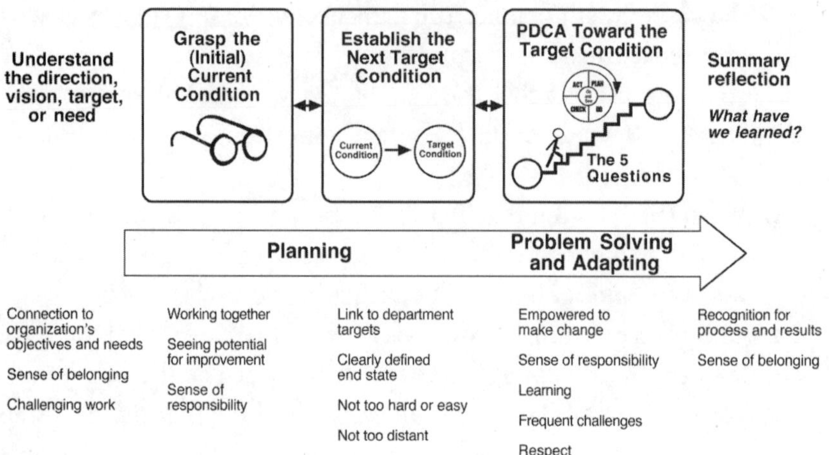

Figure 9-10. Example opportunities for successes throughout the improvement kata routine

Making a Plan

Once the advance group has spent a few months learning by applying the improvement kata at some processes, there will be a need for a plan to begin wider development of improvement kata behavior. The time horizon for such a first plan should not exceed 12 months, since at this stage you are on a steep learning curve and your grasp of conditions is likely to change appreciably. Because of our limited experience, our flashlight does not shine very far ahead.

Creating such a plan is the same as any A3 planning process as discussed at the end of Chapter 8:

- The advance group needs a mentor to whom it will present its planning efforts iteratively in coaching cycles. In developing this plan, the group focuses on one section heading at a time, since one section sets the framework for the next. Until the plan is signed, however, it is acceptable to go back and make adjustments to prior sections.

- Much of the benefit of the plan lies in the iterative planning process, because it forces you to get facts and data and repeatedly think through—deeper and deeper each cycle—what you are doing. The objective is not just to have a plan, but to go through the step-by-step effort to create the plan.
- It takes time to develop this kind of plan, easily two months. Continue practicing the improvement kata and testing ideas while the plan is being developed, since this helps you stay close to the real situation.

The following key points for this planning process are presented under their respective A3 headings.

1. Theme

The theme is to develop the behavior of managers and leaders toward a pattern that follows the improvement kata. However, be sure to keep the theme and activities linked to continuous improvement of production processes, since cost reduction via process improvement is the overall objective. We are not introducing the improvement kata for the sake of introducing the improvement kata. We should be improving processes and practicing (learning) the routine of the improvement kata simultaneously.

As described in Chapter 3, Toyota's improvement kata functions within an overall sense of direction, which is provided by a long-term vision. Without this you will find people going off in several directions when they hit obstacles. Thus, one of the first questions to ask yourself is, "Do we have consensus on a vision, that is, a long-term direction?"

I have witnessed several groups that went into long intellectual discussions about establishing a vision, and they typically ended up producing useless statements that protect several people's sacred cows. Developing a succinct, useful, but not overly confining long-term vision is difficult. It takes a considerable amount of time and reflection, and is not necessarily a democratic process. Also, if we are just beginners with understanding the potential of the improvement kata, then perhaps this is not yet the right time to be arguing about what might be an appropriate vision.

But you do need a vision, and if you are a manufacturer I see no reason why you should not simply adopt the same long-term vision for your production operations that Toyota strives for: "One piece flow at lowest possible cost." As we have seen in Chapter 3, this vision does not come from Toyota or Japan, and has been pursued for a few hundred years. Why not adopt this widely recognized production vision and get going?

2. Current Condition

The advance group has been gaining firsthand understanding of the current situation by trying to apply the improvement kata at the process level in the organization. Summarize what is being learned in bullet points. This summary should at least describe a) the current behavior of managers and leaders, and b) how process improvement is currently handled. You can also include any additional factors you would like. Some aspect(s) of this description of the current condition should be measurable so that you can gauge if you are making progress. (More on metrics later in this plan.)

Based on what the advance group has learned by immersing itself in the current condition, it can then establish a target condition.

3. Target Condition

What you are defining here is a condition you want to have in place at a future point in time (such as 6 or 12 months from now). Defining this takes some time and iterations, because it should be based on facts and data, and be specific and measurable.

There are two aspects to the target condition in this section of the plan:

1. Relative to process improvement activity. For example:
    - Total number of processes being managed and improved via the improvement kata
    - Measurable process improvement, such as process stability
2. Relative to leader/coaching behavior. For example:
    - What persons will have reached what capability level (Figure 9-11)

- What persons will be carrying out the improvement kata and the coaching kata, at what frequency, and at how many processes

How you intend to get to this target condition will be the subject of the next section of the plan.

Keep in mind as you define the total number of processes that, because the improvement kata is an approach for daily management, once you begin with the improvement kata at a process there is no end there. This means that, unlike improvement projects or workshops that have an end date, the number of processes being improved through the improvement kata accumulates and grows as you spread the approach to other processes. Do not overextend yourself at the start. In the beginning it is better to have picked too few focus processes, rather than too many.

In establishing this target condition, something we do is describe levels of capability that we would like individuals to reach. We have often used the three levels depicted below.

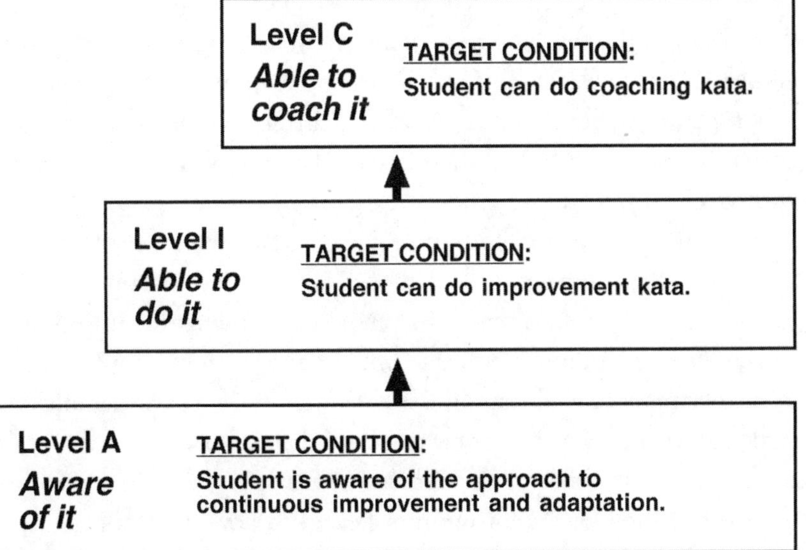

Figure 9-11. Example capability levels

Starting from the bottom of the diagram, Level A (awareness) means that the individual has a basic understanding of what the improvement kata is and how it works. Level I (improvement kata) means that the individual can effectively carry out the improvement kata. Level C (coaching kata) means that the individual can effectively carry out both the improvement kata and a coaching kata.

4. Moving from Current Condition to Target Condition

Once the advance group has defined the target condition, it should involve persons from the next level in the organization, its mentees, in planning how to move from the current condition to the target condition. The advance group should not finalize this part of the plan on its own. It is acceptable for mentors to set a target and sometimes even a target condition, but the mentees should become involved in planning how to achieve that condition. Otherwise it is akin to telling people what to do in traditional fashion.

The overall idea in this part of the plan is for people to learn the improvement kata by repeatedly practicing its routine on real processes under the guidance of a coach. In terms of tactics, this part of the plan should specify the coaching cycles in detail: who will practice when, where, and how? You might lay this out, for example, in monthly increments.

In planning how to move from the current condition to the target condition, we often linked the three levels of capability in Figure 9-11 with levels of training activity as depicted in Figure 9-12.

Starting again at the bottom of the diagram, the training activity at Level A is a classroom course with shop-floor exercises. The purpose of this course is only to create a sense of awareness about what the improvement kata is. The next training level is to practice the improvement kata, which in the diagram is called training Level I. After a person has demonstrated sufficient capability to effectively carry out the improvement kata—this is a gate—they can move to the next level of training, C, where they practice the coaching kata. Moving from Level I to Level C is not a function of time or number of practices completed, but of demonstrated capability.

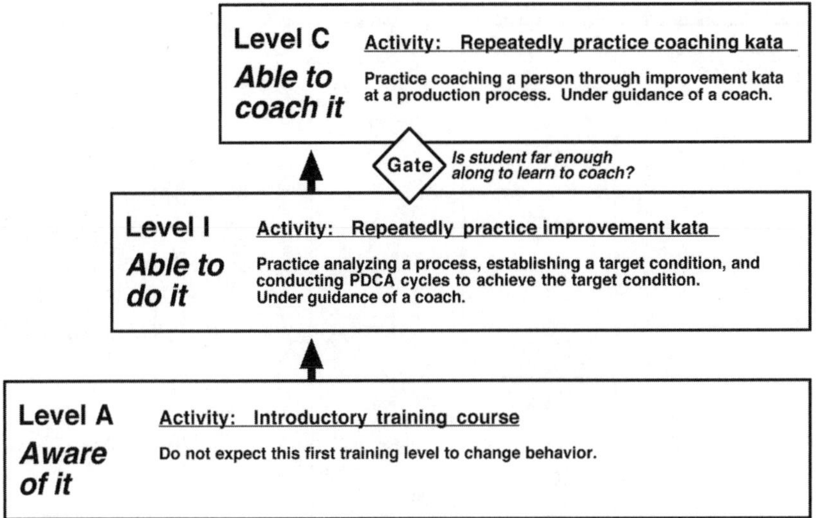

Figure 9-12. Example training levels

Within the "I" and "C" capability levels individuals will at any point in time, of course, have different skill levels. An interesting view of skill levels is provided by the "Dreyfus model of skill acquisition."[2]

The three levels of training activity, or whatever levels you may define, can then provide a framework for specifying who will practice what, when, and how. The table in Figure 9-13 is an example.

As you can see by the horizontal arrows in the table, as people move up in their level of experience, capability, and perspective, some of them teach and coach people in the next level. By coaching the next group, the higher level group can maintain a better sense of the actual situation, that is, people's true current capabilities. (See benefits of the mentor/mentee approach in Chapter 8.)

This generic table is intended to help you envision how you might move practice-based training through your organization. Real life will not be this neat and orderly, of course. What is depicted in this table will, in most organizations, also involve much more than one year. But with this sort of overall tactic in mind, you can develop your own first plan to match your situation.

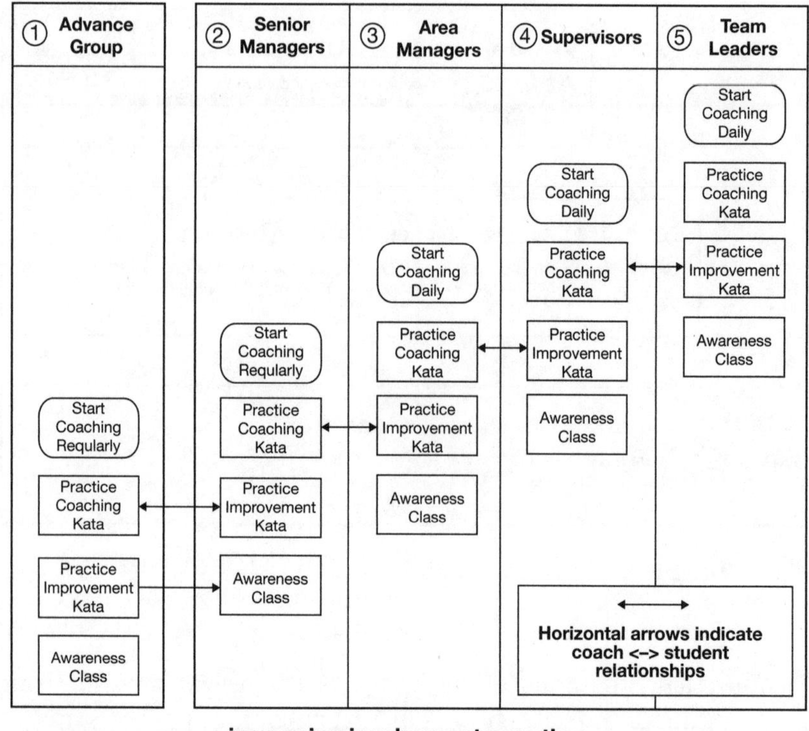

Figure 9-13. How training might be moved through an organization

5. Metrics

It is important that we can measure our progress and, in particular, lack of progress. We learn the most from our mistakes! Currently we use two categories of metrics.

1. One set of metrics has to do with coaching. These might be the start and stop times of coaching cycles, how many processes are coached, who does the coaching, how often the coaching cycles take place, and whether the next step (question five) was taken.

   However, it is entirely possible to fulfill a specified number of coaching cycles and have little to no improvement effect on the production process. Always bear in mind that the overarching objective is continual improvement of cost and quality performance at the process level.

2. Therefore you should monitor the relationship between coaching cycles (above) and a second set of metrics: to what degree the focus processes are being improved. Such improvement metrics are taken directly from the target conditions at the respective focus production processes.

   As mentioned earlier, if the coaching cycles (metric set 1) are being fulfilled as planned but the improvement in the focus processes (metric set 2) are not being reached, then you need to take a closer look at how the coaching is being done.

Also think about and define how these numbers will be obtained. Ideally this is done as simply as possible: with pencil and paper at the process. A good rule of thumb is that, if possible, you should go to the process to get the information you need. Ideally the mentee does not bring metrics to the mentor's office. It is more like a pull system, if you will, whereby mentor and mentee go to the process to obtain the necessary facts and data there.

Related to metrics, as part of their lean implementation efforts, many organizations have tried utilizing systems of point awards, or similar, to drive and assess progress. Be careful with such systems, since people often end up chasing points rather than a desired target condition. I tend to avoid such schemes.

Problems arise when awards are linked to completion or implementation of activities, which is easy to measure, rather than to attainment of a level of personal competency or of target conditions, which, admittedly, is more difficult to measure. Levels should be awarded based on the student's demonstrated capability or achievement of target conditions, not on how many courses or practices have been completed or tools implemented.

Include Reflection Times in the Plan

Keep in mind that when you execute a plan and work toward a target condition, you will need to make adjustments based on what you are learning from the unforeseen obstacles and problems you discover along the way. This is one of the reasons we prepare a plan: so we can see what is not going as expected. The advance group should reflect regularly and make adjustments as necessary. Build this into your plan by scheduling advance-group reflection times, for example, every two weeks.

By conducting reflections—that is, PDCA checks as you work to develop improvement-kata behavior across the organization—you will learn what you need to work on to achieve that behavior. You can conduct reflections in an uncomplicated fashion. Go through the five questions and record on a flip chart what is going as planned (+) and what is not working or not going as expected (−). The inputs for the reflection can come out of the more frequent coaching cycles, which are a kind of process metric.

However, one lesson I have learned is to begin any reflection session with (1) a restatement of the overall theme (for example, "To develop improvement kata behavior in the organization"), and (2) a reiteration of "why we experiment," in order to calibrate everyone's thinking before conducting the reflection. In a reflection, people may feel pressure and start defending why they were not able to complete a step as planned. This, of course, inhibits PDCA. It is useful to remind everyone that you are experimenting in order to see obstacles and to learn from them what you need to work on in order to achieve the target condition. You are not looking at individuals and evaluating them, and our success depends upon the reflection being a depersonalized, open, and data-based dialogue.

One more point to reiterate for conducting reflections. We know that the improvement kata is scientific and that it works. If process improvement results are not as expected, then it is not the improvement kata that is faulty but something in our coaching that is still incorrect. Practicing the improvement kata over and over should produce results. If they do not come, then something is wrong in our teaching.

Common Obstacles

In our experimentation there have been many obstacles, many ah-has, and many course corrections. Here are some common obstacles, just as an example. You will find more.

- It is hard for people to resist making a list of action items.
- The five key questions are often difficult for senior leaders to internalize.
- We like doing but not checking and adjusting.
- We jump into solutions and skip over careful observation and analysis.
- People do not understand Toyota-style coaching. Both mentor and mentee mistakenly believe that the mentee needs to figure out what solution the mentor has in mind.
- The unclear path to a target condition is uncomfortable for many people. People like a clear plan in advance even though that is actually only a prediction.
- Iteration (redoing steps) is uncomfortable. People feel like they did something wrong when they are asked to look again or repeat a step, yet this is very important for learning and seeing deeply.
- Many people will view this effort as just another project, rather than as developing a new way of managing. At the start, it naturally seems like this effort means adding more work on top of daily management duties, as opposed to it being a different way of conducting daily management.
- At the start, coaching cycles often take too much time and thus become burdensome. Once a target condition has been established, a coaching cycle can often be completed in 15 minutes. Less is more. As discussed earlier, rather than making a list of steps, just take one next step and then see where that takes you. Conduct your coaching cycles standing up at the process (target condition information and process data will need to be at the process), and do not let them turn into endless talk sessions. Go through the five questions, find the next step, and that is then the end of the coaching cycle. Take the next step as soon as possible.

Lifelong Practicing

In this chapter we have been talking about developing capabilities and behavior patterns, which, in Toyota's view, represent the strength of an organization.

The ongoing challenge of kata training is to strive for mastery and perfection, and even the most accomplished Toyota engineers, leaders, managers, and executives will say they are still working toward that goal. The sports metaphor is again appropriate here. Just like athletes, even advanced students and senior leaders will need to keep practicing the katas they learned as beginners, under guidance of a coach. The never-ending need for improvement and evolution of our processes and products gives us the opportunity to keep honing our skills while working on actual issues and toward real target conditions. While doing so, we should listen to our coaches and others who may detect a bad habit.

The elegant trick in this is that while you are practicing, you are also doing something real, always to the best of the current level of your abilities. This is an interesting way to manage continuous improvement and adaptation, and a fascinating way to manage an organization.

Notes

1. I am indebted to Mr. Ralph Richter for his input on this diagram.
2. This model, by Stuart Dreyfus and Hubert Dreyfus, proposes five stages of skill acquisition: Novice, Competence, Proficiency, Expertise, and Mastery.

Conclusion

We admire Toyota's ability to thrive in different environments and in changing, challenging conditions. Yet it is not necessarily a problem that organizations sometimes come and sometimes go. The economist Joseph Schumpeter saw this as a process of *creative destruction*, and suggested that it accounts for a lot of the vitality in the most vibrant and dynamic economies on Earth.

In the late 1980s when I was starting to research how manufacturing companies can retain or regain competitiveness, a Buddhist colleague surprised me with an observation. He pointed out that by conducting that research and trying to assist manufacturers, it is possible that I was interfering with natural selection, artificially prolonging untenable situations and, thus, in the long run, perhaps even causing more rather than less suffering.

Yet despite Mr. Schumpeter and my Buddhist colleague, I do find myself caring if an organization survives or not, and if your organization survives. This is not because I fear change or have a special affinity for the organization. It is because the unplanned decline or collapse of an organization suggests to me that we as humans were somehow unable to sense in a timely fashion what was happening, react appropriately, and adapt elegantly. I do not lament the loss of the organization so much as I regret the failure to use our human capability—our capability to keep adapting—to its fullest extent. In fact, if we more fully use our capabilities to adapt, then there will be plenty of change as organizations keep intentionally modifying and evolving themselves, their products, and their services, to suit dynamic conditions.

With success, business organizations may shift too much of their focus away from serving customers and society, to simply making money, trying to preserve a status quo or maximizing short-term shareholder value. Consequently, it can become more likely that progress—through improvement and evolution of processes, product, or service—will occur outside these organizations. In contrast, Toyota's improvement kata helps keep an organization's attention on what it needs to do to continue improving and evolving how it provides value for customers and society.

Financial targets and results are vital, of course, but for long-term organization survival the question "How do we achieve those financial results?" should often be preceded by the question "What do we need to do with our processes, product, or service in order to meet customer needs?"

In the space between these two questions lies much resourcefulness and creativity, which are available to any organization that has a kata that taps and channels those abilities.

If we know and can master how to proceed through unclear territory, then we need not fear many of the challenges, changes, and unknowns we encounter in any of our endeavors. Rather than trying to hold on to what may be a false sense of certainty, which can lead to trouble because we then act with a mistaken sense of reality, we can learn a means for dealing with uncertainty. This is why I continued to study Toyota and why, as the research progressed and the findings became clearer, I decided to write this book. I hope that Toyota will stay with us long enough so that many of us—in business, education, politics, and daily living—can learn from this unique company about how we might better utilize our human capabilities. Thriving in the long term, the fundamental purpose of the Toyota organization, is to me a sign of good concerted use—good management—of our human ability and potential.

Six years ago I began the research that led to this book thinking, like just about everyone else, that the story was about techniques and other *listable* aspects of Toyota. Today I see Toyota in a notably different light: as an organization defined primarily by the unique behavior routines it continually teaches to all its members. Due to the linear nature of the book format, some of my descriptions of the improvement kata are necessarily too mechanical, as compared with how this kata is utilized in every day's work at Toyota. Fortunately, the improvement kata, even as presented here, will readily accommodate reality.

Toyota's improvement kata and coaching kata are largely invisible when we benchmark Toyota. Yet these two kata play perhaps the major role in Toyota's ability to achieve ambitious targets, keep improving, and adapt. I have worked with these kata extensively now and I am intrigued by their capacity to help us move through the unpredictable paths ahead and achieve beyond what we can see (Figure C-1). When you look behind the curtain at how Toyota manages itself, you realize that Toyota has achieved not only a commercial but also an intellectual accomplishment.

The response by business leaders when they learn about Toyota's improvement and coaching kata has been overwhelmingly, and even surprisingly, positive. As if it were something we have been waiting for. When skepticism is expressed, it tends to revolve around two thoughts: that the step-by-step improvement kata and coaching kata seem to proceed slowly, or that it will take a long time to develop such behavior patterns.

In regard to the first comment, Toyota's approach may indeed appear slow, but in fact the continuous improvement and adaptation it generates is in sum both faster and more effective than our current approach of periodic attempts at improvement and adaptation. It is perhaps a classic example of the race between the tortoise and the hare.

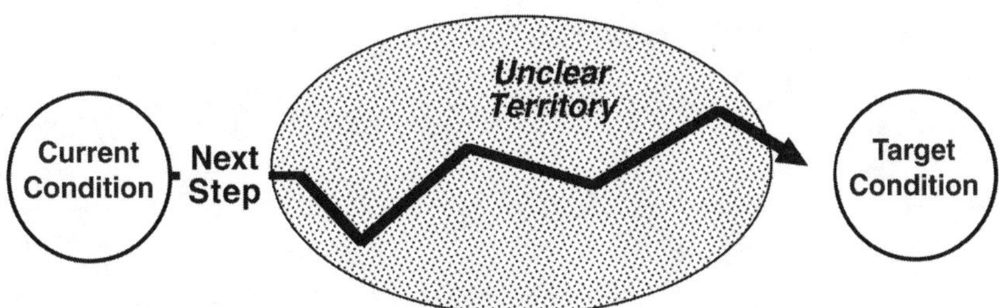

Figure C-1. Beyond what we can see

In regard to the second comment, I would agree that developing new behavior patterns across an organization involves a more far reaching effort, and probably more time, than a supposedly quick-fix solution. But a quick fix does not alter the underlying management system, and—the conclusion is becoming unavoidable—some aspects of our prevailing management system need to be changed.

Permanent pressure to adapt can keep an organization fit and healthy, if it has a systematic way—a kata—of responding to that pressure. This book does not describe everything about Toyota, but it provides more than enough information and detail for you to begin developing—through experimentation and practice—your own continuous improvement system like Toyota's. You can even see your organization as part of human history through your efforts to bring continuous improvement and adaptation into it. This is because each step in that direction not only benefits your company, it also helps move our society forward because it mobilizes our capability.

Does the way ahead for developing improvement kata behavior in your organization seem unclear? Are you unsure about what you will need to do to achieve successful culture change? Well, that is exactly how it should be, and if so, I can assure you that you are already on the right track. We cannot know what the path ahead will be, but the improvement kata shows us a way to deal with and perhaps even enjoy that unpredictable aspect of life. That latter sentiment is my wish for all of us, and, with that in mind, I will end with a question:

What is your improvement kata?

Appendix 1

Where Do You Start with the Improvement Kata?

Ideally, every production process would have a target condition. Leaders would be able to check and mentor improvement activity by going from process to process daily, observing, and asking the five questions at each stop. Certainly no process in a production facility should operate without a defined standard that it is striving to achieve. However, it would be overwhelming and infeasible to begin by applying the improvement kata at many processes simultaneously.

One common answer to the question of where to start is at the loop in the value stream with the greatest potential for improvement. In the simplified value stream map in Figure A1-1, clearly the stamping loop, with its eight days of lead time, has greater improvement

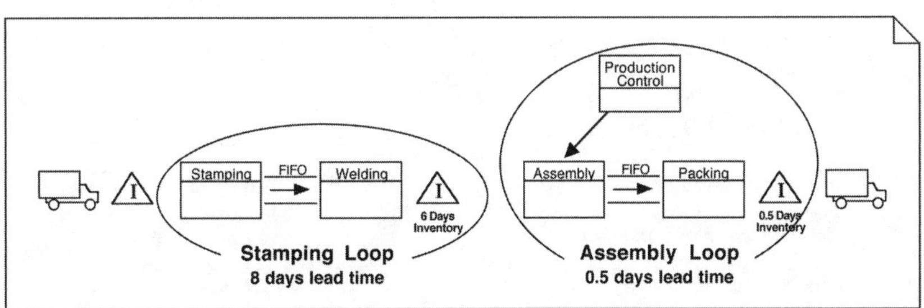

Figure A1-1. A value stream with two loops

potential than the assembly loop, which generates only a half day of lead time. Many of us would logically begin in the stamping loop.

As part of the research leading to this book, I studied how Toyota works with its suppliers. One thing I observed is that after Toyota supplier support personnel walk a value stream for some time—in order to gain a broad understanding of the overall situation—they usually began by focusing on the assembly loop of a value stream, even if it had far less inventory and lead time than the upstream loops. In the value stream depicted in Figure A1-1, Toyota would most likely begin in the assembly loop. Why?

In Toyota's way of thinking, the first place in the value stream to establish and drive toward a target condition is at the "pacemaker process," rather than at upstream "fabrication" processes. The pacemaker process, or loop, in a value stream is the set of downstream steps that are dedicated to a family of products, and where that family of products is finished for the external customer. The external-customer takt time applies to this process. Often this is an assembly process and its associated scheduling process (Figure A1-2).

Note that a pacemaker process means something different than a bottleneck process, although they could by coincidence be the same process.

Toyota tends to begin at the pacemaker loop because it occupies a critical position in a value stream and is worthy of special attention. Fluctuation and instability in the pacemaker loop can quickly affect the just-downstream external customer, and simultaneously cause hard-to-follow, amplifying demand fluctuations for the upstream processes.

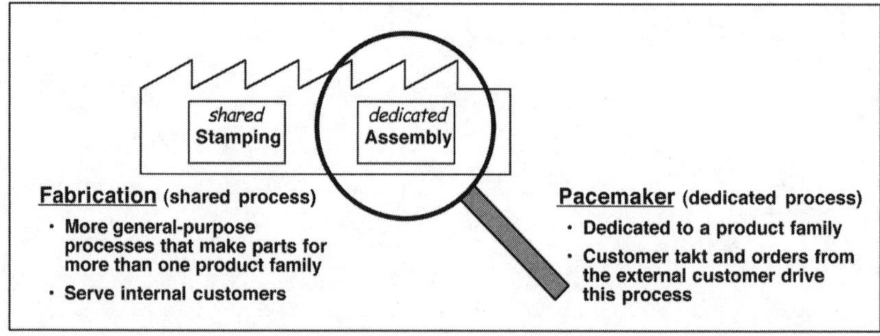

Figure A1-2. Pacemaker and fabrication processes

I first came across this effect when I visited a plant and was told that the biggest problem was the upstream machining area. The assembly process could often not fulfill its production schedules because it was frequently running out of machined parts. Yet when we got to the machining area, a few calculations revealed excess capacity there. The machining supervisor cleared things up when he said, "Yes, we have enough capacity here, but no one can expect us to keep up with assembly the way they constantly change their production schedule." At that point we went back to assembly—in the pacemaker loop—and started taking a closer look there.

Many problems in the upstream processes of a value stream actually have their origin in a poorly operated pacemaker loop. If the pacemaker is operating in a unstable or unleveled manner, it becomes difficult to discern where problems in the value stream are actually coming from. Problem solving and improvement are difficult. Toyota's improvement strategy here is to strive to develop a stable, leveled pacemaker process *first,* and then see what problems remain in the upstream processes and migrate there *as needed.*

Sometimes, of course, you cannot start at the pacemaker loop because there is a show stopper problem at an upstream process. What Toyota often does in this situation is to fix this upstream problem quickly, within a few weeks at most—even by temporarily increasing inventory there—and then get back to concentrating on the pacemaker.

A special focus on pacemaker processes, particularly at the start, may take some practice and extra effort to bring it into an organization. At one company I know, the vice president of manufacturing regularly visits the manufacturing facilities; a common practice for manufacturing VPs. Despite having been instructed on the pacemaker focus, plant managers would invariably want to walk the visiting VP through the factory to show "all the improvements we have made"; that is, to show scattered point improvements made at many places in the factory. To change this and get people more focused, it took the VP saying, "For the near future when I visit your plant, I will go to your pacemaker processes first, where I will be asking the five questions."

As you continue to focus on the pacemaker process and strive to achieve successively tighter target conditions there, the causes of obstacles

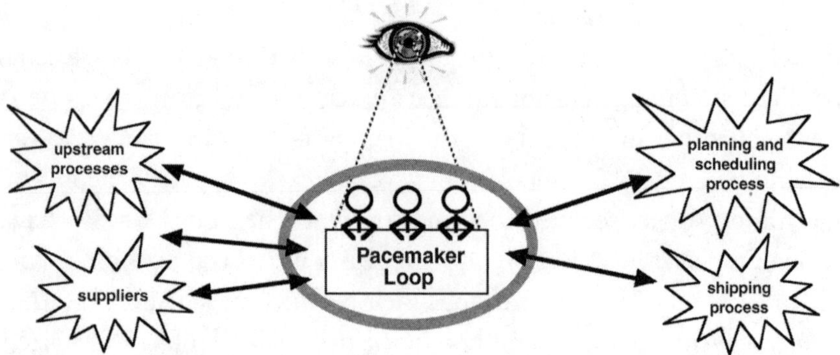

Figure A1-3. Migrating into the value stream and other areas as needed

will increasingly lie up- or downstream of the pacemaker or even elsewhere in the organization. When conditions in other processes and areas become the obstacles preventing you from achieving the next target condition at the pacemaker, you can migrate to them (Figure A1-3). This is an elegant way to expand into the value stream—following where the problems lead you—because then you are always working on what you need to work on, and individual improvement efforts tie together. Eventually you will be striving for target conditions at all processes, but in a connected and concerted way. And as you move into other processes, the value stream mapping tool will prove helpful for understanding and planning how you would like the flow to tie together next.

Appendix 2

Process Analysis

The purpose of this appendix is to show you a procedure for analyzing the current condition of a production process. This is done to help obtain the facts and data you need in order to define an appropriate process target condition.

I have used this process analysis on a wide variety of production processes; some more automated and some less automated. In some cases adjustments will be necessary in order to fit the analysis to the characteristics of a particular type of process, but the basic concept as presented here is usually about the same.

The purpose of the process analysis is *not* to uncover problems or potential improvements, but to grasp the current process condition (Figure A2-1) and obtain the facts and data you need for establishing an appropriate next process target condition. This is an important point. This is not a hunt for waste in the process. Going through the steps of this process analysis is intended to force you to look into and confront the details of a process, so you can define how the process should be operating. Once you have a target condition, then you can strive to move toward it, ask the five questions, and identify what you need to work on.

The process analysis and establishing a target condition take some time, but once a target condition has been established, the coaching cycles can be frequent and short. Try practicing the steps of this process analysis, establishing a target condition and applying the rest of the improvement kata. Once you understand the thinking and pattern behind this process analysis, you may well decide to modify it to better suit your environment.

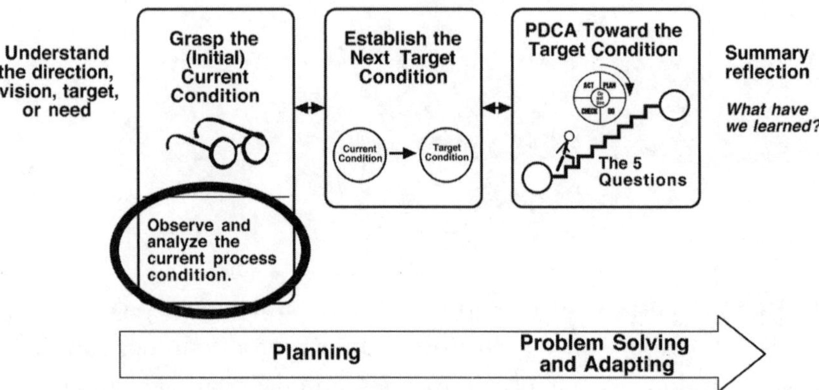

Figure A2-1. Process analysis helps you grasp the current condition

Start with the Value Stream

Improvement happens at the process level, but conducting at least a "value stream scan" is a prerequisite before conducting a process analysis and establishing a first target condition. Such a scan helps you understand the overall flow from dock to dock and to identify the segments or "loops" of a value stream.[1]

A value stream scan often does not take too much time, typically one day or less. Do not try to get all the details, just a basic overview of the value stream by asking the questions below. You can add detail to this value stream map later, as you begin to gain a deeper understanding of the pacemaker process.

Questions for a Value Stream Scan

1. Which value stream (product family) have you selected?

2. What are the processing steps? (Figure A2-2)

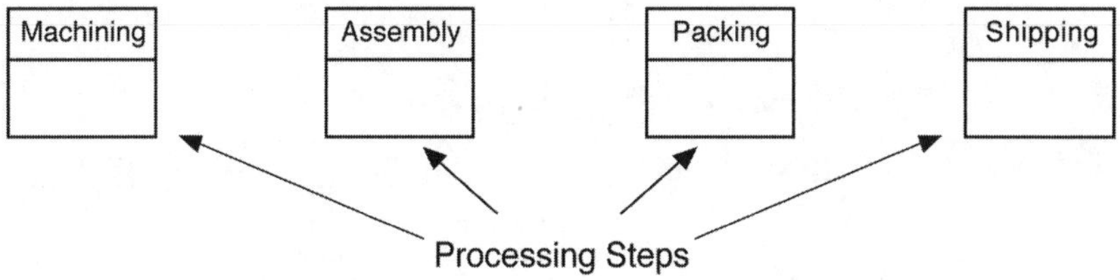

Figure A2-2.

3. Is the process dedicated (D) or shared (S)? (Figure A2-3)

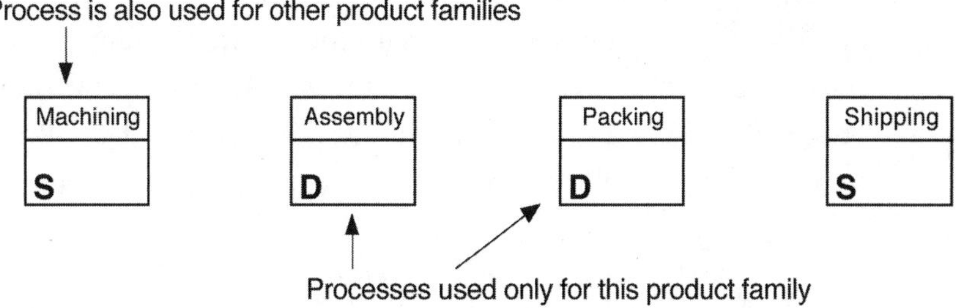

Figure A2-3.

4. At what points along the value stream is inventory kept? (Figure A2-4)

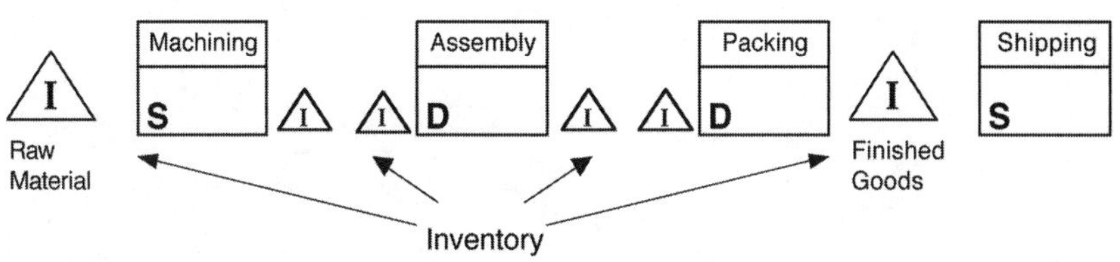

Figure A2-4.

5. How does each process know what to produce (information flow)? (Figure A2-5)

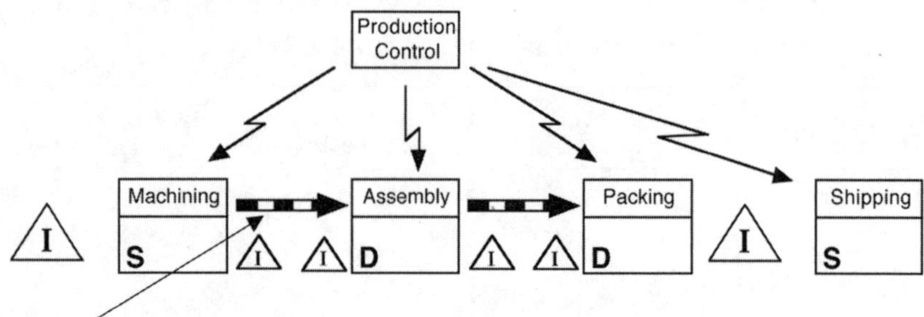

Figure A2-5.

6. At what processes are changeovers needed? (Figure A2-6)

   What is the changeover time, current lot size, current number of changeovers per day, and the estimated EPEI at those processes? (Every-Product-Every-Interval: this is the interval of time over which a process produces every high-volume product it makes.)

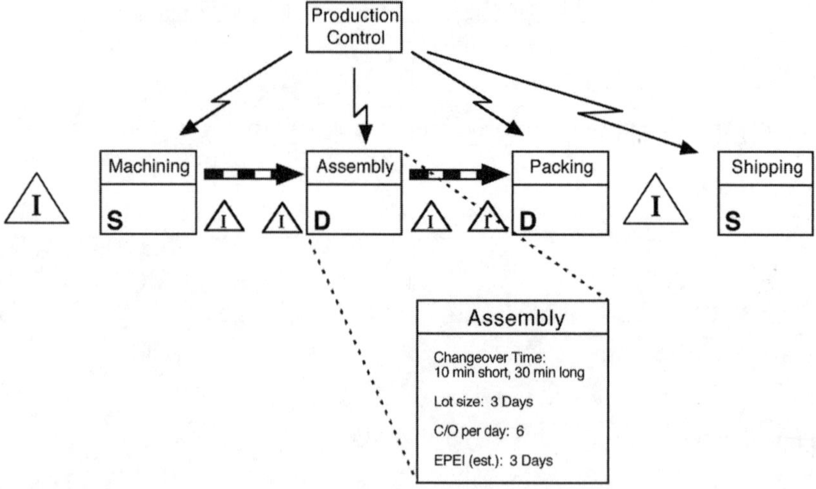

Figure A2-6.

7. What are the "loops" in this value stream? (Figure A2-7)
   Which loop is the pacemaker loop? (See Appendix 1 for an explanation of the pacemaker process or loop.)

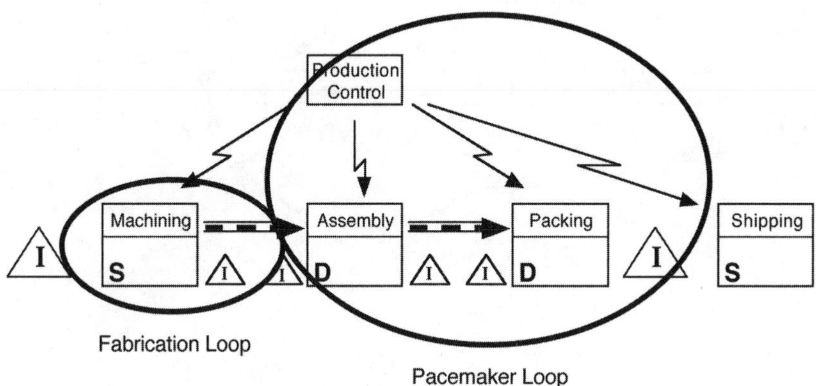

Figure A2-7.

8. With a one- to two-year time horizon in mind, where:

Do you think 1x1 flow should be possible?

Do you think inventory should be replaced with a Pull or FIFO system?

Now Focus On One Process in the Value Stream

You are now dropping down from the value stream level to the process level, to conduct the process analysis. Start at the pacemaker loop and stay focused on it. Often this means you will be analyzing an assembly or similar process (Figure A2-8).

There is a logic behind the order of these steps. However, the effort quickly becomes iterative. As you move through the analysis, you will often have to go back and review or recalculate an earlier step based on what you are learning as you move forward. This is normal. You are trying to get a deep understanding of the current condition.

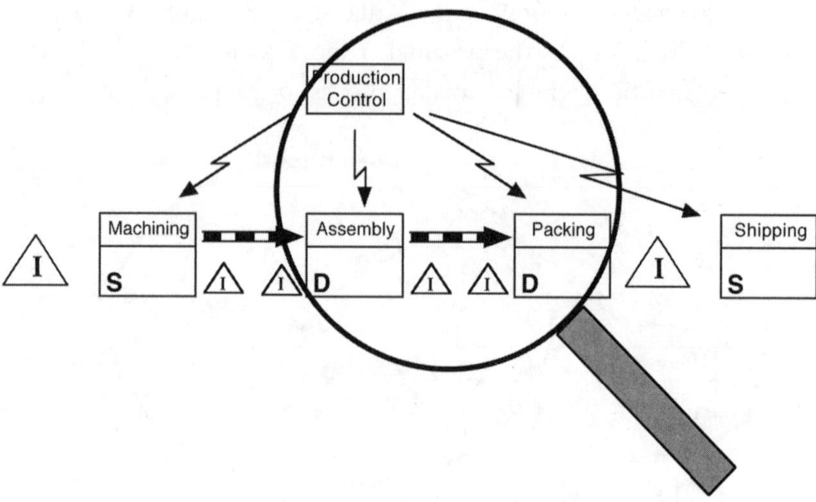

Figure A2-8. Start at the pacemaker loop

STEPS OF PROCESS ANALYSIS

Assess customer demand and determine line pace

- Customer takt
- Planned cycle time

First impressions of the process

- Get to know the process by sketching a block diagram of it.
- Is there a 1x1 flow?
- Are each operator's work steps the same from cycle to cycle?
- Is line output consistent?

Is machine capacity sufficient?

- Can the equipment support the planned cycle time?
- What is current capacity?
- How many shifts?

☹ No ☺ Yes

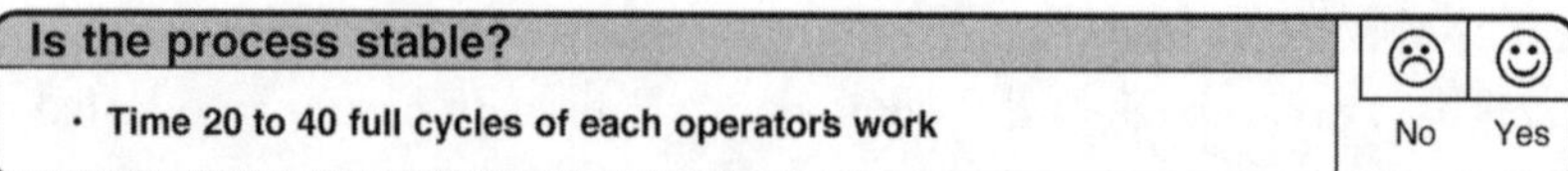

What is the necessary number of operators if the process were stable?

- Calculate number of operators

Figure A2-9. Steps of process analysis

The only equipment you need to conduct a process analysis is:

- A stopwatch that measures seconds
- Graph paper
- Pencil
- Eraser
- Calculator

Do not forget shop-floor courtesy:

- Approach the process via the team leader or supervisor

  Introduce yourself
  Explain what you are doing
  Do not interrupt the operators while they are working

- Explain that you are watching the work, not the operator. (People will not believe you when you say this, but if it is what is in your heart, eventually they will.)
- Show any notes you've taken.
- Say "Thank you" before you leave.
- Perhaps keep your hands out of your pockets on the shop floor. People are working hard here, and hands-in-pockets sends a too casual message. A better message is: "We are all working hard for the customer."

Assess Customer Demand and Determine Line Pace

Here are two numbers you should know (Figure A2-10).

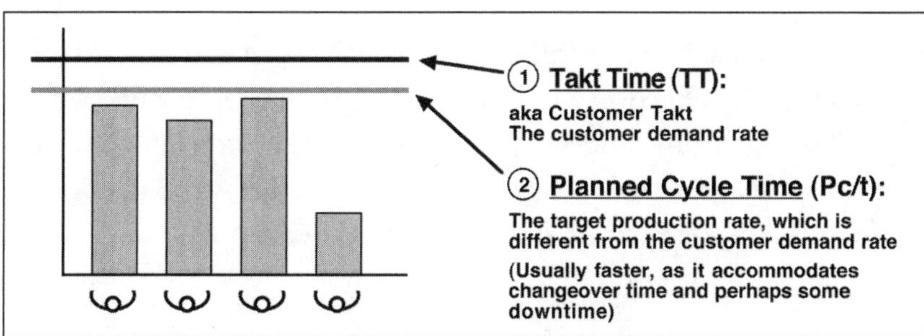

Figure A2-10. Takt time and planned cycle time

Takt time (TT). This is the rate of customer demand for the group of products produced by a process. Takt time is calculated by dividing the effective operating time of a process by the quantity of items customers require from the process in that operating time. You can see the formula in Figure A2-11, and an example in Figure A2-12.) "Effective operating time" is the available time minus planned downtimes such as lunches, breaks, team meetings, cleanup, and planned maintenance. *Unplanned* downtime and changeover times are not subtracted, because they are variables we want to reduce.

$$\text{takt time} = \frac{\text{your effective operating time / shift or day}}{\text{average customer requirement per shift or day}}$$

Figure A2-11. The takt time calculation

Example:

$$\frac{\text{26,100 seconds available time}}{\text{450 pieces required}} = \text{58 seconds takt time}$$

Figure A2-12. Example takt time calculation

Interpretation of the example: The customer is, on average, currently buying one unit every 58 seconds. (Of course, customer demand rates change over time. For example, Toyota recalculates takt time every 30 days and reviews it every 10 days.)

Planned cycle time (Pc/t). Once you have calculated takt, then also subtract changeover time and, perhaps, other losses, such as unplanned downtime and scrap and rework rates, from the operating time to arrive at the planned cycle time (Pc/t). This is the actual speed at which the line should be running.

a. *Changeover time.* In your first Pc/t calculation you can simply use the number of changeovers currently done per day, and the total time that currently takes. You can also calculate with other patterns of changeovers and changeover times, in order to explore different scenarios.
b. *Downtime.* There are two kinds of downtime: short stoppages throughout the day that add up, and rarer but longer-lasting catastrophic failures. In calculating Pc/t, we are concerned with only the small stoppages. You cannot cover for occasional catastrophe with a faster Pc/t.

   Toyota subtracts changeover time in calculating Pc/t, but not unplanned downtime. This is because Toyota factories maintain a time gap after each shift, which is used to make up for small stoppages that occurred during the shift. If you do not currently have that option, then you will probably have to accommodate for some unplanned downtime in calculating the Pc/t.

   One tactic is to strive for a Pc/t that is only 15 or 20 percent faster than takt, and prescribe that changeover time and other losses should be controlled to fit within that 15 or 20 percent gap.

The following simple capacity analysis using the L-shaped stack chart is an exceptionally useful tool for calculating planned cycle time, which you should master.

- In the stack, show each category of losses individually, rather than, for example, combining them in an OEE figure (Overall Equipment Effectiveness). This way you can better understand the issues.
- Start with a one-day interval to make the Pc/t calculation.
- If you are seeking Pc/t, calculate *down*. If the Pc/t is fixed, say because of an unchangeable machine cycle, then calculate *up*.
- Use the optimal changeover sequence to minimize total changeover loss.
- Always put changeover time at the top of the stack.

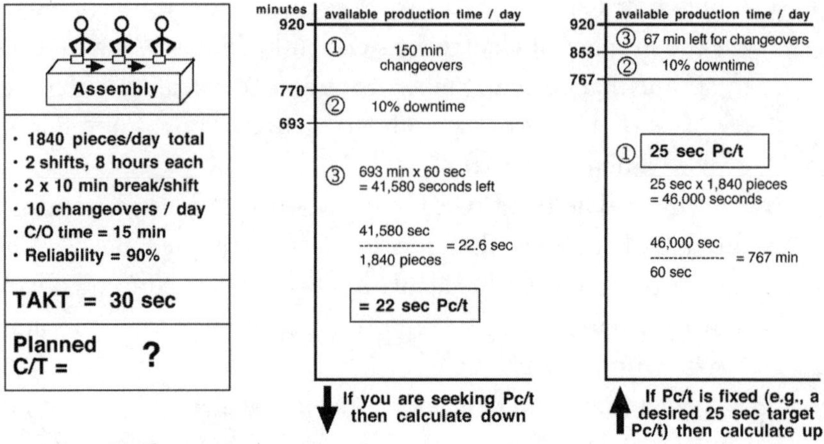

Figure A2-13. Capacity analysis

Figure A2-13 includes an example of using capacity analysis to determine Pc/t.

First Impressions of the Process

What do you see?

- Get to know the process by trying to sketch a block diagram of it. Draw a straight-line sketch of the workstations in the process. Do not draw to scale or worry about the shape—the layout—of the line. Simply make each box about the same size as shown in Figure A2-14. Each box equals one workstation or machine. This sketch can get messy as you see deeper and deeper into the process. That's ok.

Now observe the process and try to answer the following three questions. Write down your observations. You can ask questions, but do not interview people. Learn to see and understand for yourself.

pump assy	harness & filter	flange assy	harness	test	assy	tank assy	tank weld	assy	sender assy	auto tester	label & pack

Figure A2-14. A block diagram sketch of a process

- Is there a 1x1 flow?
  - Do parts move directly from one value-adding step to the next?
- Are each operator's work steps the same from cycle to cycle?
- Is output consistent at the end of the process?
  - Use a stopwatch to time 20 successive cycles at the output end of the process. Select a point and time how often a part comes by this point. Chart the individual times as shown in Figure A2-24. Do not calculate or use averages.

Check Machine Capacity

What is meant here by "machines" is automatic equipment that runs even if an operator walks away. A drill press that is operated by a person, for example, is not automatic. A drilling machine that drills by itself after a person unloads and loads it is automatic.

The questions we are trying to answer with this step of the process analysis are:

1. Can the automatic equipment in this process meet the planned cycle time?
2. What is the fastest planned cycle time that the automatic equipment can currently support? (This is current process capacity.)

Theoretically, an automatic machine's cycle time has to be right at or faster than the planned cycle time. For example, if the planned cycle time for a process is 20 seconds, then the automated machines in the process would need to go through their full cycle in 20 seconds or less. In practice, however, this is not quite correct.

Every machine has a certain small fluctuation from cycle to cycle. Sometimes the time to unload and load the machine varies slightly, or the machine cycle itself varies a small amount. Due to this "personality" of machines, a close-coupled 1x1 flow will not be sustainable if any of the automated machines in it require the full Pc/t interval to complete their cycle. In a 1x1 flow, if one machine goes over the planned cycle time, then this variation can telegraph up- and downstream and disrupt the 1x1 flow.

For this reason, automatic machines should finish their cycle a little before the planned cycle time is up, at the latest. A guideline—only a guideline—is that the total machine cycle time for any automated equipment in a 1x1 flow should be no longer than about 90 percent of the planned cycle time. This guideline applies only to machines, not operators. Operator work should ideally be filled up to the planned cycle time. Looked at another way, the fastest planned cycle time with which a line is able to consistently run a 1x1 flow is depicted in Figure A2-15. This quotient represents the current capacity limit of a 1x1 flow process.

$$\frac{\textbf{Longest total machine cycle time}}{\textbf{0.90}}$$

Figure A2-15. Current capacity limit of a 1x1 flow process

Insufficient machine capacity is a show-stopper issue, which is why there is a smile/frown check in this step in Figure A2-9. If machine capacity is insufficient, then you must address this first, before going on and making other improvements, because in that situation other improvement efforts will not stick. We must provide the factory floor with a process that is capable of supporting the planned cycle time.

To check machine capacity, draw a machine capacity chart as in Figures A2-16 through A2-19.

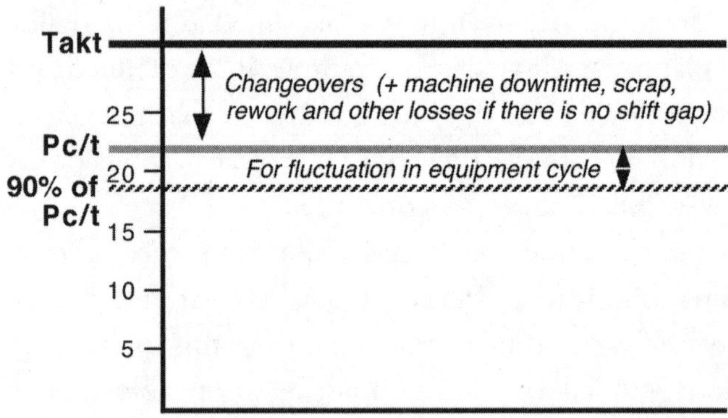

First draw in lines for the takt time, planned cycle time, and 90% of planned cycle time.

Figure A2-16. Step 1

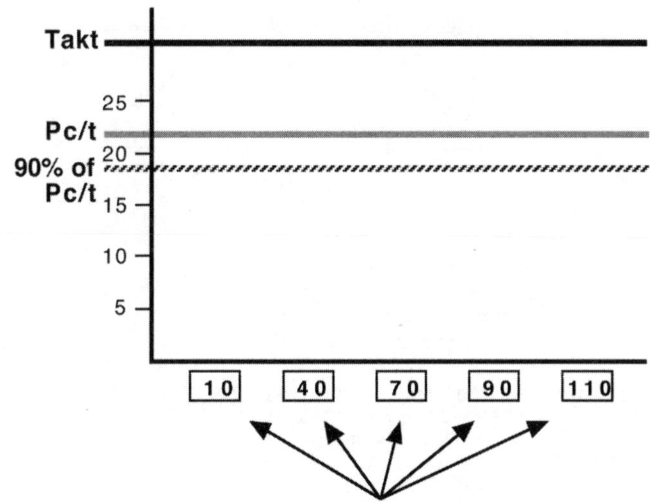

Figure A2-17. Step 2

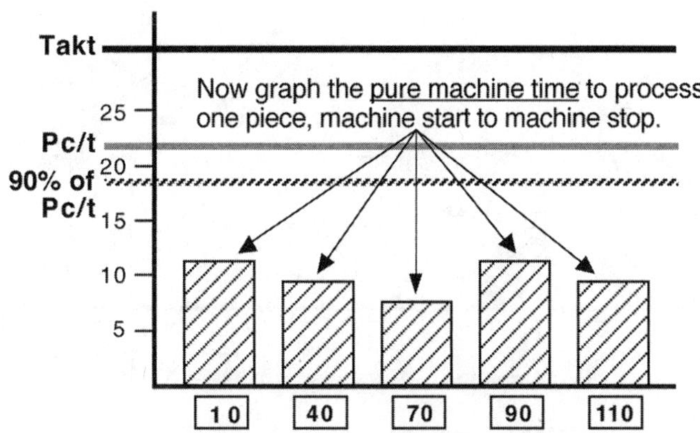

Figure A2-18. Step 3

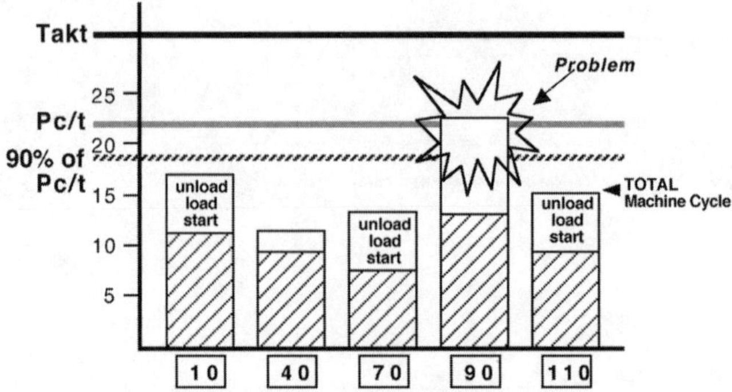

Figure A2-19. Step 4

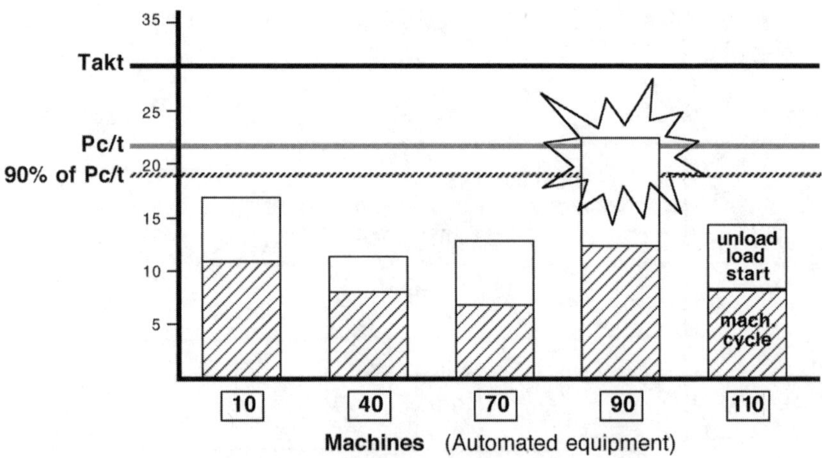

Figure A2-20. Example of a machine capacity chart

Interpretation of the machine capacity chart. The first thing a machine capacity chart shows you is if you have any equipment that currently cannot support the planned cycle time. As you can see in the example in Figure A2-20, machine 90 has a total cycle time that is too long for the planned cycle time. This must be addressed before going on. Tactics for dealing with this obstacle fall in three successive categories, the first category being preferable to the next, and so on.

1. *Category 1: True improvement.* Work hard to achieve this before going on to the next category.
   - Shorten unload and load time.
   - Reduce the gap between takt time and planned cycle time, which makes the Pc/t slower.
   - Find capacity in the machine cycle. For example, reduce empty machine cycle time, such as "cutting air." How much of the machine's cycle time is actually spent processing?
   - Split up multifunction machines, if this can be done inexpensively. Single function machines have more capacity.
   - Make machine and unload/load times occur in parallel. For example, put the part fixtures on a turntable so the operator can unload and load while the machine is running and processing another part.
   - Speed up the machine (quality cannot be compromised).
2. *Category 2: Compensating. Not true improvement.*
   - Add a small standard work-in-process buffer up- and downstream of the machine, to isolate its "personality" from the rest of the 1x1 flow. This only works if the total machine cycle time is at or below the planned cycle time.
   - Move work to other processes, which slows down the takt time and planned cycle time for this process.
3. *Category 3: Buy more capacity. The last resort option.*
   - A Toyota person once told me, "If we are resourceful and creative we can almost always find ways to get more capacity out of a machine."

A machine capacity chart can also help you see the current natural capacity level of a process. In Line A, Figure A2-21, there is a capacity problem, but it only involves two machines. If we can reduce the total

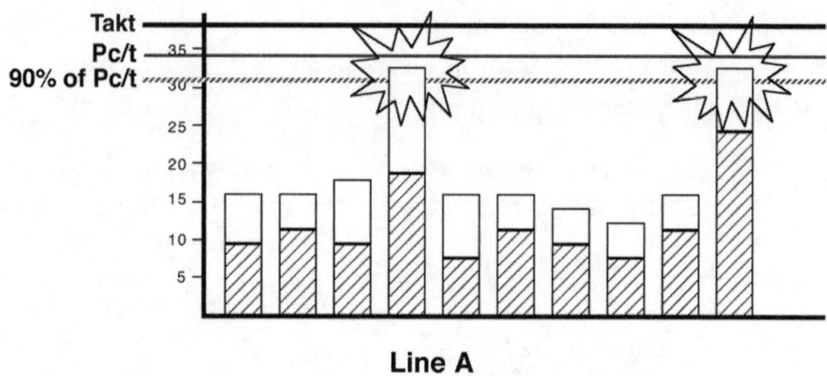

Figure A2-21. Line A is not yet at its natural capacity limit

machine cycle time for these two machines, the planned cycle time can be met. There is capacity available in this line, and perhaps, with some creativity, additional products can be added to it.

In Line B, Figure A2-22, two machines also cannot currently meet the planned cycle time. However, most of the other machines here are near their current capacity limit. There are of course things we can do to free up more capacity in this line, but increasing capacity in this process would involve nearly all the machines. Line B is close to its current natural capacity limit.

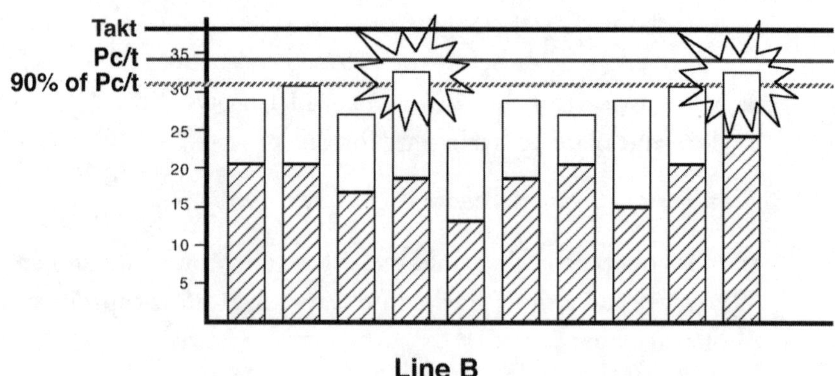

Figure A2-22. Line B is close to its current natural capacity limit

How many shifts? In conjunction with checking machine capacity, you should also consider the number of shifts. The clearest way to see what the options are is to prepare a table, as shown in Figure A2-23.

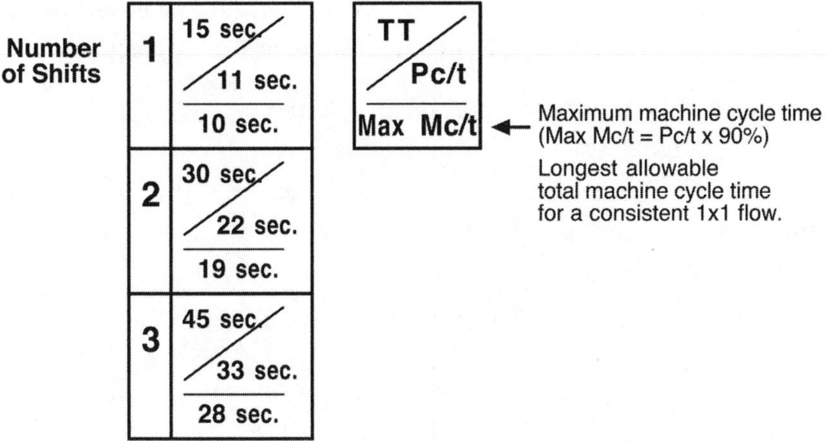

Figure A2-23. Consider the options for number of shifts

Is the Process Stable?

When you start applying the improvement kata to a production process, as well as again and again after process changes are made, the target condition often includes establishing cycle stability. Process stability, or lack of it, is another show-stopper issue.

- If a process is not stable, you will need to address this before trying to make other improvements, because without a stable process, further improvements will often not stick.
- Whenever production processes are unstable, especially pacemaker processes, the entire organization (shop floor, administration, planning, logistics, sales and after-sales service, customers, etc.) will experience waves of fluctuation, variation, and extra activities. The total extra effort and cost generated by this variation in production is called the "hidden factory." The extra

expense is not measurable because there are too many intangibles, but such variation has been estimated to add 20 to 30 percent to cost. The more stable and level you can get your processes, the leaner the entire organization can be.

Note that a stable process does not mean there are no problems, but that the process operates in a consistent manner from cycle to cycle.

Time 20 to 40 cycles of each operator's work. You can check process stability by measuring individual cycles, hourly output, and daily output. The most revealing of these measures is individual cycles, from one piece to the next, because it is a process metric that makes process details visible (Figure A2-24). Fluctuation in hourly output is also interesting, but is determined after the fact, and fluctuation in total output from day to day is only an outcome metric, that is, simply too coarse and too late for process improvement.

To check process stability, time 20 to 40 successive cycles of line output and do the same for each operator's work. Graph the results as shown in Figure A2-24, including lines for the takt time and planned cycle time. Time full cycles: select a single reference point in the cycle for starting and stopping your stopwatch and let the stopwatch run until the operator returns to this point in the cycle. Distinguish between work cycle time and waiting time as much as possible, and graph the work cycle time. Finally, do not use averages, because they conceal instability.

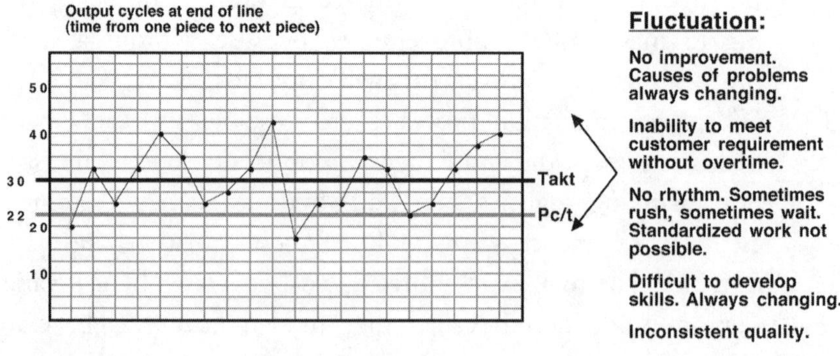

Figure A2-24. Measuring process stability

On this graph you should also note the lowest repeatable work cycle time for each operator, which is a figure you will use in the next step. In the graph above, for example, the lowest repeatable operator work cycle time seems to be 24 seconds.

What Is the Necessary Number of Operators If the Process Were Stable?

The more unstable a process, the more extra operators it will need in order to make target output. Unfortunately, overstaffing a process leads to even greater inconsistency, as lightly loaded operators naturally (and with the best intentions) assist one another with problems, work ahead to build batches, and work differently from cycle to cycle. Such increased variability actually generates more problems and makes understanding the causes of problems even more difficult. A vicious cycle.

Keep in mind, however, that if you operate even a stable process with the correct number of operators, you will need to have a way of responding quickly from outside the line when problems occur (see Chapter 7). Problems will happen.

Calculate the number of operators. Determining the necessary number of operators for a process involves measuring the total operator work time required to process one piece from start to finish. This can be done by watching and timing each operator's work, and adding the times together. (Avoid standard timetables here, as they take you away from observing the real situation.)

There is also a quicker and simpler way, which is sufficient for this process analysis: Simply use the lowest repeatable operator work cycle times from the 20 to 40 cycle graphs of the previous step. In this process analysis the initial operator times you use do not need to be exact, because you will quickly notice imbalances, overlooked wait times, and problems, and adjust as you work toward the target condition and carry out PDCA cycles. Do not waste time trying to obtain and agree upon perfectly accurate operator times now, up front, because the situation will change anyway as soon as you start taking steps toward the target condition.

The theoretically necessary number of operators for a process is determined with the formula in Figure A2-25.

$$\text{correct number of operators} = \frac{\text{Total operator cycle time to process 1 piece}}{\text{Planned cycle time}}$$

Figure A2-25. Number of operators required

Figure A2-26 is an example of this calculation.

Operator	Lowest Repeatable Time	Notes
1	15 seconds	
2	13 seconds	
3	16 seconds	Estimated total in-cycle operator work time to process one piece
4	25 seconds	
	Σ = 69 sec	

$$\frac{\text{69 sec. total time}}{\text{22 sec. Pc/t}} = \text{3.2 operators}$$

Figure A2-26. Example calculation to determine necessary number of operators

Currently, the process has four operators, and the calculation shows 3.2 operators. So four operators are necessary today. Since four operators are underutilized, however, one stretch aspect of a target condition for this process, if it is stable, could be to run with three operators.

Summarizing the Current Condition

One purpose of the process analysis is to make you spend time observing the real situation at the process, and the information and data you have obtained at this point may be sufficient for outlining a first target condition for this process. You may see what would be an appropriate next target condition and be anxious to start working toward it. However, be sure to make a simple written summary of the current condition before you start to define the next target condition.

Figure A2-27 is one example of a current-condition summary in a one-page format from a German company. I encourage you to develop your own format.

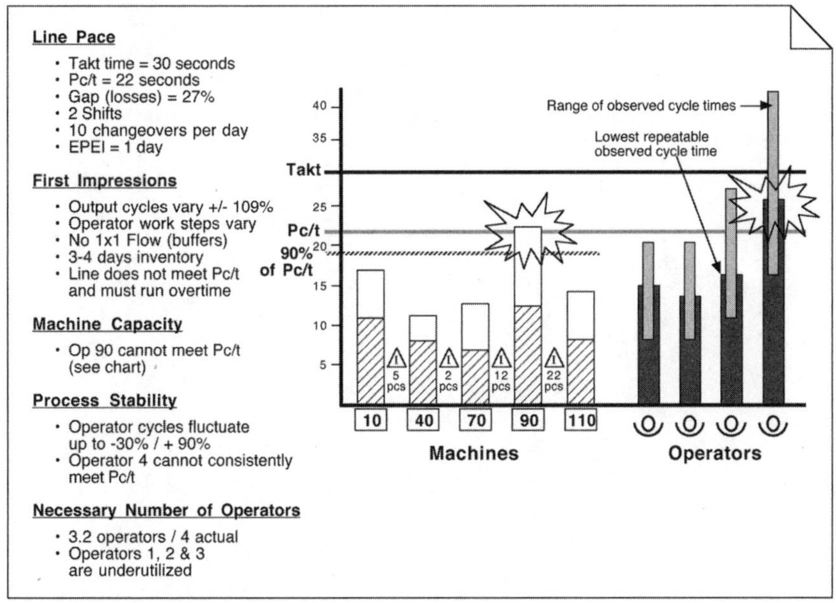

Figure A2-27. Current condition summary in one-page format

Notes

1. For more on value stream mapping see: Mike Rother and John Shook, *Learning to See* (Cambridge, Massachusetts: Lean Enterprise Institute, 1998), and www.lean.org.

Bibliography

Although this book is largely based on hands-on research, there was also considerable secondary research. The following publications were particularly helpful or influential.

Austin, Robert D. *Measuring and Managing Performance in Organizations.* New York: Dorset House Publishing, 1996.

Austin, Robert, and Lee Devin. *Artful Making, What Managers Need to Know About How Artists Work.* Upper Saddle River, New Jersey: Financial Times Prentice Hall, 2003.

Biggs, Lindy. *The Rational Factory, Architecture, Technology, and Work in America's Age of Mass Production.* Baltimore: Johns Hopkins University Press, 1996.

Carse, James P. *The Religious Case Against Belief.* New York: Penguin Press, 2008.

Cusumano, Michael A. *The Japanese Automobile Industry, Technology & Management at Nissan and Toyota.* Cambridge, Massachusetts: Harvard University Press, 1985.

DeMente, Boye Lafayette. *Behind the Japanese Bow, an In-Depth Guide to Understanding and Predicting Japanese Behavior.* Chicago: Passport Books, 1993.

Deming, W. Edwards. *Out of the Crisis.* Cambridge, Massachusetts: MIT Press, 2000. (Originally published in 1986.)

Dewey, John. *Human Nature and Conduct.* New York: Prometheus Books, 2002. (Originally published in 1922.)

______. *The Quest for Certainty.* New York: Perigee Books, 1980. (Originally published in 1929.)

Gilbert, Daniel. *Stumbling on Happiness.* New York: Alfred E. Knopf, 2006.

Henry Ford Tax Case Manuscript Collection. National Automotive History Collection, Detroit Public Library. Transcripts of Testimony of Peter E. Martin (vol. II, pp. 846–904), Fred H. Colvin (vol. II, pp. 929–47),

Edward Grey (vol. III, pp. 1230–50), and Fay Leone Farote (vol. III, pp. 1158–1229, 1250–69, 1387–1400).

Hounshell, David A. *From the American System to Mass Production, 1800–1932.* Baltimore: Johns Hopkins University Press, 1984.

Johnson, H. Thomas. "Lean Dilemma: Choose Systems Principles or Management Controls, Not Both." Unpublished paper, 2006. (Later published as: H. Thomas Johnson, "A Systematic Path to Lean Management," *The Systems Thinker*, vol. 20, no. 2 [March 2009], pp. 2–6).

Johnson, H. Thomas, and Anders Bröms. *Profit Beyond Measure, Extraordinary Results Through Attention to Work and People.* New York: The Free Press, 2000.

Kleiner, Art. *The Age of Heretics, a History of the Radical Thinkers Who Reinvented Corporate Management*, 2nd edition. San Francisco: Jossey-Bass, 2008.

Malone, Patrick M. "Little Kinks and Devices at Springfield Armory, 1892–1918," *Journal of the Society for Industrial Archeology* (1988): 14:1.

Mintzberg, Henry. *Managers Not MBAs. A Hard Look at the Soft Practice of Managing and Management Development.* San Francisco: Berrett-Koehler Publishers, 2004.

Ohba, Hajime, and Cindy Kuhlman-Voss. "Leadership and the Toyota Production System," presentation at Association for Manufacturing Excellence Conference, Chicago, Nov. 2002.

Pascale, Richard Tanner. "Perspectives on Strategy: The Real Story Behind Honda's Success," *California Management Review*, Spring 1984.

Perrow, Charles. *Normal Accidents. Living with High-Risk Technologies.* New York: Basic Books, 1984.

Popper, Karl R. *The Logic of Scientific Discovery.* London: Hutchinson & Co., 1968. (Originally published in 1959.)

Shewhart, Walter A. *Statistical Method from the Viewpoint of Quality Control.* New York: Dover Publications, 1986. (Originally published in 1939.)

Shimizu, Koichi. "Reorienting Kaizen Activities at Toyota: Kaizen, Production Efficiency, and Humanization of Work," *Okayama Economic Review,* vol. 36, no. 3, December 2004, pp. 1–25.

Spear, Steven J. "The Toyota Production System: An Example of Managing Complex Social/Technical Systems. 5 Rules for Designing, Operating, and Improving Activities, Activity-Connections, and Flow-Paths," Ph.D. dissertation, Harvard University Graduate School of Business Administration, 1999.

Watts, Alan. *The Way of Zen.* New York: Vintage Books, 1989. (Originally published in 1957.)

Womack, James P., Daniel T. Jones, and Daniel Roos. *The Machine That Changed the World: The Story of Lean Production* New York: HarperPerennial, 1991.

26 15 8 26 21 15 12 1 8 15 10 20 14 5 20 21 15 24 21 20 12
15 1 8 15 2 4 15 16 10 20 14 26 21 15 20 15 17 20 14 7 23 4
26 15 16 12 1 8 15 10 20 14 24 21 20 12 3 20 17 16 14 17 4
15 1 8 15 25 14 16 15 8 26 21 15 16 20

22 8 17 24 15 12 8 26 21

The key to this TK puzzle is hidden in one of the illustrations in this book.

Index

Locators with "n" refer to note.

C

D

N

O

Q

R

S

T

About the Author

Mike Rother is an engineer, a teacher, and a guest researcher at the Technical University Dortmund. He was formerly an associate in the Department of Industrial and Operations Engineering at the University of Michigan and a researcher at the Fraunhofer Institute in Stuttgart and at the Industrial Technology Institute in Ann Arbor. He began his career in the manufacturing division of Thyssen AG. Mike's work has brought him to numerous companies and hundreds of factories, where he collaborates with people to test ideas and share lessons learned. He splits his time between Ann Arbor, Michigan, and Cologne, Germany.

THE IMPROVEMENT KATA

A SCIENTIFIC PATTERN FOR EVERYONE

Let's face it—we have a natural tendency to jump to conclusions without realizing that our unconscious predispositions are influencing what we see, think, and do. You can make scientific, creative working a habit and get more comfortable with uncertainty by practicing the repeatable, four-step pattern called the *Improvement Kata*.

A **Kata** is a routine you practice to make its pattern a habit.

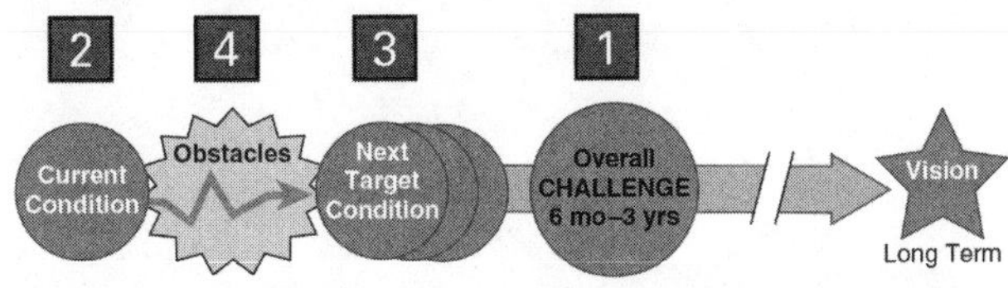

START HERE 1

Describe the overall challenge you're striving for, in a meaningful way.

What new situation do you want to have six months to three years from now?

Future-state mapping is a useful tool here.

USE THE OVERARCHING CHALLENGE AS A FRAME FOR THE FOLLOWING STEPS

2 **Current Condition:** Study the facts and data of where you are now. You're trying to see, sketch, measure, and understand the current pattern, as an input to Step 3.

3

Next Target Condition: Now describe where you want to be *next* on the way to your challenge. It will usually take a series of target conditions to reach your challenge goal. Be sure the target condition is measurable in some way and has a specified achieve-by date between one week and three months out.

4 **Experiment Toward the Target Condition:** You can't foresee the exact path to the target condition. The obstacles you encounter show you what you *need* to work on to get there. Find the path by conducting experiments daily, using the *experimenting record* and asking the *five Coaching Kata questions* after each experiment.

The point at which you have no facts and data is the *threshold of knowledge*. There's always a threshold of knowledge.

To see further, conduct your next experiment there.

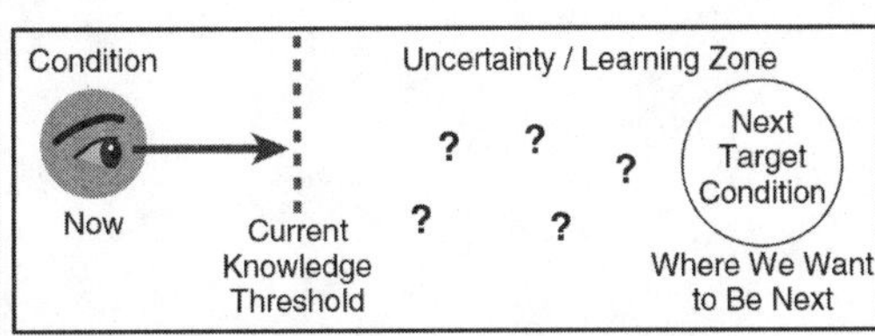